W9-BIY-232

IF ONLY WE KNEW

Also by John Willinsky

Technologies of Knowing:
  A Proposal for the Human Sciences

Learning to Divide the World:
  Education at Empire's End

Empire of Words:
  The Reign of the OED

The Triumph of Literature/The Fate of Literacy:
  English in the Secondary School Curriculum

The New Literacy:
  Redefining Reading and Writing in the Schools

The Well-Tempered Tongue:
  The Politics of Standard English in the High School

IF ONLY WE KNEW

Increasing the Public Value
of Social-Science Research

John Willinsky

ROUTLEDGE
a member of the Taylor & Francis Group
New York and London

Published in 2000 by
Routledge
29 West 35th Street
New York, NY 10001

Published in Great Britain in 2000 by
Routledge
11 New Fetter Lane
London EC4P 4EE

Routledge is an imprint of the Taylor & Francis Group.

Printed in the United States of America on acid-free paper.
Design: Jack Donner

Library of Congress Cataloging-in-Publication Data

Willinsky, John 1950–
    If only we knew : increasing the public value of social-science research /
    John Willinsky.
        p.   cm.
    Includes bibliographical references and index.
    ISBN 0–415–92651–3 – ISBN 0-415-92652-1 (pbk.)
        1. Communication in the social sciences—Technical innovations.
    2. Knowledge, Sociology of. I. Title
    H61.8 .W543 2000
    306.4'2–dc21   00–035275

In memory of Irene Samuel and A. I. Willinsky

As they spoke to me in the public interest . . .

Contents

Acknowledgments

This work, like the book before it, emerges out of a vital and ongoing dialogue with Vivian Forssman about technology, knowledge, and public purpose. The book has also received helpful readings and much-appreciated support from Richard Brown, Charles R. Green, Edgar Z. Friedenberg, Shula Klinger, Kara Macdonald, Ranjini Mendis, David Peerla, Tan Phan, Miriam Orkar, and Anne White. I would also acknowledge the contribution of the University of British Columbia's Public Knowledge group, with Glynis Andersson, Vivian Forssman, Richard Gutter, Shula Klinger, Henry Kang, Lisa Korteweg, Brenda Trofanenko, and Paul Woltenholme. The book itself has been especially well-served by my encouraging and patient editor at Routledge, Heidi Freund, and, once more, by the ever-exacting copy editor, Tammy Zambo.

I first undertook the research for this book with the generous support of the Wm. Allen Chair in Education at Seattle University and the inestimable assistance of Jennifer Hoffman, to whom I remain grateful. In addition, this work has been generously supported by the TeleLearning National Centres of Excellence and the Pacific Press Professorship of Literacy and Technology at the University of British Columbia.

A note on the footnotes: Following my interests in the public's engagement with scholarship, the publisher has agreed to place the footnotes at the bottom of the page, rather than use the more common endnotes that are placed at the back of the book. To minimize the interruption of the reader in this book's integration of text and notes, I have placed the footnote number, covering cited material and further comments, at the end of the relevant paragraphs. This note is itself supplemented by chapter 9, which is devoted to why footnotes matter and could matter more.

A Public-Knowledge Project   1

When the well-known science writer and Harvard biologist Stephen Jay Gould was told in 1982 at the age of forty that he was suffering from abdominal mesothelioma, an "invariably fatal" form of stomach cancer, he was as unsure as any of us would be about where to turn for consolation. He was fortunate enough, however, to have his faith. In his case, it was a faith in knowledge, more specifically a faith in the knowledge of numbers and statistics. In his book *Full House*, which is one of the rare occasions on which he has written about this illness, he makes clear the immediate and lasting consolation he found in learning what was known of the disease. What saved his spirit, oddly enough, was the discovery at his neighborhood university library that this abdominal cancer had a "median mortality" of eight months.[1]

As the shock of this sudden and harsh death sentence sank in, he began thinking about what this median mortality limit meant for the individual cancer patient. Eight months was not necessarily *his* death sentence, he realized. And with each subsequent insight, he lets the reader know how consoled, empowered, and just plain delighted he was by this unfolding understanding, as he writes of "my initial burst of positivity . . ."; "the key insight that proved so life affirming . . ."; "the most precious of all gifts. . . ." All of this emerged out of his growing understanding of how the median mortality was skewed toward a short time frame by the those who died quickly from the disease, as opposed to the other half of those with the disease, who lived on, many into old age, due to circumstances that Gould realized he had in his favor: "I was young, rarin' to fight the bastard, located in the city offering the best possible medical treatment [with the resources to use them], blessed with a supportive family, and lucky that my disease had been discovered relatively early in its course." Still, he recognized that "this insight gave

---

1. Stephen Jay Gould, *Full House: The Spread of Excellence from Plato to Darwin* (New York: Three Rivers Press, 1996).

[him] no guarantee of normal longevity." As it turned out, fortunately, he has continued to live a vital life to this day, in part perhaps due to his learning of and undergoing an experimental treatment. On his way however, he was obviously steadied by his ability to hold in his hands and contemplate what was known about his illness.[2]

Now, Gould is no ordinary man, it is safe to say, when it comes to knowledge. But his manifold intellectual gifts notwithstanding, it has long been his project to make the fascinations and consolations of knowledge a greater part of the public domain, under the copyright of his popular science writing. He has succeeded, judging by how widely read his books on zoology, evolution, and the millennium are, with the weight of his achievement never more apparent than when he addresses the evil that science can do, as he has in the award-winning *Mismeasure of Man*, which is on the history and consequences of race science. Gould is proudly part of a more general public-knowledge project that is inspired by the pleasures and responsibilities of sharing a sense of scientific wonder and the importance, if not always with the same dramatic consolation, of knowing what is known.[3]

My book makes a related case for improving the quality of public knowledge by drawing on social science research in such areas as health, education, justice, welfare, politics, and families. My approach is not to rely on a Stephen Jay Gould of the social sciences, who, after conducting his research by day, in the evening writes reader-friendly articles and books about his work. My approach is to make the research itself more widely available and accessible for the public. This book is about why and how that can be done. It is about how and why the social-science research community could create far more of a public and political resource than it currently does. It is about extending the public benefit of what is largely a publicly funded body of knowledge, within an increasingly omnivorous information economy. It is about using the Internet, already so vital to commercial knowledge services, to build a better source of knowledge for citizens and the curious, rather than for clients and consumers.

The public has already demonstrated a considerable appetite for

2. Ibid., 49ff. Gould: "My initial burst of positivity amounted to little more than an emotional gut reaction—and would have endured for only a short time, had I not been able to bolster the feeling with a genuine reason for optimism based upon a better analysis of papers that seemed so brutally pessimistic.... I then had the key insight that proved so life affirming at such a crucial moment. I started to think about the variation.... This insight gave me no guarantee of normal longevity, but, at least I had obtained the most precious of all gifts at a crucial moment: the *prospect* of substantial time": ibid., 48–50; my emphasis.
3. Stephen Jay Gould, *The Mismeasure of Man* (New York: Norton, 1981).

online sources of medical and health information, digging into research articles that had previously been the exclusive purview of medical researchers and dedicated physicians. The *New York Times* estimates that 25 million Americans will turn to the Internet for health information in the first year of the new millennium, much of it firsthand research. A popular site that has deeply impressed me with what it offers equally to researchers, physicians, and the public is OncoLink—a cancer-information resource run by the University of Pennsylvania Cancer Center, which is currently visited by 150,000 people a month. The Internet has become many things to many people, but one of those things is definitely a new way into forms of knowledge that matter to people, and not only when it is a matter of their life or death.[4]

The knowledge that strengthened, inspired, and comforted Stephen Jay Gould, as he stood before the ultimate question mark of his own imminent mortality, was his understanding of probability. He came to understand how that concept is used in epidemiology (originating in the study of epidemics) to analyze the chances of survival and death in certain medical and social circumstances. Epidemiology is at the crossroads of medical science and social science, and social science is where I have spent my career as a researcher and scholar. In my position as professor of education, I do social-science research on the nature of learning and teaching within institutional settings such as the schools. In this I share in the responsibility for the public standing of social-science research, as we in this field assume, not surprisingly, that our intellectual activity brings a certain light to the world for the benefit of students, teachers, parents, and people generally. This sense of responsibility, as scholar and educator, has led me to wonder whether the entire field of social-science research could not prove itself a better source of knowledge for the public, and whether this knowledge could not play a greater role in public and personal arenas of understanding and action— "greater" implying something between Gould's urgent reading of a statistical death sentence and his fascinating inquiry into a panda's thumb. In my dual role, I have come to wonder why the vast body of social-science scholarship concerning how we live does not offer greater educational value for the world at large.

---

4. OncoLink, http://cancer.med.upenn.edu/. Another powerful health-information site is Clinical Trials Listing Service, operated by CenterWatch, a Boston-area publishing company. As I write, the CenterWatch site is visited each month by 85,000 patients, as well as those looking for a little research money, who are able to search through some 7,000 clinical trials of new drugs and procedures, including, for example, 423 listings for hypertension and 73 for HIV: CenterWatch (September 1998), http://www.centerwatch.com.

My project with this book, then, is to explore why the time is right for social scientists to explore ways of improving the contribution that their research makes to public knowledge. As the table of contents suggests, I go about this project by first asking how our concept of knowledge stands with the idea of "public," how it works within the new economy of information, and how it has been housed and ordered to increase its value. I then turn specifically to the social sciences, exploring four aspects that bear on the contribution of this field to public knowledge: what social science owes to the public; what its public impact has been up to this point; how chance and risk frame what it knows; and how ancient and new devices, such as the footnote and the hyperlink, can pull together what otherwise flies apart within those fields of intense inquiry. I then conclude where I began, with the political potential of a public knowledge backed by the diverse, eclectic reach of social-science inquiry.

My aim is to open the door on a relatively cloistered body of knowledge that claims to have some bearing on each of our lives. Imagine just how many professors around the world are working in anthropology, economics, political science, psychology, and sociology, as well as in professional schools of law, commerce, education, and health. Then consider how the vast majority of them are engaged in researching how people live for better or worse, coming up with not only the median mortality of abdominal cancer but also a greater understanding of what happens in families and schools, street gangs and golf clubs, prison cells and courthouses, voting booths and on shop floors. The resulting wealth of recorded knowledge, carefully screened by academic journals, now amounts to more than all but the richest university libraries can afford. The result is an oft-mentioned crisis in scholarly publishing, resulting from the proliferation of journal titles amid wildly escalating subscription rates. Meanwhile, a new publishing medium looms on the cyberspace horizon.[5]

Given this vast and complex accumulation of knowledge, it may seem simply crass to ask about the public return on this considerable financial and intellectual investment. Although there is no simple way to value this

---

5. To give an idea of scale, the *Social Sciences Citation Index* works with 1,700 titles in English; the British Library for Development subscribes to 5,000 journals related to economic and social development; and the Harvard University Library, with the largest serials holding in the United States, has 90,000 titles covering all fields: *Social Sciences Citation Index* (Philadelphia: Institute for Scientific Information, 1998); Maureen Mahoney, "Overcoming Information Poverty: The Research Information Shared Pilot Scheme," *Information Development* 15, no. 1 (March 1999): 44; "The Crisis in Scholarly Publishing," University of Waterloo Electronic Library, Scholarly Societies Projects (September 1998), http://library.uwaterloo.ca/society/crisis.html.

knowledge, there are many ways of improving its worth. This knowledge could do more than it now does for the decisions and deliberations by which people live, and more in helping them assess the risks and possibilities they face. This knowledge speaks, in all of its partiality and diversity, to what people tend to identify in polls as "the most important problem facing the country today." And it could do more than it has in the past because we have new technologies that can vastly improve public access to such knowledge. Few people may possess the depth of Stephen Jay Gould's faith in science as a way of understanding the world, but whatever their beliefs, they possess the right to know what is known as a result of the scientific endeavors conducted in their name. The benefits could work both ways, for doing more to engage the public in this knowledge project would, I believe, improve both social-science research and public knowledge.[6]

This sense of "doing more" to engage the public calls for rethinking every phase of a research project, from how a study is conceived, initiated, and funded, through how it is designed and operated, on to the data gathering and analysis, and into the writing-up and publication of the results. Each of these steps has an impact on how a study makes sense of a social issue and on how a study relates to other studies, past and present. Each of these steps needs to be rethought with an eye to how the coherence and intelligibility of the research enterprise could be improved for a wider public. Fortunately, efforts are under way on many fronts to enhance what we might take as the coherence of social-science research: collaborative and multidisciplinary studies are taking place on a global scale; large data-sets are being developed for shared use among research teams; websites are testing research applications of hypertext and virtual reality, e-journals and indexing services; and what I would call "public-knowledge sites" are being built to connect research, policy, and practice, as well as the people who work in each of these areas.[7]

---

6. In a 1999 Gallup poll, the most important problems facing the country were identified as "ethics, morality, family decline" (18 percent), "crime, violence" (17 percent), "education" (11 percent), and "guns, gun control" (10 percent); thus, 56 percent of respondents selected the top four categories identified in the poll. In 1980, by comparison, 99 percent of the people selected the top four categories (foreign policy, inflation, energy, and unemployment): "What's the Problem?" *New York Times*, August 1, 1999, WK4.

7. For a summary of recent developments in educational research, see Roy D. Pea, "New Media Communications Forums for Improving Education Research and Practice," in *Issues in Education Research: Problems and Possibilities*, ed. Ellen Condliffe Lagemann and Lee S. Shulman (San Francisco: Jossey-Bass, 1999); and Jeremy Roschelle and Roy D. Pea, "Trajectories from Today's WWW to a Powerful Educational Infrastructure," *Educational Researcher* 28, no. 5 (June–July 1999), http://www.cilt.org/html/publications. html.

This book supports these initiatives by working out the details of a public-spirited philosophy devoted to understanding knowledge as a public resource. It addresses the prospects of creating online public spaces that integrate sources of knowledge with my focus on social-science research as a way of exploring the ongoing relationship between democracy and technology (dating back to the invention of the printing press). My hope is that this discussion will contribute to a renewed sense of public purpose and public support for research. The goal is to encourage the social sciences to play a much more vital role in the public sector of a knowledge-based economy, perhaps leading to equally developed knowledge-based politics. I recognize that such talk of greater coordination and coherence within the research enterprise needs to be approached cautiously if we are not to lose the risky and rigorous, creative and critical tensions that are the bases of the contribution of research to knowledge. Can we introduce more coordination and coherence among studies, as well as a greater connection between research and other forms of public understanding, without reverting to social-engineering models of social-science research, without assuming that knowledge possesses an underlying unity that we can now realize, and without taking the public value of research as a given?

First of all, I do not presume that the social sciences could readily dispose of social problems if they just got their act together. Nor do I see research as dictating a course of action, determining a policy, or otherwise being used to undermine the political and public processes that decide how people's lives are governed. The driving image here is not one of coordinated teams of researchers swarming in and cleaning up social dilemmas like a spandexed set of superheroes. Rather, it is, I imagine, the social sciences making it relatively easy for the public to consult the range of relevant and diverse research that supports their working through the challenges they face. Researchers can improve their contribution to public understanding without assuming that their mandate is to engineer social solutions. This relationship between research, understanding, and action leads to the second distinction that I need to make.

These efforts at improving the coherence and coordination of social-science research are *not* about uncovering the underlying unity of knowledge or of scientific research. Although, I return to this theme in chapter 11, let me state here that my interests in improving the coherence and comprehensibility of the social sciences is not about achieving a Grand Unifying Theory of human behavior. Rather than seeking to put together the pieces of a single puzzle called the True Knowledge of the World, this project is about helping people appreciate the different ways we have developed for understanding social phenomena. It is about how or whether this diverse body of research can improve its value for a broader public as a way of understanding, discussing, debating, making judgments, and taking action. The improvements I propose are aimed at enabling greater connections and comparisons to be made both within this body of research activity and as this research relates to policies, practices, and programs in the larger social world. So this public-knowledge project is not about rendering the whole of the world intelligible in any singular or monolithic sense.

Finally, I wish to make it clear that I do not assume that the world is really waiting with bated breath for all that social-science research has to offer. What has yet to be tested and proved is whether the public value of this knowledge can be improved and whether access to this knowledge can support democratic participation, improve professional practices, and help people make greater sense of the world and act on that world. While research processes within the social sciences are not perfect or complete in themselves, my hypothesis is that the public could be better served by this research and by the existing resources and talents devoted to it. I could be wrong, and in more than one way. I could be wrong about whether more of this knowledge can be shared with the public than is currently shared, and I could be wrong about the value of this sharing for both the public and researchers. But I can't help thinking that I am right about the importance of exploring and testing whether social-science research can offer people more than it currently offers to our knowledge of what is human and what is just and fair within the scope of that humanity.

Now, I also realize that I am presuming a great deal about the intent of the social sciences. Social scientists are often a little vague about the intended audience of the knowledge they so eagerly produce. They may unfailingly intend their work to benefit humankind. But how exactly do they expect that to happen? The common assumption is that the application of this knowledge is best left up to others, to professionals (policy makers, legal professionals, teachers, physicians, social workers, etc.) who are equipped to make it work on behalf of humankind. Little thought is given to what the social sciences owe directly to the public and to public knowledge. What would it take, I am asking, for people to be able to turn to social-science research as easily as they turn to other sources of information on say, finance or sports.

It will take some doing, I realize, to help people see that although social-science research does not provide definitive answers to what can be done about school-yard bullies or working conditions in overseas factories, it can help people judge the scope and scale of such problems, while providing a critical guide to what has been done and what could be done. In turn, this new level of public access may lead people to direct questions and challenges about the work back to the research community. Such access is now easy to imagine. To this end, the Public Knowledge team—consisting of Vivian Forssman, Henry Kang, Lisa Korteweg, and Brenda Trofanenko—that I am currently working with at the University of British Columbia has built a prototype Public Knowledge website, described later in the book, which links related studies, forums, policies, and practices on the topic of technology and education. Sites such as this one can point to books and other traditional sources, providing a gateway between technologies while enhancing access to them.[8]

As things now stand, the exchange between the public and social scientists is too often a fount of frustration for both parties. On the one hand, the public feels that it simply cannot get a straight answer from social scientists. It doesn't seem to matter whether the question is how to reduce the problems some children have with reading, how to break the cycle of poverty in families, or how to foster racial integration in communities. The answer often seems to be some combination of, "It depends," and, "More research is needed." On the other hand, social scientists grow tired of a media-driven public attention limited to sound-bite scholarship that cannot help but distort and trivialize hard-won ideas. Researchers' vanity may flourish in the media's bright lights, but the research itself continues to be directed largely toward interested colleagues who have time and reason to pursue it through journals and conferences.

Even where social-science research is ostensibly meant to inform professionals working in education, justice, health, commerce, and social work, there is still a sense of an interested public poorly served by what that research has to offer. Practitioners fondly refer to this as the great divide between research or theory and practice—"Well, that may be what the research says, but *I* know ..." They are no less put off than the

---

8. Vivian Forssman, Henry Kang, Lisa Korteweg, Brenda Trofanenko, and John Willinsky, Public Knowledge Project, in conjunction with the *Vancouver Sun* (1999), http://www.educ. ubc.ca/faculty/ctg/pkp, and with Glynis Andersson, Shula Klinger, Paul Woltenholme, and the British Columbia Teachers Federation (1999), http://www. pkp.bctf.ca. Both websites are currently being maintained as demonstration sites, as they were both tied to specific events. They will have links to new versions of the project.

public by the complicated jargon and rarely reconciled contradictions within bodies of research. In my field, education, teachers often come back to graduate school to learn more about schooling and to improve their credentials, only to be struck by the seeming irrelevance of educational research. A number of education professors have responded by getting teachers to conduct their own loosely structured inquiries in the name of "action research." Such is the search among professionals for the relevance of our pursuit of knowledge.

In this book I focus on the contribution of the social sciences to public knowledge, rather than to professional expertise, for two reasons. The first is the rather obvious point that, in most cases, if I can convince social scientists to increase the public value of their research—by improving its organization, connections, coherence, and intelligibility—its value is bound to be enhanced for the related professions, as well as, in all likelihood, for other researchers. The second reason for focusing on the public rather than the professional quality of the knowledge is political. Any improvements in professionals' access to research might ultimately benefit the public, but I would not want to increase public dependence on professional authority. Going public with our knowledge, for all of the challenges it poses, is about better equipping people to participate in a civil and democratic society, to steer a steady course through the current state of information glut and knowledge fragmentation.

This public-knowledge project addresses a particular malaise of the times, much in line with Harvard professor of government Michael J. Sandel's analysis of "democracy's discontent." For Sandel, the anxiety and frustration that beset us stem from a "fear that, individually and collectively, we are losing control of the forces that govern our lives," a fear related to an unraveling of the moral fabric of our community, from family to nation. We can read about this discontent in the press and feel it on the street. Although, the social sciences are just one among many sources of understanding this malaise, they are so thoroughly devoted to a close and considered assessment of both "the forces that govern our lives" and the fabric of local and global communities that it seems absurd that so little is done to ensure that the knowledge they have to offer is a source of greater control for people. In a theme I return to in the final section of this book, the social sciences need to offer more to the processes of public deliberation that Sandel and others feel are critical to extending the elements of self-government in our lives.[9]

---

9. Michael J. Sandel, *Democracy's Discontent: America in Search of a Public Philosophy* (Cambridge: Harvard University Press, 1996), 3.

Central to this idea that the social sciences could be far more publicly engaged is the emergence of the Internet. Whereas some are quick to identify technology's increasing surveillance and management of our lives, I join with those who hold that the future is yet to be determined rather than already set by the machines we live by, and that the social sciences have the opportunity to explore and to demonstrate just how these new information and communication technologies, like the printing press before them, can extend scientific inquiry, public knowledge, and democratic participation. And while I argue the need for the social sciences to experiment with new sorts of public spaces for its knowledge to operate within, some may interpret the very proposal to experiment as yet another threat posed by these technologies to the quality of the knowledge by which we live.[10]

I argue in this book, however, that humankind's work with knowledge has always entailed innovative technologies of order and access. Many historically critical developments in information technology (IT)—the papyrus scroll, the printing press, cheap paper, the penny post—have been imaginatively used both to increase the store of public knowledge and to expand its reach. Take the electric light, for example, which, as Marshall McLuhan pointed out some decades ago, is every bit an information technology. This may seem rather a strange thing to claim, even for McLuhan, until we consider that one of the first large buildings to be fitted with this IT at the turn of the twentieth century was the New York Public Library. Still today, with the recently refurbished Rose Reading Room at the library, which is equipped with reproductions of the original reading lamps as well as high-speed Internet terminals, it represents one of the city's most magnificent architectural tributes to public knowledge, as well as a vital contributor to that knowledge.[11]

What, then, of the contribution of this new, ubiquitous technology to knowledge in the social sciences? It can be safely said that the professor's

10. See, for example, Andrew Feenberg: "Technology is one of the major sources of public power in modern societies. So far as decisions affecting our daily lives are concerned, political democracy is largely overshadowed by the enormous power wielded by the masters of technical systems: corporate and military leaders, and professional associations of groups such as physicians and engineers": "Subversive Rationalization: Technology, Power, and Democracy," in *Technology and the Politics of Knowledge*, ed. Andrew Feenberg and Alastair Hannay (Bloomington: Indiana University Press, 1995). A public-knowledge project such as mine should also be able to add to "the democratic politics of technology" advocated by Richard Sclove, founder of FASTnet (Federation of Activists on Science and Technology Network) and author of *Democracy and Technology* (New York: Guilford, 1995), 197–238.

11. Julie V. Iovine, "Open for Travel in Realms of Gold," *New York Times*, November 5, 1998, D14. Marshall McLuhan, *Understanding Media: The Extensions of Man* (New York: Signet, 1964).

ever-upgraded home and office computers have sped up the research process of locating and applying for grants, gathering and analyzing data, writing up and circulating studies. So we have more studies being published by more people in more journals. Yet this bulking up of the body of knowledge can also be seen as slowing it down, whether as a source of understanding or wonder or inspiration or action, because of the extra effort needed to bring related work together and to connect it with the larger world. This is what leads me to propose that, rather than simply being used to increase rates of scholarly production (a process that, if nothing else, increases the stakes for tenure and promotion among professors), these technologies should be directed toward creating new ways of organizing and connecting research; creating fields of greater coherence; connecting critiques, responses, and reconsiderations; aligning alternative perspectives among works; and engaging larger communities in the social sciences' knowledge project.

Of course, it is not unusual for a new generation of technologies to be used initially to speed up old processes, amounting to a brief and false first step before the new technology reshapes those processes. When Gutenberg, the goldsmith-turned-printer, began to turn out page after page of the Bible in Mainz, Germany, midway into the fifteenth century, he still needed to send the freshly printed, unbound pages to a scriptorium to be illuminated by hand, creating a hybrid work caught between epochal technologies of bookmaking. (This might be compared to how researchers and their editors now prepare almost every aspect of their texts online to meet the printed-page requirements of bound journals.)

In the decades that followed Gutenberg's invention, European printers, who originally acted as publishers, editors, graphic designers, author agents, and booksellers, began experimenting with new page designs that not only were suited to printing-press technology but also were far easier to read and more economical to produce with its clean, crisp page and font design, albeit with the loss of the intricate beauty of the illuminated manuscript page. It must have been hard to imagine, in Gutenberg's fifteenth-century world of Latin literacy, that reading and writing would ever become a common skill among people. But, of course, the search for a broader market for print led to massive publishing in the European vernacular languages even before literate standards of spelling and grammar were developed for them. Although it took until the end of the seventeenth century for Latin to lose its hold on scholarly publications, by then Bacon, Descartes, and others had made it apparent that plain and ordinary language, "naked and open" to the world, best served scientific claims of veracity. The reverberations of this greater public engagement with the written word, through book or pamphlet, broadsheet and bal-lad, changed the world of politics, religion, literature, science, and scholarship. Still, the long, hard struggle for universal public education and literacy was to stretch well into the final decades of the nineteenth century, for, among other things, the idea of this knowledge in the hands of the many was rightly feared by the powerful few as posing a threat to their comfortable hold on the world.[12]

The close of the nineteenth century saw two terrific gains in public knowledge in the West—public education and public libraries. Public schooling may have been as much about a declining market for child labor and a desire to assimilate immigrants and the industrial classes as it was about using print technologies to expand democratic capacities. And while one may similarly want to question the reasons behind the heavenward intentions of Andrew Carnegie's generous funding of some 2,500 public libraries around the English-speaking world between 1890 and 1920, his action still adds up to an extremely large, single-handed contribution to the store of public knowledge. Carnegie sought "to help those who [would] help themselves; to provide part of the means," and this philanthropic theme of investing in character is bound to remain an aspect of such provisions for public knowledge. But more than a few of those children walking home with their checked-out library books even-tually became far more than was dreamt of in Carnegie's philosophy, and we may expect the same from the children who now leave the libraries in "under-served rural and urban areas" that Bill Gates's Library Initiative is equipping with computers and Internet service, with plans to extend support to 13,000 libraries in Canada and the United States over the next five years.[13]

What the printing press did for expanding the community of readers, the Internet stands poised to do again as it is directed toward the inter-ests of public knowledge. A converted olive press in Mainz did not determine the Reformation, the rise of nationalism, or the spread of democracy. It only provided a means for doing with the word what had not been done before. It took the imagination and commitment of thou-sands among future generations to realize just what this technology could

---

12. Francis Bacon, cited in Robert N. Proctor, *Value-Free Science: Purity and Power in Modern Knowledge* (Cambridge: Harvard University Press, 1991), 34. On mass literacy, see Patrick Brantlinger, *The Reading Lesson: The Threat of Mass Literacy in Nineteenth-Century British Fiction* (Bloomington: Indiana University Press, 1999); and my *The Triumph of Literature/The Fate of Literacy* (New York: Teachers College Press, 1991).

13. Andrew Carnegie, cited in Abigail A. Van Slyck, *Free to All: Carnegie Libraries and American Culture, 1890–1920* (Chicago: University of Chicago Press, 1998), 10; Sam Howe Verhovek, "Elder Bill Gates Takes on the Role of Philanthropist," *New York Times*, September 12, 1999, A1.

mean for the balance of power in people's lives. Many of the resulting cultural and political changes took place, it is well to remember as we move into a new era, amid deadly and massively destructive struggles. We can hope that we are all somewhat wiser today, but we can only wonder whether the knowledge at issue is less volatile this time. There's no predicting how things will unfold, yet that offers little excuse for sitting back and waiting to see.

By briefly calling up the drumbeat of history like this, with more detailed analysis of critical historical moments and figures to follow, I mean only to suggest the reasonableness of considering, at this juncture, what the new generation of information technologies offers for rethinking and redesigning the representations of knowledge in one area of academic inquiry. It has become clear over the last few years that this sense of impending change is not just the digital soapbox oratory of technoenthusiasts. And when it comes to scholarly communication, it is becoming clear that the Internet is going to be the publishing medium of choice.

What is this technology doing to the nature of academic knowledge? As I write, the web is being used, in an experiment with the British Library for Development, to create global access to scholarly materials that were once the privilege of industrialized nations. It is also being used to mount primary documents behind works of history, such as Avner Cohen's *Israel and the Bomb*, which supports the argument that Israel became a nuclear power in the 1960s despite the country's denials. "I am saying, 'Look at my raw material on line," Cohen, a senior research associate at the National Security Archive in Washington says. "You don't have to buy my interpretation. Here are the documents. Judge for yourself." For Tom Blanton, director of the National Security Archive, associated with George Washington University, "this is the beginning of a new era in this kind of endeavor for people to be able to see primary sources unmediated, together with the advantage of the mediation. You have them side by side." Archivist Blanton may have forgotten those medieval biblical and Talmudic traditions that filled the margins of their primary sources, namely, biblical texts with endless streams of commentary done in many hands. Which is only to point to how the knowledgeable goals are the same, even as the means and scope change.[14]

---

14. Mahoney, "Overcoming Information Poverty"; Cohen and Blanton cited in Ethan Bronner, "A Ticking Bomb on the Web," *New York Times*, October 31, 1998, A21. The Research Libraries Group, an international alliance of 160 libraries, is attempting to create a directory for online archives, including the 4 million digitized items of the Library of Congress, and London's Public Records Office, with materials dating back to the eleventh-century Domesday Book; Jo Thomas, "Web Surfers Jump onto Archivists' Bandwagon," *Toronto Globe and Mail*, December 17, 1998, D2.

Douglas C. Bennett, vice president of the American Council of Learned Societies, speaks of how council members "believe the technologies of digital networks will plow up and replant the worlds of scholarship and education." Bennett also shares my hope that the digital network will work against "the context of disconnection" that currently dominates scholarly activity and is especially noticeable in "the sharp separation of scholars from the general public." The isolated journal article will be replaced, he hazards, by more connected and more coherent forms of publication, and the tired tradition of shrouding scholarship in obscurity in the name of academic freedom just isn't going to cut it anymore.[15]

In 1665, when Henry Oldenburg set out the mission of the first English academic journal, the *Philosophical Transactions* of the Royal Society, he insisted that publishing in this way would assist new ideas to reach a wider circle going beyond the world of scholars: "Whereas there is nothing more necessary for promoting the improvement of Philosophical Matters, than the communicating to such, as apply their Studies and Endeavors that way, such things as are discovered or put in practice by others; it is therefore thought fit to employ the *Press*, as the most proper way to gratify those, whose engagement in such Studies and delight in the advancement of Learning and profitable Discoveries, doth entitle them to the knowledge of this Kingdom." Just as this expansion of audience was seen as vital to knowledge's project in Oldenburg's day, I am looking in ours to extend the circle of communication, for the social sciences, to include a wider public. The Internet has already proven to be a source of public knowledge across a wide range of areas, from personal health to consumerism. Yet, for all of social sciences' use of this technology, as well as for all that the social sciences are doing to expand what is known of how people live, love, play, work, and die, I keep coming back to two questions: Why aren't the publicly funded aspects of this knowledge available to those with an interest in them, when the means for such access appear to exist? What would happen to this headlong production of research if the public were a greater part of the reason it exists?[16]

---

15. Douglas C. Bennett, "New Connections for Scholars: The Changing Missions of a Learned Society in an Era of Digital Networks," *Occasional Papers*, no. 36 (Washington: American Council of Learned Societies, 1997), http://www.acls.org/op36.htm.

16. Henry Oldenburg, cited in Jean-Claude Guédon, "Electronic Academic Journals: From Disciplines to 'Seminars,'" in *Computer Networking and Scholarly Communication in the Twenty-First Century*, ed. T. M. Harrison and T. Stephen (Albany: State University of New York Press, 1966), 336.

This public knowledge project falls within a long history of public-broadcasting efforts that have proven fundamental to the growth of democracy and the struggle for greater equality that it represents. However hard it is to gauge what is achieved by these technologically enabled increases in the freedom of expression, the sense of an informed public, aware of the issues that unite and divide us, can be taken as a good in itself. So, this call for strengthening public knowledge is not so much radical or innovative as inevitable. Yet against this gradual sense of inevitability is the current situation, in which information technologies are devoted, in large measure, to developing the private and commercial side of this knowledge economy, resulting in vastly improved resources for investors, consumers, travelers, and above all, sports fans.[17]

To place this historic opportunity and challenge in perspective, I ask you, the reader, to look not only ahead, to what can be, but also back, to a no less speculative time from whence we came. For according to one substantial source in the Judeo-Christian tradition, in the beginning, before there were data and information, there was the temptation of knowledge. We would do well to let Francis Bacon be our guide in this line of thinking, given that he did more than a little to inspire current datamongering by giving rise to modern conceptions of science. Bacon saw that in biblical days, "the aspiring to overmuch knowledge was the original temptation." It certainly proved an apple too many for Eve and Adam. Bacon also reminds us that it was not long before the likes of such wise men as King Solomon were complaining "that there is no end of making books, and that much reading is weariness of the flesh," adding for good measure the warning, "He that increaseth knowledge increaseth anxiety."[18]

When Bacon himself set about increasing knowledge and anxiety by launching the modern scientific project, in his own foretaste of the tree of knowledge's Newtonian apple, he proposed avoiding the prideful knowledge of good and evil—thus challenging God's order—in favor of what he called "the pure knowledge of nature and universality." Such was to be the dominion of the sciences, and the pursuit of this new knowledge order became the work of the Royal Society that received its charter within decades of his death. These ambitions soon propelled

---

17. "The World Wide Web has served the sports fan even better than the sex addict.... The Internet extends his access to databases on which he thrives as well as to a variety of sources from which to draw opinions. Chat rooms and bulletin boards have given him the chance to test (or steal) assertions": Douglas Rushkoff, "Sports May Be the Internet's 'Killer Application,'" *Toronto Globe and Mail*, February 3, 1999, C9.

18. Francis Bacon, *The Advancement of Learning and the New Atlantis* (1605; reprint, London: Oxford University Press, 1906), 1.1.2.

imperialism's great scientific expeditions around the globe, carrying naturalist-adventurers who eagerly harvested scientific specimens and recorded data for European museums, laboratories, and universities, as well as traveling circuses and private collectors. From biblical Eden to Renaissance Europe, each era had its own sense of knowledge surfeit, each era its worries about the public purposes to which that knowledge should be turned. Each era also seems to afford a few minds the privilege of worrying about the harnessing and ordering of this overweening knowledge; this book will consider the contributions of Bacon, Leibniz, Pascal, Diderot, Dewey, and Borges, among others.[19]

There has been a constant tension between those who spin out prolific amounts of information and knowledge in all directions, and those who seek to anxiously reign this abundance in, trying to give it order and a center. This tug-of-war continues within both the big and the small forces of knowledge in the social sciences, whether the topic is global economic systems or infant–mother interactions. Today, as research results fill libraries and swell databases, it seems only reasonable to wonder whether information technologies might introduce new levels of order, integration, and accessibility that could stem the increasing fragmentation that is reducing the overall value of this research proliferation. Today's great epistemological dilemma, for all of the postmodern fervor over the death and dearth of truth, is no different from the dilemma that Solomon and Bacon faced—how to bring some greater order to what we know, however we name that knowledge. For the real prize comes of the ordering, which reveals junctures, gaps, tensions, alternatives. "The political problem during the final years of the twentieth century," as sociologist Irving Louis Horowitz names it, "is much less the amount of scientific information and technical material available than the integration and accessibility of the value of that information."[20]

Horowitz fears we are falling "behind in the orderly processing of data and information as such." I tend to think this has always been the case and it has continually provided the impetus for new ways of working with knowledge, from libraries and encyclopedias to networks and databases. Yet where I see the need to extend the technologies of knowledge, Horowitz sees machines as posing "a near insoluble problem ... [which] is less with [their] totalitarian capabilities than [their]

---

19. Ibid., 1.1.3. Some time after Bacon, David Hume pointed out how the Baconian passion for discovering the secrets of nature was "so agreeable to the natural vanity and curiosity of men": *The History of Great Britain*, vol. 2 (London, 1757), 454.
20. Irving Louis Horowitz, *Communicating Ideas: The Politics of Scholarly Publishing*, 2d ed. (New Brunswick, N.J.: Transaction, 1991), 23.

anarchical consequences." I hold that those consequences, at least in some small part, lie in our hands. Thus arise my hopes and plans for directing more of this silicon toward just the sort of "integration and accessibility" that Horowitz sees as wanting. We need to see how technology can help us extract greater value and connection from this information overload, or else we face what Horowitz characterizes as the "purely narcotizing dysfunction" and the "increased chance of anomie and normlessness" that come of facing simply too much information.[21]

So much information and so little sense of how it works together and where to go with it is part of our current epistemological malaise. What this looks like in the social sciences might be imagined by returning to the image of the beautiful Rose Reading Room at the New York Public Library. At nearly the length of a football field, it is furnished with two long rows of massive oak reading tables. Now imagine that each table has been assigned to three or four of the hundreds of different social concerns, from infant care to geriatric support. At the tables, researchers are carefully cutting out jigsaw pieces, representing their own studies, while at the same time copies of other jigsaw pieces, representing related studies, are continually being dropped off. The pieces would seem to be cut for a great number of puzzles or perhaps (some suspect) for one great puzzle, with the researchers who are working on their studies always uncertain about the consequences of their cuts. When these people pause from their cutting to arrange the pieces, they find that some pieces readily snap together, while other pieces, it is obvious from the expression on some of the faces, bring the very idea of the puzzle into question. And always there are too many pieces arriving at the table, as in truth roughly three thousand articles are published each month in the social sciences. Then there are all the papers presented at the endless stream of conferences staged around the world, the unpublished research reports commissioned by governments and private agencies, and on and on it goes. Now, what's missing from this picture are the public, although they are welcome to come in and watch, as they are welcome to use the university libraries where much of this work is ordinarily stored.[22]

What I am asking is that we explore whether we can improve the way we do and work with research to help to connect the puzzle pieces in

---

21. Ibid. The Holocaust Museum in Washington, D.C., exhibits the totalitarian capabilities of information technologies by showing that, in the 1930s, the Nazis were using early versions of IBM computers for the automated tracking of Jewish populations through census data.
22. *Social Sciences Citation Index.*

ways that make greater sense for the the public, related professions, researchers, and students. Current returns on public investment in the social sciences are bound to seem more difficult to defend in the face of corporations' deployment of technologies to manage, distribute, and increase the value of their knowledge resources in ways that help them and their clients know more of what needs to be known. And then there is the current push among conservative governments to compel public universities to use performance indicators and productivity measures to improve their accountability, which will only offer a finer take on the problem of what social-science research knowledge is about if it is not working in and on the world that exists beyond the careers of social scientists.

In this book I set aside the question of corporate organization and technological design, which I pursued in *Technologies of Knowing: A Proposal for the Human Sciences,* to explore the historical and epistemological reasons for using technology to improve the social sciences' contribution to public knowledge. This book asks how, within this emerging information economy, the academy can better support knowledge's public sector. It works through technology's potential contributions to what has been made and what can still be made of books and libraries, indexes and footnotes, encyclopedias and databases as vehicles of public knowledge. The driving ethic of this book remains deriving more good from what has already been produced in the public interest. It is not the same thing as convincing the public to invest in a new strain of unproven wheat, hoping it will produce another green revolution; it is, rather, that the social sciences are already producing warehouses full of what is claimed to be golden grain, grown for the benefit of humankind, but what, for all intents and purposes, merely feeds and seeds its own kind. If we really were to get knowledge onto people's tables, only to find that it fails to feed their minds and souls, and this is a real and pressing possibility, then we would need to stop and rethink what we are doing in the name of the social sciences. Such are the assumptions of this project on increasing the public value of the social sciences.[23]

My approach is to work with issues and instances, including foster children, science teaching, and crime rates, to pursue the possibilities of a more coherent and more comprehensible body of knowledge. My aim is to inspire discussion and action among both social scientists and the public. The lessons I draw from this historical and contemporary analysis are directed at increasing the flow between social-science research

---

23. John Willinsky, *Technologies of Knowing: A Proposal for the Human Sciences* (Boston: Beacon, 1999).

and public knowledge in ways that would further the place of knowledge within the democratic project, as a means of increasing people's participation in decision-making processes. Yet let me reiterate that neither the public value of social-science research nor the political force of coordinated bodies of information is a given. These ideas need to be thought through and tested. New formats, genres, apparatuses, and technologies for making more of the knowledge at hand need to be explored.

This book deals in the long-standing potential and promise of knowledge. I have no doubt that the public value of social-science research can be improved, if only in small increments, through the imaginative use of new technologies, matched by corresponding changes in how we go about doing social-science research. The very working out of these new forms is bound to change the nature of knowledge and, in turn, the basis of democratic self-determination. Given that the global expansion of democratic systems is underwritten by information economies that have a rather different agenda for knowledge than do the majority of those working in the social sciences, it seems a time for the defenders and benefactors of the public (knowledge) sector to ask whether there is not more that these knowing machines—this technology of systematic inquiry—can do for all of us.

Section I
Knowledge

Public Knowledge 2

I take "public knowledge" to fall somewhere between common sense and studied expertise. It is the knowledge picked up from newspapers and television, books and magazines; it's found in public libraries and on the web; it's what has survived from our school days. The laws, taxes, and other systems that work upon our lives count as public knowledge. So do familiar ideas of history, culture, and science. Some of it is trivial—like the fact that Bach and Beethoven were both German—and some of it helps make greater sense of the world—like knowing one's rights under the law. The public knowledge that interests me here, derived from the social sciences, is intended to bring that world into greater focus while identifying risks and possibilities, inequities and injustices. Think of how we imagine that "if this were known, no one would stand for it," or, "justice must be seen to be done." Public knowledge, then, is not only about what people can be generally expected to know, but also about their very right to know. Democracy depends on the quality of public knowledge. Public knowledge requires a certain freedom of expression, just as it depends on organized efforts to make that expression publicly available.[1]

Sometimes public knowledge breaks across the public's consciousness like a wave, often a wave generated by the full force of the media, as in the death of a celebrity or a health scare. Sometimes a considerable effort is needed to carry an idea into the public sphere. Think of the belated government response to the AIDS epidemic, which was finally triggered by such political and public theater as the "Silence = Death" campaign; or the web-based attack on Nike's treatment of overseas workers, which finally resulted in more vigilant operating policies for the corporation,

1. The *Index on Censorship*, a magazine dedicated to that critical component of public knowledge known as freedom of expression, publishes a national index on abuses of free speech, which currently begins with the Algerian murder of Berber singer Lounés Matoub and ends with the Zimbabwean government's virtual monopoly over the media: http://carryon.oneworld.org/index_oc/.

even as its president complained about being the poster boy for globalization.[2]

The value of taking social-science knowledge public dates to the early nineteenth century, although public knowledge has always been a political issue. In the United States, those conducting research for the social-reform movements discovered that government programs could be secured for impoverished children and widows by publicizing the case studies and statistics they had assembled on those who were suffering. These organizations took advantage of the growth in public communication that came with the development of a far more affordable press, educational outlets such as *National Geographic*, and greater access to public schooling. These reform efforts were supported by the public-spirited mission of the American Statistical Society—founded in 1839 with a constitution stating that "every rational reform must be founded on thorough knowledge"—and the Social Science Research Association, founded in 1865.[3]

The reform campaigns of the late nineteenth century were matched by "a complementary hunger for information and understanding at the grassroots level," according to historians Dietrich Rueschemeyer and Theda Skocpol, with "craftsmen, workers, and farmers, as well as professionals and businessmen engaged in self-education, creat[ing] reading groups and study groups, and us[ing] private and public libraries to advance their understanding of social change and social reform." Of course, there was a newness to such learning then, and that helped to infuse this near-golden era of public knowledge with a sense that a shared understanding could form the blueprint for a better world. It was also a time before social research was largely channeled into the closed loop of academic publication, a time before bureaucracies knew enough to guard knowledge of their operations closely.[4]

Today, social-reform movements take the form of special-interest groups, many of which adeptly mobilize public funding, opinion, and action through public-relations campaigns and media presence. The press's coverage of a critical issue can end up consisting of interviews

---

2. On more recent methods of virtual sit-ins conducted by "hacktivists," see Amy Hamon, "'Hacktivists' of All Persuasions Take Their Struggle to the Web," *New York Times*, October 31, 1998, A5.

3. Mark C. Smith, *Social Science in the Crucible: The American Debate over Objectivity and Purpose, 1918–1941* (Durham, N.C.: Duke University Press, 1994), 16–17.

4. Dietrich Rueschemeyer and Theda Skocpol, conclusion to *States, Social Knowledge, and the Origins of Modern Social Policies,* ed. Dietrich Rueschemeyer and Theda Skocpol (Princeton, N.J.: Princeton University Press, 1996), 298. See Rueschemeyer and Skocpol also on Émile Durkheim's idea of sociology and blueprints and Max Weber's insight on bureaucracies and knowledge (302, 308).

with the official spokespersons of the relevant and opposed interest groups serving as gladiatorial combatants in democracy's official spectator sport. If the issue is building logging roads through the wilderness, then expect to find the Wilderness Society pitted against the Intermountain Forest Industry Association, with the U.S. Forest Service in the middle. Meanwhile, Mothers against Drunk Driving (MADD) has proved to be an effective legislative force, and the Campaign for Working Families seems adept at putting late-term abortions at the forefront of strategically chosen election contests. The Children's Defense Fund uses elaborate economic models to show that investment in the health of children reduces government medical bills. The half-million-strong Sierra Club is divided in its drive to take a stand on immigration as an environmental issue, with extensive websites supporting both sides of the issue. There are now how-to books available on "policy entrepreneurship," which makes a business out of getting the public behind desired changes in government policy.[5]

Interest groups form around social and political issues with a refreshingly plainspoken partisanship of the sort that most politicians, carefully guided by their handlers, shy away from. The politics of public knowledge, then, is very much about the power of these interest groups. A front-page story in the *New York Times* tells it all: "So many independent interest groups are poised to spend large sums on advertising to influence elections ... that Republicans and Democrats alike fear the candidates may find themselves playing bit parts in their own campaigns." These interest groups use research and conduct polls; they undertake publicity campaigns and hire political lobbyists to give their views the currency of public knowledge; and they direct donations to candidates, knowing that spending the most wins in 94 percent of congressional races.[6]

Interest groups sponsor referenda, plebiscites, and ballot initiatives that amount to single-issue information campaigns directed at convincing people to act on what they now know as a result of the accompanying public-relations campaign. As a result of such activism prior to the 1998 elections, Alaska voted on making English the state's official

---

5. Marian Wright Edelman, "The Status of Children and Our National Future," *Stanford Law Policy Review* 1, no. 1 (fall 1989); John H. Cushman Jr., "An Uncomfortable Debate Fuels a Sierra Club Election," *New York Times*, April 5, 1998, A6; Nancy C. Roberts and Paula J. King, *Transforming Public Policy: Dynamics of Policy Entrepreneurship and Innovation* (San Francisco: Jossey-Bass, 1996).

6. Richard L. Berke, "Interest Groups Prepare to Spend on Campaign Spin," *New York Times*, January 11, 1998, A1, A14; Dale Bumpers, "How the Sunshine Harmed Congress," *New York Times*, January 3, 1999, WK9.

language, while Washington State considered whether to ban state-sponsored affirmative action, legalize medical uses of marijuana, criminalize late-term abortion, and raise the state's minimum wage. Such initiatives have proliferated in the 1990s, leading four states—Mississippi, Missouri, Oregon, and Wyoming—to place initiatives on the ballot that would make the referendum process itself more difficult. Interest groups are proving to be the vehicle of choice for getting behind political issues, for civic action, and for financial donation. The politics of sponsored public knowledge forms its own arguments for improving the general public's access to highly intelligible forms of social-science research. It could raise the level of argument among interest groups. It could provide or check on the misuse of research. It could serve those who harbor doubts while wondering whether there is not another perspective on the question at hand.[7]

THE SENSE OF "PUBLIC" AND "KNOWLEDGE"

This changing political landscape defines one of the "public" dimensions of the knowledge to which the social sciences could well make a greater contribution. We see that newspaper readership has been slowly going down, book sales have slipped (but only very recently), television still rules (if across more channels), and Internet use is accelerating rapidly. I do not attempt here a demographics of who is most likely to be interested in this contribution to public knowledge. My contention is principled—people have the right to know what is known in the publicly sponsored sense of social-science research—and markedly pragmatic—the knowledge is only as good as it works on, and is worked on, by public interests.

That what the social sciences do is already a form of public knowledge is also a concern of this project. Just how much public influence there is on research becomes apparent only in looking back over two or three generations of researchers. To appreciate what is "public" about the knowledge that the social sciences afford, one has to return to when, from the our vantage point, the tendency of social scientists to work *from* public knowledge and prejudices is readily apparent. Take the social-science research on "race relations" from between the world wars. Frank Füredi, a sociologist at the University of Kent, describes how during the 1930s in the pages of the distinguished *American Journal of Sociology* scholars were contributing to the "marginality" of colonial intellectuals.

---

7. Sam Howe Verhovek, "Growing Popularity of Ballot Initiatives Leads to Questions," *New York Times,* November 2, 1998, A20.

One *AJS* article from that period, "Eurasian in Shanghai," by H. D. Lansom, for example, concluded that "an intellectual training had been provided which enabled [colonial intellectuals] to understand Western ideas, but not the character formation which enabled them to function adequately in a dynamic competitive society." At best, Lansom could be said to bring a certain sympathetic aspect to this framing of what was otherwise a common prejudice in the public knowledge of the West at the time. When British anthropologist Bronislaw Malinowski wrote against "racial mixture" in the *Listener* during this period, his concerns lay not with common-enough themes of race purity and pollution but with the "social degradation" that people of mixed race suffered, although he also observed, sociologically speaking, that a "mixed race does not rise to the level of the higher parent-stock."[8]

From our vantage point, this work seems more than a little mired in the biases of the times. It is as if, in Marx's sense of ideology, the work of the researcher really was to take the common flow of ideas and anxieties among the ruling classes and dress them up with all the trappings of knowledge, which did, on occasion, introduce precious incremental gains on the side of reason and justice. The research could as easily represent a channeling and burnishing of popular prejudices, giving them a refined legitimacy on which policies and programs can be more firmly and more comfortably based. In this way, the social sciences have always taken their bearings from the public world and have always been engaged in nothing but creating forms of "public knowledge" for each age. My concern is that what the social sciences give back, in a public sense, is little except in the official contexts of the public world, such as government programs, court cases, and school-board deliberations. This becomes especially critical for the researchers who dare to determine and challenge popular and official prejudices, for, as engaged as they are in public knowledge, they can be safely ignored as blowing their horns of warning for their own ears.

Looking back over the research should also temper traditional ideas about the scientific accumulation of knowledge, with research contributing to increasing depth and breadth of understanding. The social sciences' particular engagement with public thinking tends to move on with the times. Its date stamp runs within a generation or two of researchers. I do not mean that there is no lasting scholarship or research in the social sciences. The social thinking of the dead, such as Marx and

---

8. H. D. Lansom and Bronislaw Malinowski, cited in Frank Füredi, *The Silent War: Imperialism and the Changing Perception of Race* (New Brunswick, N.J.: Rutgers University Press, 1998), 146, 150.

Malinowski, can serve us well as we rethink what is being made of our own times and how our own public concerns stand in relation to their thinking and times.

What is critical to the place of the public in knowledge is that researchers appreciate how, in effect, they are engaged in public-works projects, testing the quality of roads much traveled in ways that should help with democratic deliberations over where we should be headed. Researchers may imagine themselves to be working on permanent, lasting contributions to knowledge, and a few may well be doing so, but such aspirations need to be integrated with current responsibilities to advancing public knowledge, where their work is most likely to do some lasting good. The knowledge lives not as it accumulates, in some sort of continuous streaming forward, but only as it is reworked, rethought, and reinterpreted. Malinowski took what now seems to be a very small step on the question of race, but such points of analysis are part of how progress in public and academic knowledge is measured. Researchers work by the light both of the past and of their own lives in framing, articulating, and modeling, in the name of knowledge, what might otherwise be the blur of public traffic. My own generation of researchers, the flower children of the 1960s who worked their way into university positions a decade or two later, found their discipline's statistical determinations of the world simply wrongheaded. They favored forms of personal knowledge and adopted techniques such as ethnography, narrative, and life history to create a research paradigm around what was once a counter-culture frame of mind as an alternative to statistical and experimental research methods.

If this provides some sense of what is "public" about the public knowledge of concern to the social sciences, the reader may still ask, What then makes it "knowledge"? To say that something is "public knowledge" is to point to its widespread acceptance as fact. Public knowledge, in this sense, is wrapped up in traditional notions of the true and the real. What makes it knowledge, rather than information, is a judgment call that has to do with, perhaps, how well what is known fits within a greater understanding of some phenomenon. One person's knowledge may well be another's information, while connecting different sources of information may increase the chances of arriving at what seems like more of a body of knowledge. Fostering a public understanding of what divides researchers in their analysis of a social issue can augment public knowlege by providing a greater sense of the scope and factors potentially involved in such issues. There are, of course, many other public sources of understanding, if one thinks about the array of cultural experiences people turn to in giving meaning to their lives. The public knowledge that I am concerned with, especially as it could be better informed by the social sciences, then, is best thought of as but one of many resources in our efforts to fathom what life might be all about. I am tempted to claim that public knowledge makes a special contribution to the life of a democracy that sets it apart from other forms of knowing. But I think it more realistic to say that it is simply a way of identifying a particularly promising point of entry for the social sciences to improve their contribution to democratic forms of life.

If these are not the best of times for public knowledge, on occasion they are among the most interesting. I am thinking in particular of how special prosecutor Kenneth Starr's investigation of President Clinton produced a public-knowledge spectacle of stupefying proportions. Simply stated, people had unprecedented access to the minutiae of this legal investigation, including the subpoenaed videotaped testimony of the president of the United States before a grand jury, normally a confidential process. Starr's investigation ushered in another "era of betrayal with its public unfolding of the tender linen of our little lives," as poet Robert Kelly has described the McCarthy debacle of the 1950s. This, in the name of public knowledge.[9]

In this case, we might say that never have so many people known so much about a political situation, in all of its public and private dimensions. Never have people had such direct and unmediated access to the original sources of that knowledge. Four million people, not waiting to hear the highlights on the news, directly accessed Kenneth Starr's 445-page *Report of the Independent Counsel* on the Internet, and an additional 6 million people tuned in to the Internet broadcast of the president's videotaped testimony. This flow of information created a level of public knowledgeability that made the usual lineup of media commentators all the more redundant. All that exposure to the evidence put people in a position to judge, and judge they did, with the continuous polling and publication of their opinions adding to the public-knowledge loop.

Those behind the investigation and the report believed, it appears, that making a man's failings so thoroughly public could not help but destroy that man. Yet this relentless publicizing of every sordid detail finally led to a widespread public sense of "enough already!" This, in turn, led Republican politicians, determined to pursue the impeachment

---

9. Robert Kelly, "Are You Now or Have You Ever Been . . ." *New York Times Book Review,* October 11, 1998, 7.

of President Clinton, to turn their backs on the polls, offering their own check on this increasingly powerful form of public expression. Like a river whose course is permanently changed after the hundred-year flood, this torrent of public knowledge, even as it finally subsided, is bound to affect the public interest in knowing and acting on that knowledge. I take it as part of the ongoing democratic experiment in public knowledge and information technologies to which this book seeks to make its own modest contribution on behalf of the social sciences.

But let me leave aside the scandals of public knowledge for less sensational but no less important developments within the realm of knowing. Take Carl Malmud, an economist and Internet-software developer, who among his earlier nonprofit ventures launched a campaign that successfully persuaded the United States government to make public records available on the Internet. As a result of Malmud's efforts, what began as a trickle of documents placed online by the Securities and Exchange Commission and the U.S. Patent and Trademark Office soon grew into a steady stream in response to public interest in having ready access to this knowledge. The web is setting a new standard in public access to knowledge at an opportune time. The American Library Association has been expressing concerns over declining access to government materials and has called for a national information policy "to ensure the right of access." Ralph Nader, through his Public Citizen group, has sued the National Archives and Records Administration over the printing out and deletion of electronic records, arguing that keeping them in electronic form makes them far more easily searched by the public. Debates are ensuing over the race to map the human genome as the Cambridge University labs, freely publish their results while the American company, Human Genome Sciences, keeps what it finds secret and proprietary. The struggle over what knowledge belongs in the public domain will only grow with the development of new technologies that make it that much easier to offer up what is known on a global basis.[10]

When it comes to the question of how much knowledge humankind can bear, it is easy enough to conclude that apart from scandals, not a

---

10. John Markoff, "Eyes for the Mouse, Wheels for the Joystick," *New York Times*, September 23, 1998, C7; *Less Access to Less Information by and about the U.S. Government: A 1994 Chronology, January–June* (Washington: American Library Association, 1994); *White House Conference on Library and Information Services* (Washington: U.S. Government Printing Office, 1980), 42; Laurie Flynn, "Archives Wins Reprieve in Storing Electronic Records," *New York Times*, October 5, 1998, C4; Nicholas Wade, "Cambridge Laboratory Keeps Britain Ahead in Genome Stakes," *New York Times*, October 6, 1998, B12.

whole lot. People prefer keeping things simple. Public knowledge might be thought to suffer accordingly. However, when it comes to judging the intellectual capacities and interests of the public, the best-seller phenomenon can always be held up. The social sciences may be inspired to undertake a public-knowledge project by at least three examples I have come across recently.

First, there is the still unlikely example of Cambridge cosmologist Stephen Hawking, who explicated big bangs and black holes in *A Brief History of Time*, which rode the *London Times* best-seller list for 237 weeks, longer than any other book in any category. The success of the book, which is now available in thirty languages, surprised Hawking as much as anyone, given that, in his estimation, the book could serve as a good cram for a Ph.D. in theoretical physics. Certainly, many who purchased it have not read it, or at least not much of it, but Hawking has been convinced by the many readers who have spoken to him that they have picked up the "flavor of the intellectual quest for the basis of rational laws." Hawking goes on to argue for the democratic importance of this public interest. Given his faith that scientific progress is bound to continue at an ever-increasing rate, he feels "it is vital that we all take part in the debate about where we are going." He then adds, "We don't want the knowledge and the decisions to be left to a few experts." Such is my claim regarding why we need to do more to improve what the social sciences make available to public knowledge—not through the extraordinary success of a best-seller, mind you, but on a regular and systematic basis.[11]

A second instance, in striking contrast but nonetheless speaking to the public's appetite for greater knowledge, is the book series that began with *DOS for Dummies* in 1992. This initial title sold 4 million copies in thirty languages, and now there are some four hundred books in the series, laying out the intricacies of everything from the Internet to sex, with *Shakespeare for Dummies* about to be launched as I write. In seven years, John Kilchun, CEO of International Data Group Books Worldwide, has turned the concept into a way to achieve, in his words, "mass market literacy" based on people's drive to know. He sees the books as enabling people

---

11. Stephen Hawking, "Time Marches On," *Toronto Globe and Mail,* August 15, 1998, D5. Hawking's impact can be compared to the mixed findings of a recent National Science Foundation survey, in which 70 percent of the two thousand Americans questioned expressed an interest in science and technology—an increase over past surveys—while only 48 percent knew that the earth goes around the sun once a year: "Interest in Science High, but Knowledge Still Poor," *Chronicle of Higher Education,* July 17, 1998, A22. Not to be outdone by Cambridge, Oxford has made Richard Dawkins the Professor of Public Understanding of Science.

to do what they otherwise feel unable to do. "They all say the same thing," in Kilchun's estimation. "'I don't know where to begin, I don't have time to go to a classroom, I have to get something done now—today. What's going to handhold me through the process?'" Although a *Social Sciences for Dummies* has not yet appeared in the series, comparable, if intellectually upscale, series offer books on sociology and postmodernism, as well as Foucault, Marx, and other related figures.[12]

My third runaway-best-seller instance of the public's intellectual appetite is pure social science. University of Toronto economist David K. Foot's *Boom, Bust, and Echo: How to Profit from the Coming Demographic Shift* topped Canadian nonfiction charts for more than two years, standing head and shoulders above books on murder, adventure, and mayhem. Of course, Foot immodestly claims that "demographics explains two-thirds of everything," applying the principle to the impact of different cohorts— including Depression babies, baby boomers, and baby busters—on product demand, school enrollment, crime levels, house prices, and drug sales. The book works with concepts of probability and participation rates, offering readers formula-less appendixes on statistical forecasting techniques for demographics, products, and activities. This may be primarily social-science-for-profit, yet Foot moves the discussion from real-estate investments to the political questions Canadians face, particularly the constitutional negotiations between Quebec and the rest of Canada.[13]

Foot's position is that "demographics are too useful a tool for explaining the world to remain underground." So let it be said of the social sciences generally, especially when there are signs of public interest in a larger world of practical, political, and scientific ideas. Still, it took federal and provincial subsidies and a business journalist, Daniel Stoffman, to help Foot turn his demographic research into public knowledge. I would not want to see an end to such books, but I believe that there are other ways of realizing this vision that valuable sources of understanding from the social sciences should have more than an underground existence.[14]

---

12. John Kilchun, cited in Gordon Pitts, "Empire Building for Dummies," *Toronto Globe and Mail*, March 5, 1999, B5; see Richard Osborne and Borin Van Loon, *Sociology for Beginners* (Cambridge, England: Icon, 1996); and Jim Powell, *Postmodernism for Beginners* (London: Writers and Readers, 1998).
13. David K. Foot with Daniel Stoffman, *Boom, Bust, and Echo: How to Profit from the Coming Demographic Shift* (Toronto: Macfarlane Walter & Ross, 1996), 2. The book acknowledges the support of both federal and provincial granting agencies that subsidize literary and scholarly books in the public interest.
14. Ibid., 195.

PUBLIC RELATIONS AS PUBLIC KNOWLEDGE

Despite these encouraging signs of public interest in new sources and fields of knowledge, the prospects of public knowledge in this age of information should not be taken for granted, certainly not according to Herbert Schiller, a very active communications professor emeritus from San Diego State University. Schiller argues that rather than facing an information glut, as some would argue, what the public really suffers from is a form of "data deprivation" that keeps people from exercising greater control over their lives. In yet another instance of a world divided between the haves and the have-nots, corporations and governments collude against the interests of public knowledge, as Schiller sees it, to sustain the "largely invisible deficit of socially necessary information."[15] The increasing concentration of corporate control over communication channels as a result of deregulation is matched by the legacy of government secrecy, which according to Schiller, costs Americans some $14 billion annually.[16]

The reader may recognize Schiller's tune as one that MIT linguist and political gadfly Noam Chomsky has been playing to sizable audiences for some time. Chomsky insists that the corporate goal "from the beginning, perfectly openly and consciously, was 'control the public mind.'" To Chomsky, it seems obvious that "the public mind was seen as the greatest threat to corporations, from early in the century," with the corporations responding by hiring the likes of Edward Bernays—the original spin doctor and self-proclaimed inventor of the public-relations industry. On first setting up his consultancy in the 1920s, Bernays became convinced

---

15. Herbert I. Schiller, *Information Inequality: The Deepening Social Crisis in America* (New York: Routledge, 1996), 43. "The diminution of public expression and influence that can be found is not the consequence of a decline in national creativity or some other organic disability. It is the result of deliberate and successful efforts to reduce, even eliminate, the public realm in favor of the corporate sector" (67). Schiller notes how his case against corporations differs from the one Bill McKibben makes in *The Age of Missing Information* (New York: Random House, 1992) that the TV world that so many turn to fails to recognize both the sustainable limits of the larger world and its sensual pleasures. A second aspect of deprivation, this time following the global pattern of inequities, is found in William Wresch, *Disconnected: Haves and Have-Nots in the Information Age* (New Brunswick, N.J.: Rutgers University Press, 1992). And on information excess, see David Shenk, *Data Smog: Surviving Information Glut* (San Francisco: Harper, 1997).

16. Schiller, *Information Inequality*, 50. Schiller's point has recently been reinforced by U.S. senator Daniel Patrick Moynihan's denouncement of the government's cultish devotion to secrecy. Among other things, Moynihan points to the government's annual production of nearly a half million "top secret" documents, and this since the cold war ended: *Secrecy: The American Experience* (New Haven: Yale University Press, 1998).

that, as Chomsky puts it, "the manipulation of organized habits and opinions of the masses is the central feature of a democratic society." Yet Bernays's life speaks eloquently to just how complicated a mix exists between market capitalism and democratic rights, a mix that has much to do with what absorbs and constitutes public knowledge, just as it does with whether people are to be judged fooled or foolish.[17]

On Easter Sunday in 1929, to take a sterling example of Bernays's approach, he arranged for ten women in their Easter finest to stroll down New York's Fifth Avenue openly smoking cigarettes, which is precisely what decent women did not then do in public. His planted spokeswoman among them made it clear to reporters covering the Easter parade that this seemingly spontaneous "Torches of Freedom" march was a puff, if not a blow, for women's rights. He was, I should add, in the employ of Lucky Strike at the time. The publicity stunt made the front page across the country, and Bernays's employer was very happy at how, without the least tipping of its hand, women had been encouraged to smoke in public and smoking was associated with the fundamental American quality of freedom. This cigarettes-and-suffragettes association has since been recycled, of course, through the Virginia Slims ad campaign of the last decade. Today, young women are still blowing far too much smoke in the face of the official antismoking message, mainly it appears out of a drive for thinness, itself yet another gift of Madison Avenue public relations. Bernays may have claimed that public relations was all about "regimenting the public mind," but I see his work far more as a massaging of that mind, playing on its inclinations toward freedom and fashion in this case while changing what people knew of the world. Manipulation or persuasion, public relations or public knowledge—I realize that it can be a little hard to sort out at times.[18]

Where is the free press in this public relations' pursuit of public knowledge? Paid newspaper circulation in the United States is down 10 percent since a 1984 peak of 63.3 million readers, with the country's

---

17. Noam Chomsky, "Propaganda and the Control of the Public Mind," in *Capitalism and the Information Age: The Political Economy and the Global Communication Revolution,* ed. Robert W. McChesney, Ellen Meiksins Wood, and John Bellamy Foster (New York: Monthly Press, 1998), 180–81; Joseph Goebbels was among the readers of Edward Bernays's *Crystallizing Public Opinion* (1923): see Larry Tye, *The Father of Spin: Edward L. Bernays and the Birth of Public Relations* (New York: Crown, 1998); Malcolm Gladwell, "The Spin Myth," *New Yorker,* July 6, 1998.

18. Edward Bernays cited in Gladwell, "Spin Myth," 64. When Bernays was hired by Simon and Schuster and Harcourt Brace in 1930, he pulled a wonderful indirect marketing ploy for the book industry and the growth of public knowledge by encouraging architects and builders to construct bookshelves in new homes; Tye, *The Father of Spin,* 52; Carolyn Abraham, "Teen Girls Fight Fat with Fire," *Toronto Globe and Mail,* August 3, 1998, Al.

130,000 reporters now outnumbered by the roughly 150,000 PR consultants. The public relations industry spends roughly $10 billion a year to sustain America's attention and interest in its message. But then too, by some estimates as much as 40 percent of the day's news is drawn straight from press releases. Seeing the press and the public-relations industry as being in opposition may no longer be appropriate. For example, Liss Jeffrey, journalist and associate director of the McLuhan Program in Culture and Technology at the University of Toronto holds that "journalism, business, government and public relations are converging within a fundamental culture of marketing that is so pervasive it's invisible." They all have a message to market, and marketing today is all about pushing information into the public realm so that it sticks. Still, when *New Yorker* writer Malcolm Gladwell recently reviewed the "spin myth" of the public-relations industry, he was led to wonder whether "it makes just as much sense to assume ... the reason spin is everywhere today is that it *doesn't* work."[19]

Another reason for concern about the assault on "public expression and influence" that Schiller and Chomsky portray is the increasing corporate concentration that exists within the publishing industry. This economic control speaks to the need for new channels of public knowledge. Something has been lost, as Chomsky suggests at one point, with the disappearance of, for example, so many of the eight hundred union newspapers that were still printing well into the 1950s, in which workers talked about their struggles and frustrations, recipes and ball games, voicing as well, in too many cases, a certain lack of support for racial integration and women's rights. Creating vital sources of public knowledge, whether in new or old mediums, can renew and strengthen what unions have always stood for, if always imperfectly, in the fight for social justice and human equality.[20]

Yet another source of undue public-relations influence on the state of public knowledge today is the Public Broadcasting Service (PBS), which I took as something of a model for a "corporation for public knowledge" that I proposed in my earlier book. In a recent critique by B. J. Bullert, a professor of communications at the American University, PBS has been accused of shirking its original mandate under the weight of increasing corporate sponsorship. As a proof of what is at risk, Bullert holds up the report of the original Carnegie Commission that gave birth

---

19. Audit Bureau of Circulations, cited in Felicity Barringer, "Paid Circulation in U. S. Continues to Decline," *New York Times,* November 3, 1998, C7; Liss Jeffrey cited in Guy Crittenden, "Flack Attack," *Toronto Globe and Mail,* October 31, 1998, D3; Gladwell, "Spin Myth," 67.
20. Chomsky, "Propaganda," 187.

to PBS in 1967, which declared the intent to offer "a forum of controversy and debate." Some thirty years later, Bullert sees the network offering significantly diminished opportunities for independent, controversial, and provocative documentaries, such as *Waco: The Rules of Engagement,* because they are judged unlikely to attract corporate support. He responds with his hopes for reviving "the dream of a genuinely non-commercial oasis in a profit-driven society." Such are the goals of public-knowledge advocacy.[21]

Clearly the viability of public knowledge as a political and democratic force is nothing to be complacent about. The struggle for people's hearts and minds among the Edward Bernayses and Noam Chomskys, at this point calls for innovative measures that keep the question of public knowledge before people as an important issue. It is not that corporate logos or pizza commercials should be dismissed as inherently antithetical to public expression or democratic processes, but that what gets sponsored and funded needs to be continually challenged for what it makes of and gives to public knowledge.

PUBLIC PARTICIPATION

One can be forgiven for turning to the Internet as a source of hope for public knowledge, given that it is still in its formative years. It is certainly proving to be the inspiration of strange new political creatures, such as "E The People," that would electronically restore the voice of the people in government processes. This project recently had Alex Sheshunoff touring the United States with a bus and a laptop, selling people, newspapers, nonprofit organizations, and corporations on the value of the E The People website, which enables citizens to sign existing petitions, create new ones, or write to officials at any level of government, thanks to the site's handy identification of who's who among the many bureaucratic structures, both at the local level and in Congress. As I write, forty-five newspapers have agreed to link their websites to E The People, which could open the flow, one imagines, from the public knowledge offered by the press to the political action of letting one's voice be known among government officials. It will be interesting to see whether people's political participation will increase as more and more such links are in place, and the world shrinks to no more than six mouse-clicks of separation.[22]

---

21. B. J. Bullert, "Public TV: Safe Programming and Faustian Bargains," *Chronicle of Higher Education,* September 18, 1998, B7.
22. Rick Lyman, "Got a Cause and a Computer? You Can Fight City Hall," *New York Times,* October 3, 1998, A12; E The People, http://www.e-thepeople.com.

There is still much to be said in favor, as well, of the continuities of traditional public spaces for public knowledge. Along with the libraries and bookstores, especially the used ones, I am thinking of such places as, in my case, Yoka's Coffee, where I often end my afternoons sometimes quietly, sometimes amid the café's flow of ideas about urban development, aboriginal rights, linguistic origins, educational decline, lunar eclipses, and the grinding of herbs. But the highly political coffeehouse forums that flourished in a thousand shops in early-eighteenth-century London are not what the Starbucks coffee franchise is merchandizing these days, and my encounters at Yoka's are, at best, at the margins of a public sphere of influence and impact, compared to those earlier forums.[23] Whether in electronic or store-front settings, we now seem far better served as a republic of consumers than as an engaged public of concerned citizens.

The question of what to make of a disengaged public was raised by the political commentator Walter Lippmann earlier in the twentieth century when he named the "phantom public" that had come to inhabit American democracy. The question for Lippmann was "whether it is possible for men to find a way of acting effectively upon highly complex affairs by very simple means." This is really to ask whether democracy is possible, assuming, as Lippmann did, that people's "political capacity is simple." As a result of such doubts, he began placing his hopes in elected representatives working with the expertise of the newly emerging professional classes, representatives whom Lippmann could not resist making wonderfully Caesarlike: "They initiate, they administer, they settle." Against such powers, all that democracy can ask, according to Lippmann, is for a little accountability in plainly recording and objectively measuring, as he put it, the acts of public officials and industrial directors. Public accountability, within this vision of social engineering, might increase the political participation of the social sciences, but it would surely reduce what public knowledge might do to increase people's political capacities and democratic participation.[24]

By contrast, I am calling on the social sciences to create a freestanding resource out of social-science expertise that both politician and public can readily consult. If I seem to exaggerate people's political capacity, as Lippmann might claim, I can respond only by asking, how else are we

23. On coffeehouse society, see Jürgen Habermas, *The Structural Transformation of the Public Sphere: An Inquiry into a Category of Bourgeois Society*, trans. Thomas Burger (Cambridge: MIT Press, 1989), 32–33, 42–43.
24. Walter Lippmann, "The Phantom Public," in *The Essential Lippmann: A Political Philosophy for Liberal Democracy* , ed. Clinton Rossiter and James Lare (New York: Random House, 1963), 89–90, 92; Walter Lippmann, "The Dilemma of Liberal Democracy," in *The Essential Lippmann*, 22.

to test and expand that capacity if not by experimenting with ways of increasing the store of public knowledge and observing what happens? I think social scientists also have a good deal to gain by rethinking how their knowledge is currently managed, directed, coordinated, and distributed. This public-knowledge project for the social sciences is about improving the quality of knowledge as well as providing for greater participation in the public sphere and democratic processes.

Two things have changed since Lippmann first worried about how much reality the public can bear, let alone act upon. The first is that we have seen and felt what can come of expert control over the planning, management, and completion of public projects. I'm referring here not to European fascism but to some of the best-laid ideas of American urban planners that have gone awry, leaving such overwhelming monuments of miscalculation as Chicago's Robert Taylor Homes project. Initiated in 1959 and stretching across a mile of urban landscape, this project is now home to some 11,000 people, most of whom feel trapped there. After it was built, the experts moved on to other ideas, and the project was essentially abandoned along with its residents, who had little choice but to ride its spiral of decline. The project is now among the 100,000 apartments across the United States that are scheduled to be razed under the federal program hauntingly known as Hope VI.[25]

The second thing that has changed since Lippmann's day is how we understand this thing known as the "public." In a recent collection of essays on the "phantom public sphere," Bruce Robbins, an English professor at Rutgers University, calls for the recognition of "alternative publics" and "counter-publics" made up of those who are excluded from the phantom of a homogeneous whole public. This was no less so when Lippmann wrote, but it has taken a sharply articulated politics of identity to make this range of publics critical to the democratic project. How this diversity works and how it can continue to move toward greater democratic means and ends would be measures of what the social sciences have to offer public knowledge. The very diversity of knowledge that the social sciences represent is one starting point in supporting alternative and counter-publics. As I've stated, what I seek, within the social sciences and beyond, is not the great and singular unity of knowledge but only a way of improving the comprehensibility of this diverse understanding among a wider public.[26]

25. Pam Belluck, "Razing the Slums to Rescue the Residents," *New York Times,* September 6, 1998, A1.
26. Bruce Robbins, introduction to *The Phantom Public Sphere,* ed. Bruce Robbins (Minneapolis: University of Minnesota Press, 1993), xvii. Robbins also points to Jürgen Habermas's historical tale of how the public sphere was once the creation of

But will anyone care? The question is something of a constant in this project, and although I will return to this theme in chapter 10, on the politics of knowledge, my first response is to acknowledge that, no, people don't as a rule ask what's new in the research these days. I think people have learned not to expect a comprehensible, engaging exchange of ideas with the social sciences, just as the producers of this knowledge have learned to direct their work to a select band of colleagues. Yet there are those encouraging examples of people who have proved interested in the qualities of public knowledge offered by the social sciences and related disciplines. As I write, for example, the residents of Framingham, Massachusetts, are celebrating the fiftieth anniversary of the Framingham Heart Study, in which ten thousand residents of this New England town volunteered to participate in what became a multigenerational study that has outlived its original twenty-year plan. The very term "risk factor" was coined out of this study, which is sponsored by the United States Public Health Service. Framingham resident Elaine Prince, who went with her father for the first heart study in 1948, summed up her experience with pride: "Mainly, it's an honor to participate in something that's going to benefit people long after we're gone.[27]

The Framingham Heart Study represents something of a research bargain, even as a $47 million government investment over half a century. Close to a thousand scientific papers, many using social-science techniques, have resulted from the study, reporting major findings on the impact of smoking, cholesterol, obesity, diabetes, high blood pressure, exercise, and menopause—all of which have contributed much to the public's knowledge of health and well-being. People do care to know, and they do take to heart the knowledge supported by major public-education campaigns. The Framingham research is credited with contributing to a 50 percent reduction in fatalities from cardiovascular disease over the last thirty years. We live with the research results every day through public campaigns on eating right that have become part of our daily publicity diet.

What needs to be noted, and perhaps celebrated, here is that public knowledge itself proves to have been the magic pill in this successful fight against heart disease. One finds former U.S. surgeon general C. Everett Koop building a health-information website on the motto, "No prescription is more valuable than knowledge," only to run into serious

the bourgeoisie, a democratic promise won and then lost, although Robbins allows that this is "a usefully mobilizing fiction."

27. Carey Goldberg, "A Town of Guinea Pigs Celebrates Its Contribution to Longer Life," *New York Times,* September 27, 1998, Y12.

questions about the financing of that advice. And how is all of this public knowledge working for people's health? One doctor, Lloyd M. Krieger, writes that "patients who see me are quoting from medical articles they found on the Internet as often as they are citing commercials for a wonder drug."[28]

If the most massive of public-knowledge health campaigns has yet to put an end to smoking, we can still claim that getting the word out on cigarettes, as well as on diet, exercise, and safety, may be as effective at saving lives as any given medication or treatment. Such life-saving knowledge forms only a small part of what the social sciences have to offer the public, principally through the field of epidemiology, and I suggest that the public have a much wider range of interests and activities than the critical work of maintaining their health.

Examples abound of the influence of research on public knowledge that go well beyond what it takes to stay healthy. Think of the idea of "significant others" and the related concept of peer pressure, first introduced by social psychologist George Herbert Mead in the early 1900s. Anthropologist Margaret Mead's work from the 1930s helped people to appreciate cultural diversity among families, creating a basis for multiculturalism. Sociologist Robert K. Merton's work from the 1950s has given us the common caution against "self-fulfilling prophecies." I will have more to say on the impact of the social sciences, but let me just state here that the public is willing and able to take up the results of scholarship and research that help it make sense of the greater and lesser worlds in which we all live. People are interested in new ways of handling challenges, whether how communities support the homeless or how running-shoe manufacturers treat their overseas labor force.[29]

However, I am not content to leave this process alone. Something seems missing from how this knowledge goes public, something that has to do with a convergence of public knowledge, democratic rights, and new technologies, something that has to do with people's right to know. On this theme, Rabbi Julia Neuberger recently turned the Institute of Information Scientists Annual Lecture in London into a passionate plea for making health information more widely available. She insists that

---

28. C. Everett Koop, http://drkoop.com; Lloyd M. Krieger, "What's Right about Drug Ads," *New York Times,* December 7, 1998, A27. Krieger also sees that the $1.2 billion spent annually on advertising by the pharmaceutical industry contributes to the education of patients.

29. George Herbert Mead, *Mind, Self, Society* (Chicago: University of Chicago Press, 1934); Margaret Mead, *Sex and Temperament in Primitive Societies* (New York: Morrow, 1935); Robert K. Merton, *Social Theory and Social Structure,* rev. ed. (New York: Free Press, 1968).

"we still barely recognize the need that exists for information to be made freely available if the public is to be able to make proper decisions about health and other issues, for that matter, in the public sector." She is equally concerned about patients' rights to their own medical records, as well as to the latest research related to their conditions. Only when these rights are granted can we begin to talk about people playing a meaningful part in their own health care. Neuberger has actively promoted innovative ways of getting the word out on research, such as the King's Fund Consensus Conference on breast cancer, which brought together researchers and the public in the mid-1980s, "leading to changes in practice and certainly changes in patient attitude." This is more than aiding the already educated, as Neuberger is also concerned with providing much better information about breast cancer for people with "learning difficulties," as she puts it. This seems to me an exemplary instance of a responsible information service, and, as she notes, it can make a significant difference in how a life is lived: "The attitude which said that people with learning difficulties must be told what to do, and not given choices does seem to be gradually disappearing."[30]

Here, then, is an ethic for public knowledge. People have the right to consult the available sources of knowledge and understanding; they have a right to expect some light from such sources. Although the vigilant application of research ethics in both medical research and the social sciences has vastly improved over the years, its focus remains on protecting the research subject rather than protecting the public's right to gain from the proposed value of the research.

Research on health issues has been an area in which public access to knowledge has seen considerable growth. Ten years ago, ABC World News Tonight gave little coverage to personal health, but it now regularly devotes 5 percent of its broadcast time to such items. Many newspapers have taken to running weekly health columns for their readers under the theme of "news you can use." Doctors can now get daily medical updates delivered to their desktop computers, while being assured that "everything known to medical science is now available in this new form." Medcast Networks is one such service that offers "just-in-time Continuing Medical Education and split-second access to trial recruitment and pipeline updates," as well as a "patient-tutorial system that instantly provides animated graphics of disease-states, as well as surgical devices, and pharmacological treatment options." This new service, with its claim to millions of dollars of development and years of research, promises to

---

30. Julia Neuberger, "Information for Health: Whose Information Is It?" *Journal of Information Science* 24, no. 2 (1998): 69, 70, 72.

make both doctor and patient party to a subscription-based channel directing medical research into the reservoir of public knowledge.[31]

Health research may be leading the way not only with patients' information rights but also with the ethical responsibilities of the research community and the technologies that can help get the word out. Still, I see no reason why these same sensibilities should not be applied to social-science research on matters of governance, justice, welfare, education, and culture, especially as the knowledge is often generated at public expense. As it now stands, this research reaches the public, if at all, through a middle person—a knowledge broker who searches, synthesizes, and summarizes the relevant work in a newspaper article, a commissioned report, or a book. These helpful guides are necessary to the degree that public access does not figure in the thinking of the research community. These act as a buffer, leaving the research community to continue talking among themselves. By contrast, I hold that more direct channels of communication between researchers and the public are no less a right and a responsibility of both parties, if only for the value and meaning they bring to the knowledge at issue.

We now stand before a new medium that has the power to transform public access to knowledge by a substantial factor, much as the printing press did centuries ago. What the printing press was to the library and bookstore, so the Internet is to the home and workplace. The Internet has a potential that we need to explore and press, as if the burgeoning body of social-science research, in all of its diversity, contestation, and contradictions, might still develop into the public resource that many researchers assumed it was all about in the first place. The value of this knowledge is at stake.

The next two chapters address the current urgency and historic momentum of this public-knowledge project. Knowledge is now backed by big business in ways that obviously pose dangers to public interests in knowing, with obvious importance for the future of the universities. After considering the business of knowledge in chapter 3, in chapter 4 I offer a brief history of how knowledge has been brought to order in an age-old struggle, from the earliest libraries to the latest indexes, that calls once more for clever uses of current technologies, if these technologies are to prove a lasting friend to public knowledge.

---

31. "Bystander News," *Toronto Globe and Mail*, September 5, 1998, D6; Medcast Networks advertisement, *New York Times*, October 5, 1998, C14.

Knowbiz Economies 3

Where once cities were bound by industrial landscapes of smokestacks and rail yards, they are now marked by sealed-glass towers that tele-operate a global system of factories and plants. The new world order is all about information acting at a distance. It currently takes an annual injection of $500 billion worth of information technology (in a meld of hardware, software, and people) for the United States to hold its central place within this global order, with the IT industry now the nation's largest business. Although the current service economy certainly has a discouragingly large "Want fries with that?" sector, knowledge is at the forefront when it comes to the services of finance, media, law, health, technology, and education. The electronic network is the assembly line of the Information Age. Data are assembled into chunks of information before being machined and finished as quantities of knowledge. And knowledge is the commodity of the day. One may wonder how long it will be before forms of knowledge are listed with soybeans and pork bellies on the Chicago futures market. But all of my questions concern the fate of public knowledge in this knowledge-market economy.[1]

The initiation of a knowledge-based economy was the unsung story of the 1960s. The early years of that heady decade saw the launching of *Datamation*, a journal that made information processing its business. What were identified for the first time as "knowledge industries" by Princeton economist Fritz Machlup had by that point captured a quarter of the U.S. gross national product. It was not long before management guru Peter Drucker was pointing out that "knowledge workers" constituted the largest segment of the workforce. By the 1970s, Harvard sociologist Daniel Bell announced the coming of the postindustrial society, and it could be said that the character of knowledge, by virtue of its economic

---

1. The computing and telecommunications industry grew by 57 percent between 1990 and 1997, with sales at $866 billion. See Steve Lohr, "Information Technology Field Is Rated Largest U.S. Industry," *New York Times*, November 18, 1997, C12.

and technological place in our lives, had changed. This burgeoning knowledge trade was driven, Stanford social analyst Thomas Sowell observes, by an increasing dependence on what others know: "We are all in the business of selling and buying knowledge from one another, because we are so profoundly ignorant of what it takes to complete the whole process of which we are a part."[2]

Knowledge has become the defining term of economic development. On a global scale, the Organization for Economic Cooperation and Development (OECD) claims that its analysis of "economic and social development shows clearly *that knowledge and the way we use it* are becoming central to our prosperity and success as societies." The World Bank has adopted "Knowledge is development" as its recent theme. Its *World Development Report* for 1998 insists that countries that fail to make knowledge their top priority face the bleakest of futures. It warns against "information constraints" and "information failures," as if they were new strains of a deadly economic virus. It also holds that real diseases and health problems are best fought by knowledge. Unfortunately, the report pays little mind, according to reporter John Stackhouse, to traditional knowledge systems that are increasing in use, from organic farming to Hindu medicine. The World Bank claims that half of the considerable difference in economic growth between South Korea and Ghana over the past three decades can be attributed to the investment in the right kinds of knowledge.[3]

The "knowbiz" is the new engine of economic growth. Corporations now employ a "chief knowledge officer" to work in tandem, presumably, with the chief information officer. The "knowledge management services" industry is growing into a multi-billion-dollar enterprise. The SAS Institute of Cary, North Carolina ("Turning Data into Pay Dirt"), invests $200 million annually in research and development on decision-support software. Financial analysts who conduct research on companies' stock prospects earn salaries of $350,000 to $10 million, and a know-corp like Hoover's, which serves up mostly free information on

2. Fritz Machlup, *Production and Distribution of Knowledge in the United States* (Princeton: Princeton University Press, 1962); Drucker's statistic is based on census figures for "professional, managerial, and technical people": Peter Drucker, *The Age of Discontinuity: Guidelines to Our Changing Society* (New York: Harper & Row, 1968), 264; Daniel Bell, *The Post-industrial Society: A Venture in Social Forecasting* (New York: Basic Books, 1973), 44; Thomas Sowell, *Knowledge and Decisions* (New York: Basic Books, 1980), 48.
3. OECD, cited in Tom Alexander, "Information Needs: OECD Perspective," in *Knowledge Bases for Education Policies* (Paris: OECD, 1996), 14, original emphasis; World Bank, *World Development Report* (1998), cited in John Stackhouse, "Knowledge Key to Progress: World Bank," *Toronto Globe and Mail,* October 5, 1998, A12.

14,000 companies to some 2 million people, is valued at $160 million. The typical knowledge maven of the business world predicts that "the best forms of the future will be those in which everyone creates, shares, and uses knowledge instead of hoarding it.... Knowledge is everybody's job."[4]

Charles Leadbeater, one of the new "portfolio workers, armed with a laptop, a modem, and some contacts" who define this economy, sings the praises of this new knowing age as a convergence of economic, political, personal interests and hopes: "The goal of politics in the twenty-first century should be to create societies that maximize knowledge, the wellspring of economic growth and democratic self-governance. Markets and communities, companies and social institutions, should be devoted to that larger goal. Financial and social capital should be harnessed to the goal of advancing and spreading knowledge. That will make us better off, more in charge of our lives and better able to look after ourselves."[5]

What sort of knowledge is driving this economy? Potato chip manufacturers like Frito-Lay are finding that their competitive advantage lies not in taste or even in fat content but in the micromarketing information compiled from the sale of one hundred products placed in 400,000 stores. Similarly, Sears, Roebuck found that the way ahead in the 1990s was better information rather than better prices. "We have spent enormous time on information—even if it is bad," a vice president reports, and morale, sales, and service records all improved as a result. Sears pursued this path with such enthusiasm that it soon ran up against the limits to information and its oversell.[6]

Not to be left behind in this mad pursuit of knowbiz, my university now offers workshops on "competitive intelligence," which is not about excelling at chess or fencing but about using data mining and other knowledge-management tools that enable the "gathering, analyzing and using [of] information about competitors and the business environment." Such is the commercial success story of the social sciences in a knowledge-based economy. And such is my reason for thinking about a

---

4. Gretchen Morgenson, "So Many Analysts, So Little Analysis," *New York Times,* July 18, 1999, B1; Richard A. Oppel Jr., "A Company Short on Buzz Long on Results," *New York Times,* July 21, 1999, C1; Tom Davenport and Larry Prusak, in an interview on their new book, *Working Knowledge: How Organizations Manage What They Know* (Cambridge: Harvard Business School, 1997), in the WWW Virtual Library on Knowledge Management, http://www.brint.com/km/davenport/working.htm.

5. Charles Leadbeater, *Living on Thin Air: The New Economy* (New York: Viking, 1999), cited in *New Statesman,* July 12, 1999, 28.

6. Jessica Keyes, "The Smart Business," in *Technology Trendlines* (New York: Van Nostrand Reinhold, 1995); Jennifer Steinhauer, "Time to Call a Sears Repairman," *New York Times,* January 15, 1998, C1, C3.

political economy of knowledge in which the social sciences play a far more important role in strengthening the place of knowledge in the public sector.

The knowledge boom is not, of course, the result of some evolutionary leap forward in intelligence or wisdom on the part of humankind. It is the product of rapid improvements in the ability to move, store, process, and organize data, information, and knowledge. The dramatic drop in costs, matched by huge increases in speed, has produced an economy devoted to flipping data into information and, Rapunzel-like, spinning off knowledge. The great irony of the age of information is that this abundance is driven by technical capacity rather than intellectual desire, and this phenomenal increase in computing power has not yet led to demonstrable increases in workplace productivity. But such details are hardly going to deter those who are convinced that "there's no biz like the knowbiz"[7]

Of course, knowledge has always been the backbone of business. In fact, when was the drive to know not a basic human need? The first and most persistent question our children pose is "Why?" and surely this wanting to know why never really leaves us, even as we learn better than to ask. It persists even as the answers rarely satisfy that drive to know. If "knowledge" has always been an abiding desire and an elusive source of consolation, if it has always enabled one person to do business with another, then what is this current noise about a knowledge economy all about? More specifically, what does this change mean for the most dedicated of knowledge enterprises—the university? How can the university's traditional manner of producing and sharing knowledge continue unscathed amid such changes?

There's no question that the universities are still major players in this knowledge economy, although this news has been a source as much of despair as of delight across the different faculties of the university. My interests lie in encouraging the social sciences to join the side of the

---

7.   In 1960, the unit cost of processing 1 million operations was seventy-five dollars, but by 1990 that figure had fallen to less than one-hundredth of a cent: see Manuel Castells, *The Rise of the Network Society*, vol. 1, *The Information Age: Economy, Society, and Culture* (Cambridge, Mass.: Blackwell, 1996), 45. For a business review of the knowledge economy, see Thomas Stewart's *Intellectual Capital: The New Wealth of Organizations* (New York: Doubleday, 1997). Stewart includes figures that place the information sector of the economy at 15 percent of the total picture (from *Business Week*, 1994), down from earlier figures ranging as high as 46 percent, whereas he computes "knowledge workers" (professional, technical, managerial, sales, and clerical) at currently more than 50 percent over the labor force. His encouraging thesis: "Information and knowledge are the thermonuclear competitive weapons of our time" (ix).

public sector of this economy by gearing its production for that sector into a more conducive form for direct and immediate public consumption. For the danger otherwise is not only that the social sciences will suffer a further loss of public support but also that other segments of the university will fail to learn from this new civic-spirited approach to knowledge, thereby missing out in their efforts to make the public contribution they have always promised, if too rarely delivered. There is too much at stake for the universities to sit back, holding to their privileged, landscaped grounds, while the private sector increasingly monopolizes this knowledge economy.

In America, the 2.5 million people employed in the country's 2,125 four-year colleges (a quarter of which are private) represent more than the total workforce of the auto, steel, and textile sectors combined. The postsecondary education industry, which brings in $180 billion to $250 billion, now accounts for close to 3 percent of the country's economy, which is three times the share it held at midcentury. Higher education stands as a "mature industry," according to Arthur Levine, president of Teachers College at Columbia University. But, as if to prepare his faculty for the introduction of performance indicators and other measures once foreign to academic life, he points out that with such maturity come greater public expectations of accountability, productivity, and efficiency. Such measures are typically focused on degrees granted, levels of research funding, and publication counts, but one might also wonder how this maturity could be directed at moving the knowledge that the university produces beyond the education of its students and the feeding of further research, into more public domains, in the case of the social sciences at least. I dare not, except mockingly, name this a vast market opportunity for publicly supported, value-added research knowledge, but I do think we want to nimbly avoid the fate that follows maturity by coming to the rescue of the public sector and routing a total private-sector takeover of the "knowledge thing."[8]

One would think that a flourishing knowledge economy would delight scholars. It might seem as if the footrace planners of this economy set up the finish line across the road from the university's lemonade stand (industrial park). Yet something has changed to put many faculty off,

---

8. The college's preparatory place is secure in this new knowledge economy, with a recent Canadian Broadcasting Corporation News poll, for example, finding that 75 percent of the 1,307 people surveyed affirmed the economic necessity of college in today's world: see Karen Arenson, "Why College Isn't for Everyone," *New York Times*, August 31, 1997, El; Arthur Levine, "How the Academic Profession Is Changing," *Daedalus* 126, no. 4 (fall 1997): 2. For an exposé on workloads, see Charles Sykes, *ProfScam: Professors and the Demise of Higher Education* (New York: St. Martin's, 1990).

even if the modern university has never been as free of economic and political entanglements with the world beyond the campus as some would imagine. Once, the university was simply the benefactor of corporate patronage, which in the glory days of late-nineteenth-century American capitalism gave rise to Cornell, Johns Hopkins, Stanford, Chicago, and others. Today, one finds a different sort of corporate patronage. Faculty engage in patenting, licensing, and consulting, as well as creating spin-offs and start-ups with stock options and strategic alliances. The university's trademark protection on knowledge has lapsed, and the university's response, in some quarters, has been to declare itself, as the current phrase goes, "open for business." Knowledge has gone retail.[9]

We have come a long way since Cardinal John Henry Newman, recently appointed rector to the new Catholic University in Dublin in 1852, made liberal education the very idea of the university. "Any kind of knowledge, if it really be such," he wrote with the utmost certainty, "is its own reward." In his influential *The Idea of a University*, he set out the educational goals of "intellectual excellence" and "inward endowment" set within the common-room comforts of "a pure and clear atmosphere of thought." The university was about making gentlemen, as he put it, "of cultivated intellect, a delicate taste, a candid, equitable, dispassionate mind, a noble and courteous bearing in the conduct of life." In a masterly rhetorical stroke, he opposed the liberality of this learning to the otherwise servile concerns of what we call today "learning a living." For my part, I only want to consider whether that knowledge-in-itself could simply be made more widely available. Going public with what we know is yet another end in itself for knowledge. After all, what comes of a liberal education, according to Newman, is the fulfillment of the "duty that we owe to human society," which includes "facilitating the exercise of political power" and other "professional interests." In one sense, I ask no more of social scientists than Newman did of his students' education.[10]

Certainly, Newman's bones must have been rattled by the *Economist*'s 1997 extended survey of today's university, under the title "The Knowledge Factory." The article positioned the university as a "major agent of

---

9. Richard Hofstadter, "The Revolution in Higher Education," *Paths of American Thought*, ed. Arthur M. Schlesinger Jr. and Morton White (Boston: Houghton Mifflin, 1963), 275.

10. John Henry Newman, *The Idea of a University* (New Haven: Yale University Press, 1996), 77–78, 89–90, 119, 126.

economic growth." The federal research funding that dominates the university (60 percent of all research funding in the United State) is more and more dedicated to "mission-oriented spending," as the *Economist* put it, rather than to basic science. In the sciences, new research centers unabashedly solve problems faced by today's industries. The lab becomes an incubator for the knowledge economy while scrambling for soft, venture-driven money. The result, in the words of the *Economist*, is a multitude of "peri-university institutions—research institutes, think-tanks, consultancies, and campus-based companies—organized loosely around the campus and making opportunistic connections with each other." As a result, the breakthrough excitement on campus is often focused on the art of the (partnership) deal. The *Economist* admonishes the faculty of the new knowledge factory that "their right—no, their duty—to be accountable to no one" has lapsed, while all and all it's "nice work, so long as the taxpayers are willing to pay for it."[11]

The university's response to such talk is not so much mixed as divided across the campus between those who are and those who are not participating in this new economy. The pure and applied sciences have the advantage of ground-floor entry, as they slip into what is unimaginatively called Mode 2 knowledge production. The shift to Mode 2 is marked by problem solving rather than curiosity-driven research priorities (Mode 1). Mode 2 is transdisciplinary in focus, given to linking university and commercial interests while proving to be far more socially accountable and collaborative than previous scientific research.[12]

Yet this convergence of epistemologies and economies can prove confusing in its application. The Xerox Corporation gave a million dollars not too long ago to the business school at the University of California at Berkeley to establish a Distinguished Professor of Knowledge position. The first appointee of this endowed chair is Ikujiro Nonaka, best known for coauthoring *The Knowledge-Creating Company: How Japanese Companies Create the Dynamics of Innovation*. The question of where knowledge is created and generated is bound to unsettle those who once imagined that they had cornered the market on knowledge.

---

11. "The Knowledge Factory," *Economist*, October 4, 1997, 4, 12, 16, 19, 22.
12. Michael Gibbons et al., *The New Production of Knowledge: The Dynamics of Science and Research in Contemporary Societies* (London: Sage, 1994): "Socially distributed knowledge production is tending towards the form of a global web whose numbers of inter-connections are being continuously expanded by the creation of new sites of production" (14). Gibbons et al. also refer to a shift from the idea of intellectual coherence, which is being lost to the transdisciplinarity of this knowledge production, to institutional coherence (83).

Certainly, the idea of a professor of knowledge caught many at the university off guard. "The idea is a little bizarre," observed philosopher Murat Aydede, a reported authority on theories of knowledge. The move seemed to tread on intellectual turf and signaled the failure of philosophers to recognize that business had entered into the knowledge game without properly notifying them. "The idea of a knowledge-based society, I don't really understand what that can mean," Bruce Vermazen, chair of Berkeley's philosophy department, went on record as saying. "It makes me a little frightened about the future. I liked it better when we made steel. Knowledge seems like kind of a shaky industry." I suppose he should know, although I believe tenure still holds at his institution. It seems odd for a philosopher to fear the success of what we understand to be his lifework, which is to increase an appreciation of knowledge on the road to wisdom.[13]

Dennis Baron, professor of English and linguistics at the University of Illinois wonders, without an apparent trace of irony, "how long [it will be] before someone tries to corner the market on knowledge," and launches into a weak attack on all that the business world doesn't understand about knowledge: knowledge doesn't stand "still long enough to record and sell" (what of Baron's own books?), it isn't "a commodity to quantify and digitize" (patents and academic promotions notwithstanding?), and "it does not reside in the business school" (a fair comment?).[14]

If philosophy and linguistics departments are perplexed by this knowledge business, university administrations have generally welcomed the rising fortune of knowledge, hoping to take advantage of their colleges' cottage industry of patenting and branding. They have seen the example of both public and private institutions, like the University of California, which in 1995 received $57 million through licensing agreements on its intellectual property, while registering 122 new patents for the year, or Stanford University, with $39 million in licensing agreements and 70 patents in the same year.[15]

Typical university licensing agreements, arising from patents and other arrangements, range from the University of Florida's thirst-slaking, dollar-making Gatorade to Harvard's genetically enhanced mouse. In

---

13. Aydede and Vermazen cited in James Sterngold, "Professor Knowledge Is Not an Oxymoron," *New York Times*, June 1, 1997, E5; Ikujiro Nonaka, Hirotaka Takeuchi, and Hiro Takeuchi, *The Knowledge-Creating Company: How Japanese Companies Create the Dynamics of Innovation* (New York: Oxford University Press, 1995).
14. Dennis Baron, "Can B-Schools Corner the Market on Knowledge?" *Chronicle of Higher Education*, June 5, 1998, B7.
15. *Chronicle of Higher Education* (May 1997), http://www.chronicle.com.

1997, the total figure of such agreements reached half a billion dollars among American universities, a 33 percent increase over the year before. As a result, knowledge entrepreneurs and venture capitalists are often met at the university gates by the school's technology transfer and industry liaison officers, who are happy to pitch strategic town-and-gown partnerships.[16]

A good indication of the university's stake in this knowledge economy comes from a recent National Science Foundation (NSF) study, which reports that government-sponsored research in universities is producing more patents than the R and D initiated by private industry with much less investment. Industry has increased its R and D spending to $120 billion—twice government levels—but it is far more focused on product development than on conducting patent-rich experiments with new processes and materials. Although the whole R and D effort amounts to 2.5 percent of gross domestic product, every dollar of this investment, the NSF study calculated, adds an additional fifty cents a year to national output. Patent-generating research is clearly an important piece in the engine of this new economy. Yet within the sciences there is a concern about "creeping propertization," as Boston University law professor Robert Merges names it, which tempts science away from the public-spirited roots that led to publicly shared semiconductors, penicillin, and jet transportation. The knowledge economy's readiness to finance scientific research may not kill off science as public enterprise, but there is reason to be concerned. For the public may well grow comfortable with having the financial responsibilities of university laboratories lightened and the fruits of science come all the quicker to market.[17]

Clearly, this burgeoning knowledge business is bound to create greater suspicion, discomfort, and uncertainty within the humanities than in other areas of study. David Noble, a historian of technology at York University and cofounder of the National Coalition for Universities in the Public Interest, is among the most outspoken of those concerned about corporate influence on the use of technology in the university. In a well-known paper first published on the web, "Digital Diploma Mills,"

---

16. The University of California system tops the royalties list for universities, with $61 million annually from some five hundred licenses: Julianne Basinger, "Universities Royalties Income Increased by 33% in 1997, Reaching $446 Million," *Chronicle of Higher Education,* January 8, 1999, A51.

17. However, *R and D Magazine* (September 1998), 31, gave universities credit for only nine of the top one hundred technological developments of 1997; "The Leverage of Federal Research," *New York Times,* May 15, 1997, A28; Robert P. Merges, "Property Rights Theory and the Commons: The Case of Scientific Research," in *Scientific Innovation, Philosophy, and Public Policy,* ed. Ellen Frankel Paul, Fred D. Miller Jr., and Jeffrey Paul (Cambridge: Cambridge University Press, 1996), 145.

Noble worries about the inexorable force that "is rapidly drawing the halls of academe into the age of automation." Professional autonomy is being sacrificed to budget-conscious administrators seeking corporate sponsorships and partnerships that have become increasingly critical with the drop in government support of postsecondary education.[18]

At Noble's York University, by going on strike under the slogan "the classroom vs. the boardroom," the faculty managed to secure contractual protection from having to post corporate-sponsored webpages. Such actions are signs of an "overriding commercial intent and market orientation" for Noble, as is the push for technology transfer (from research to industry). He also deplores how the rise of the online course means that students not only are losing access to faculty but are actually risking their education, as they beta-test the online learning technologies of these educational-corporate initiatives. Certainly he is right to insist that students play an informed part in these R and D projects. Still, I fear many students would laugh at the idea that technology depresses the quality of teaching, just as I think they would welcome, in many cases, the invitation to experiment with new forms of learning. Noble solemnly concludes that "in ten years we will look upon the wired remains of our once great democratic higher education system and wonder how we let it happen. That is, unless we decide now not to let it happen."[19]

Yet it is also interesting that Noble holds more than business responsible for the academy's technological drive. In *The Religion of Technology*, Noble the historian traces back the "religious myths and ancient imaginings" that continue to inspire faith in technology and innovation, even as these technologies are now deployed by corporate interests "to discipline, deskill, and displace untold millions of people, while concentrating global power and wealth into fewer and fewer hands." Although I hope the public-knowledge project I propose falls outside of Noble's corporate-horsemen-of-the-apocalypse vision, I can see the danger of seeming to join ranks with "scientists and technologists [who] increasingly attest publicly to the value of their work in the pursuit of divine knowledge." Noble is right to decry the promises of otherworldly "deliverance" or "salvation" among techno-advocates, but

18. David Noble, "Digital Diploma Mills: The Automation of Higher Education" (November 1997), http://132.198.113.115/Notebook/digital-diploma-mills.html.
19. Ibid. I should declare that I have been party to this process, having initiated with Vivian Forssman a high-tech start-up company to build an online educational website. See Vivian Forssman and John Willinsky, "A Tale of Two Cultures and a Technology: A Musical Politics of Curriculum in Four Acts," in *Curriculum, Politics, Policy: Cases in Context*, ed. Catherine Cornbleth (Albany: State University of New York Press, 2000).

he also needs to consider how often the dedicated pursuit of knowledge possesses this redemptive character, whether it takes place inside and outside the university, and whether it uses the technology of the book or the screen. Still, the literal sense in which religious passions have inspired a technoclergy who brought us the bomb and took us to the moon is worrisome. I can only hope that, when Noble asks that we "begin to redirect our astonishing capabilities toward more worldly and humane ends," a public-knowledge project such as I am recommending will qualify.[20]

Apart from being rooted in religious and corporate fervor, the academy's defense of its intellectual position within this new knowledge-based economy has been remarkably flat and milquetoasty. From the administrative side of things, for example, Elizabeth Blake, chancellor of academic affairs at the University of Minnesota at Morris, defends the way scholarship "disseminates ideas, revealing to one scholar how another scholar *thinks*." Brian Lang, chief executive officer of the British Library and a social anthropologist, writes of how a researcher publishes "to give an account to colleagues of a new contribution to knowledge." These statements both seem to be stunningly limited visions of the quest for knowledge. Lang reduces the publication of an article to the equivalent of a birth announcement to which others might return congratulations. If this is all there is to our work, beyond the more sensational disease-curing and planet-probing knowledge-factory model of the sciences, then the university is not only operating outside of any sense of a knowledge economy of circulating goods, serving needs, and enhancing value, but is also offering a very terminal sense of Newman's Knowledge as an end in itself. Chancellor Blake and CEO Lang, in affirming the disturbing exclusiveness of research devoted to one scholar keeping up with another's progress, simply fail to credit the power and possibility of ideas to serve the world at large. In so doing they make little of both the value and the accountability of scholarship and research.[21]

Of course, Blake and Lang reflect a reclusive and self-contained scholarly tradition dating back to the ancient quadrangles of Oxford and Cambridge. The colleges of these two universities present a handsome enough face to the street, yet their real wonder lies protected within.

---

20. David Noble, *The Religion of Technology: The Divinity of Man and the Spirit of Invention* (New York: Knopf, 1998), 3, 4, 6, 206, 207.

21. Elizabeth. S. Blake, "Talking about Research: Are We Playing Someone Else's Game?" in *The Politics and Processes of Scholarship*, ed. Joseph M. Moxley and Lagretta T. Lenker (Westport, Conn.: Greenwood, 1995), 33; Brian Lang, "Bricks and Bytes: Libraries in Flux," *Daedalus* 125, no. 4 (1996): 221–34.

Beyond the vaulted entranceways, through the wooden gates, past the kindly, respectful porters stand the inner courtyards and ancient sheltered cloisters. These architectural wonders reflect a felt need to shelter the scholar and protect knowledge, to keep it concentrated on itself and away from the world. They constitute a sanctuary for knowledge, a privileged estate for an aristocracy (which only gradually became an aristocracy of the intellect) who alone walks upon those finely trimmed inner lawns. The old universities were so contained in their thinking that they almost missed out on the scientific revolutions of the sixteenth and seventeenth centuries, with Copernicus, Brahe, Bacon, Kepler, and Descartes all working outside the university, and Newton and Galileo leaving the confines of the college for other positions.

The quad was not the only design followed in collegiate architecture. The American campus is notable for its open, parklike setting, suggesting a more public landscape for knowledge. The term *campus* appears to have been first used in press descriptions of the tea-burning protests at Princeton University during the initial blazes of the American Revolution. Recall the issue of campus access during the free-speech movement not so long ago, and the Vietnam War protests at American colleges. The image of the university sitting apart from the world and cultivating knowledge at a scholarly pace had begun to dissolve long before our own fascination with the knowledge business arose. At the turn of the twentieth century, Thorstein Veblen was busy attacking business-minded faculty who posed as "captains of erudition," corrupting the university's true mission with their packaging and marketing of learning. According to the more convincing case made by University of Illinois historian Burton Bledstein, the American university of that day was already "a vital part of a culture of professionalism" promoting a business of expertise. Today's knowledge economy has only brought about a greater blurring of the distinctions between university and industry. Consider the Microsoft "campus" in Redmond, Washington, which produces a new global operating system for information processing every few years while Cambridge University negotiates a multi-million-dollar Microsoft lab and lesser colleges invest in industrial parks to attract their own set of business partners.[22]

---

22. Bledstein: "Careerism, competition, the standardization of rules and the organization of hierarchies, the obsession with expansion and growth, professionals seeking recognition and financial rewards of their efforts, administrators in the process of building empires; basically both the values and arrangements with American universities have changed little since 1900"; *The Culture of Professionalism: The Middle Class and the Development of Higher Education in America* (New York: Norton, 1976), 288–89; see also Veblen, cited in Bledstein, 287.

The pressure to "only connect" that has the university reaching out to the larger knowledge economy is being felt across the campus. Nearly two decades ago, Senator Edward Pell, who had been among the original sponsors of the National Endowment for the Humanities (NEH) in 1966, wrote that "we cannot justify the expenditure of taxpayers' money in support of the humanities, if the tendency of the program is to proliferate volumes of humanistic studies in university libraries, just for the academic humanist to read." The NEH has awoken to that idea and to its political future by, among other things, sponsoring links between humanities research and the schools, bringing the advantage of new insights and inspired teaching to schools while giving greater focus to the scholars in turn. The recently appointed director of the NEH, William R. Ferris Jr., initiated in 1998 a series of regional humanities centers intended to bring the value of the humanities to a greater part of the public. As Ferris puts it, "The objective of this initiative is to encourage Americans to observe the millennium by rediscovering the nation's history and culture and by preserving our rich heritage for the benefit of future generations."[23]

Among those pressing the university to rethink its public responsibilities is the late Representative George E. Brown Jr., who was ranking minority member of the House of Representatives Committee on Science. In speaking to the American Association for the Advancement of Science, he pointed out that the end of the cold war left America without "clearly defined values for research and technology sufficiently visionary to justify ... public confidence and support" (as if mutually assured mass destruction were a value-defining gift to the American research enterprise). It falls to scientists, he insisted, to become more actively involved in making the case for funding or to risk losing it, and that means they need to "take responsibility for any unplanned social consequences" of their work. For the social sciences (if I can ride in on Brown's influential coattails) that also means taking responsibility for ensuring that there are *planned* social consequences, namely, in the form of public knowledge. Brown called on scientists to "relate their work more closely to the values and goals of society, producing a vision of what they can accomplish that will justify public support for research," and he asked for greater public participation on policy and advisory

23. Edward Pell, cited in Ronald S. Berman, "Why His Reappointment Was Shelved," *Chronicle of Higher Education,* October 11, 1976, 9; William R. Ferris Jr., cited in Paulette Walker Campbell, "Head of Humanities Endowment Plans Network of Regional Cultural Centers," *Chronicle of Higher Education* (February 5, 1998), http://chronicle.com/che-data/news.dir/dailarch.dir/9802.dir/98020502.htm.

boards. This alone will make apparent "what [we are] getting for all the tax dollars spent."[24]

I would ask no more of the social sciences, except that they also turn the results of that scholarly vision into far more of a public resource. I realize the political danger that comes of making the vision behind a good deal of social-science research better known because the very defining of a social-science research problem can draw public censure, raising issues of academic freedom addressed in chapter 5. Yet this political and public engagement with knowledge is critical both to democracy and to research. Otherwise, my fear is, we risk having a nearly invisible body of social research intended to help humankind and another well-publicized body of research dispensing "competitive intelligence." A recent full-page ad that the magazine-publishing conglomerate Conde Nast took out in the *New York Times* featured a picture of a packed opera hall. The text in a box at the top of the ad read, in modest type, "We know which one made a million in the market today, which one came to town on the Concorde but had to borrow money for a ticket...." The text at the bottom read, "You need to know what we know about consumer attitudes about money." This is the force of social-science research that is working on the public, and that people in business are turning to for support in their work. The private sphere of research is about publishers and television producers selling their audiences to prospective advertisers, person by person. It is driven by the value of this knowledge to others, or as the management consultant Michael Treacy has identified, the changing value of useful, ready information: "The old game was having unique data or recognized leadership in filtering data. In the new game, the instant accessibility and usability of that information will be even more important." The "old game" sounds a lot like the university's traditional research paradigm, while the "new game" of increased accessibility is one for the universities to now consider, without giving up on Cardinal Newman's liberal sense of knowledge as a satisfying end in itself as well as a means of action.[25]

We have always been driven by the dream of knowing more, of coming to an understanding that makes greater sense of the world.

---

24. George E. Brown Jr., "Defining Values for Research and Technology," *Chronicle of Higher Education,* July 10, 1998, B4–B5. By the 1950s, military spending on R and D constituted 80 percent of the government's investment in knowledge, thirty times its prewar spending in constant dollars: Paul Edwards, *The Closed World: Computers and the Politics of Discourse in Cold War America* (Cambridge: MIT Press, 1996), 60.

25. Condé Nast advertisement, *New York Times,* October 6, 1997, A5; Michael Treacy, "What's Driving the Information Shakeup?" *Toronto Globe and Mail,* May 15, 1997, B10.

Insofar as the social sciences can speak to that dream, we have to recognize that they are already part of an economy of value-added knowledge. This only adds to their social scientists' responsibility for doing as much for knowledge's public sector in ways that might enable or inspire more people to use what is known as a means of greater understanding and as a basis of greater participation in, for example, shaping the social policies and practices that govern their lives. As I have already suggested and will turn to in some detail in the next chapter, one of the great challenges in going public with what we know in a field like the social sciences is the sheer quantity of information on hand. We need to be guided by how each age invents its own devices for managing and ordering the great store of knowledge that it is drawn to find and make use of, from libraries, to footnotes, to encyclopedias, to databases.

Housing Knowledge 4

While many writers turn to love and others to mayhem to find the literary truth of our lives, the Argentine fabulist Jorge Luis Borges looked to the library and the book. In giving imaginative form to our dreams of knowing, his fiction is often concerned with the spell cast by real and imagined books and includes cryptic and arcane obscurities often of his own making. His earnest and ingenious fascination with bookish knowledge often plays with the limits of our ordering of things. In one story, he ushers readers into the "Library of Babel"—a the library of all possible books. Here, suddenly, is the whole of the known world: "The Library is total and ... its shelves register all the possible combinations of the twenty-odd orthogonal symbols (a number which, though extremely vast, is not infinite): in other words, all that it is given to express, in all languages. Everything: the minutely detailed history of the future, the archangels' autobiographies, the faithful catalogue of the Library, thousands and thousands of false catalogues, the demonstration of the fallacy of those catalogues, the demonstration of the fallacy of the true catalogue, the true story of your death, the translation of every book in all languages, the interpolations of every book in all books."[1] Borges speaks of the extravagant happiness that visitors feel on discovering that the library contains all possible books. This exhilaration, however, which the reader also feels in reading the story, is inevitably followed by depression, after exhausting journeys through the library's endless galleries, shelves, and hallways as one realizes that "obviously, no one expects to discover anything." Some end up dreaming of a "Man of the Book," a librarian who has found and gone through the one book that stands as "the perfect compendium *of all the rest.*"[2]

The exhilaration over having everything and the desire to know its

---

1. Jorge Luis Borges, "The Library of Babel," in *Labyrinths: Selected Stories and Other Writings* (New York: New Directions, 1962), 54.
2. Ibid., 55, 56, original emphasis.

order (through faithful catalog and perfect compendium) represents a tension fundamental to the quest for knowledge. The tension is between wanting *completeness* and *compression* in knowledge. In imagining how the body of social-science research can offer new levels of public service, how it can offer people both a sense of the whole and an understanding of the parts, we have only these long-standing dreams of knowing to guide us. We need to find a way of helping people to move readily among all that this knowledge contains and to be able to find their bearings by a series of always partial and imperfect catalogs and compendiums.[3] In considering architectural models and other devices, real and imagined, for making something more of what we know, this chapter moves from the footnotes of Peter the Lombard, to the demonstrative encyclopedia of Leibniz, to the cyberization of the great national libraries. Each of these projects works with different bodies of knowledge directed toward different audiences or at least different versions of what I see as an ever-expanding public audience for this knowledge. For that reason, these historical initiatives represent an important inspiration and precedent, if sometimes a cautionary one, for placing this public-knowledge project within a long-standing dedication to wresting greater value from what we appear to be capable of knowing.

MEDIEVAL APPARATUSES

In a book commemorating, as he puts it, the passing in our own time of the "Epoch of Bookish Reading" and the "Epoch of the University," Ivan Illich offers a history of the way knowledge was reshaped on the page in medieval times during "the dawn of scholastic reading." Illich's principal exhibit is the churchman Hugh of St. Victor's encyclopedic guide to the art of reading and matters instructional, composed in 1128 or thereabouts. Rather than crediting the printing press as initiating the great revolution in learning, Illich holds that scribes created a secular and

---

3. Some two centuries before Borges wrote "The Library of Babel," Louis Sébastien Mercier offered his own bibliotopia in the form of the compendium. In *L'an 2440*, published in 1771, Mercier's narrator comes across the library of the king, which contains but "one small cabinet, in which were several books that seemed to be far from voluminous." The librarian explains that "as we were neither unjust nor like the Saracens, who heated their baths with masterworks, we made a wise choice: wise men extracted the substance from a thousand in-folio volumes, all of which they transferred into a small duodecimo-sized volume, somewhat in the same way that the skillful chemists who extract the virtue from plants concentrate it in a flask and throw away the vulgar liquor": cited in Roger Chartier, "Libraries without Walls," in *Future Libraries*, ed. R. Howard Bloch and Carla Hesse (Berkeley and Los Angeles: University of California Press, 1993), 40–41.

studious literacy three centuries earlier. They developed the scholarly features of text, making the knowledge that it represented more available for study and critique in the great universities of Bologna, Paris, Padua, and Oxford. Thus, Illich is inclined to credit that era with initiating its own great revolution in learning. In rethinking how to order and organize knowledge in service to the public today, we are working with variations on these earlier themes.[4]

In the first alteration of medieval texts, it was found helpful for readers of unfamiliar works to have clearly identifiable spaces between words and to mark paragraphs. Hugh of St. Victor and others went on to experiment with introductions, tables of contents, and chapter summaries as ways to support the studying of these texts. The twelfth century was also the time when the most important of scholarly tools, the book index, appeared (strangely absent, however, from Illich's own book). While these innovations enhanced the scholarly quality of the books themselves, others were assembling library inventories and concordances, all of which had the effect of creating libraries that could be readily used by visiting scholars almost from the first moment of arrival. Given how few copies of certain texts existed, the monastic collections of Europe formed a vast library system that was navigated, for the most part, on foot. The world was a long way from any sort of "public" participation in this body of knowledge, truly, but I'm drawing my lesson from the act of a monastery making its holdings that much more comprehensible to peripatetic monks.[5]

Working during roughly the same period as Hugh in the twelfth century, Peter the Lombard furthered the graphic design of the scholarly page by insisting that the calligraphers to whom he dictated his commentaries on the Psalms set off his citations of someone else's work with what we now know as quotation marks. He also asked them to add marginal references, as a form of footnote or "sidenote," crediting his sources. Peter the Lombard also used different sizes of lettering and underlining for emphasis in the text. "For him who searches," he wrote, "it be not necessary to turn the leaves of many volumes, but that he may encounter quickly without toil what he is after." Illich comments that "the new abstract beauty ... of the layout ... reflects the pleasure of projecting

4. Ivan Illich, *In the Vineyard of the Text: A Commentary to Hugh's Didascalicon* (Chicago: University of Chicago Press, 1997). As Illich has it, academics and professionals have become intellectual as well as physical commuters: "The speed of the car and the dullness of the road and the distractions of billboards put the driver into a state of sensory deprivation that continues as he hurries through manuals and journals once he arrives at his desk" (110).

5. Ibid., 30–33, 101–5.

mentally organized and quantified patterns of knowledge onto the empty space of the page." This new architecture of the page created a much more efficient and informative work space. It made the knowledge-building process that much clearer, offering both proof and invitation to others to judge for themselves. For Illich, this means that the page "is no longer the record of speech but the visual representation of a thought-through argument."[6]

The book was thus transformed from a reflection of God's or the author's word into a staging ground for working with knowledge. It was no less so for writers and teachers than for the then-limited body of read-ers and students. The urge to experiment with the graphic design of the page was the desire to bring greater order and access to the knowledge produced. In thinking about the potential of new technologies, I'm tempted to challenge Illich by asking where the scholarship that he so clearly holds dear would be today if Hugh and Peter, and those who followed in their footsteps, had not broken with their own inherited traditions. They showed little of the nostalgia toward lost practices within which Illich frames his story. They worked new devices into those bound pages of vellum to support greater ease of access and better serve the interests of scholarship. How are we to continue the good work done by these medieval scholars if not by experimenting, as they did, with old traditions through new forms? At present, the public (cyber)sphere awaits a new mix of source, resource, and reflection, with laptops set among stacks of books, as conversations over knowing and the known are conducted among texts, across tables, and around the globe. The graphic devices that Hugh and Peter experimented with continue to be developed on the page and screen, as the goal remains for the knower to "encounter quickly without toil what he [or she] is after."

BACON'S "GOODLY HUGE CABINET"

In all that Bacon did to launch the great ship of Western scientific inquiry during the early years of the seventeenth century, he had sufficient foresight to know that the resulting wondrous knowledge needed to be properly housed. "The shuffle of things," Bacon proclaimed, "shall be sorted and included." This could well be the motto of my project. Progress in knowledge, Bacon insisted, depended on not only "the books of learning" and "the persons of the learned" but also "the places of learning." Such places had the power to concentrate learning, to keep it

---

6. Peter the Lombard cited by Illich, Ibid., 98–100.

handy, and to prevent its value from dissipating, much as a cistern gathers rainwater.[7]

Bacon's blueprint for such a place included a four-part repository for knowledge and its artifacts. It was to consist of a library, a zoological and botanical garden, an experimental laboratory, and "a goodly huge cabinet, wherein whatsoever the hand of man by exquisite art or engine has made rare in stuff, form or motion; whatsoever singularity, change, and the shuffle of things hath produced; whatsoever Nature has wrought in things that want life and may be kept; shall be sorted and included." One can imagine a grandly furnished estate of knowledge in all of its baroque excesses, its artifacts and ancient books artfully stacked on antique tables, as it might appear in a Peter Greenaway film such as *Prospero's Books*.[8]

Bacon, however, had more than idle architectural aspirations for housing knowledge. He had little patience with what he named "natural curiosity and inquisitive appetite," for they were sources of "the greatest errors" in learning. He had little time for "entertainment" and "ornamentation" and cared for neither "reputation" nor the "barren" truths of scholasticism. Rather, knowledge for Bacon was about the benefit that it offered humankind: "Shall we not there be able to produce worthy effects," he wrote, "and to endow the life of man with infinite commodities?" The answer is, of course, yes, and the result of his instrumental and practical science is an infinite line of dishwashers, cell phones, and fruit drinks, as well as such "worthy effects" as improved health care and agricultural production.[9]

Bacon also had a second interesting recommendation for improving knowledge that builds on this theme of human benefit: "The corrective spice, the mixture whereof maketh knowledge so sovereign, is charity." It may be well to take charity cautiously from a man allegedly complicit in the torture of political prisoners and susceptible to bribery during his service to the court of James I. Yet whatever he made of knowledge at court, Bacon-the-scientist's stance on the charitable benefits and public good of knowledge formed a driving force in the sciences. Within the

---

7. Francis Bacon, *The Advancement of Learning and the New Atlantis* (1605; reprint, London: Oxford University Press, 1906), 2.1.3.
8. Francis Bacon, *Gesta Grayorum* (1594), cited in Thomas Markus, *Buildings and Power: Freedom and Control in the Origin of Modern Building Types* (London: Routledge, 1993), 190.
9. Bacon, *Advancement of Learning*, 1.5.11. "Worthy effects" resonates with physicist Freeman Dyson's point that science tends, in its less beneficent quality, toward making toys for the rich rather than necessities for the poor: "Can Science Be Ethical?" *New York Review of Books* 44, no. 6 (1997), 46–49.

scope of this civil philosophy of science, Bacon also spoke of the need for knowledge to provide comfort against solitude, assistance for business, and protection against injuries, in an early form of risk management for which this civil servant felt the government and empire should be responsible. It was all about the need to make "learned men wise in the use and administration of learning."[10]

Bacon also directed his attention to the graphical elements of furnishing knowledge easier to use and administer. He recommended laying out what was known in a table so that ideas could be readily ordered, aligned, and compared across the page. Here was a device on the order of Hugh of St. Victor's improvements in scholarly technology. Bacon turned the table into its own tiny house of knowledge, using it to construct helpful categorizations and comparisons in "tables of degrees" and "tables of comparison." In Novum Organum, Bacon offers the example of a table that compares how quickly various substances, from horse dung to quicksilver, absorb heat. He admits that, given "how poor we are in [natural] history," he was forced with this table to "include traditions and stories (although always adding a note as to their doubtful reliability and authority) instead of proved history and certain instances."[11]

Bacon adds that, as a result of laying things out in a table, gaps in the knowledge became apparent and he was "often also compelled to say 'Have an experiment done' or 'Further inquiry is needed.'" Sound familiar? Although "further study needed" remains a common research refrain, the table has proved to be one of the more familiar knowledge-management devices of the contemporary website, where it operates much as an index linked to a database. Tables may have been only a small part of the story for Bacon, but he recognized the double function

---

10. Bacon, *Advancement of Learning*, 1.5.3, 2.1.2. Although I and others have portrayed Bacon as a founding figure of a rapacious imperial science, Sachiko Kusukawa's trenchant analysis makes it apparent that Bacon's idea of protecting empire included not naval force but the liberal naturalization of aliens, the employment of just laws, and taxation with consent: "Bacon's Classification of Knowledge," in *The Cambridge Companion to Bacon*, ed. Markku Peltonen (Cambridge: Cambridge University Press, 1996), 66.

11. Francis Bacon, *Novum Organum* (1620), trans. and ed. Peter Urbach and John Gibson (Chicago: Open Court, 1994), 159, 168. Michel Foucault makes much of the table as situating learning in identity and difference. He calls it "the center of knowledge, in the seventeenth and eighteenth centuries," representing the sciences' great project, "however remote it might be, of an exhaustive ordering of the world": *The Order of Things: An Archeology of the Human Sciences* (New York: Vintage, 1970), 74. As Foucault see it, "The episteme of Western culture had opened up an area to form a table over which it wandered endlessly, from the calculable forms of order to the analysis of the most complex representations" (75).

of gathering and sorting that was to set in motion imperialism's great machine, intent on bringing order to all that could be known of this world.[12]

Finally, among the Baconian furnishings for the house of learning, perhaps the most versatile and expansive was the multidrawered cabinet intended to house and display curiosities and objects of interest to the knowledgeable. The cabinet of curios would eventually grow into the full-blown museum, but it was also adapted to house a library's card catalog, a tabled index to the library's holdings. Against "the shuffle of things," we have built magnificent repositories of order, an inspired knowledge architecture from library through museum to encyclopedia and scientific society.

Bacon's successful advocacy of natural and experimental science as the path to knowledge was based on the claim that "the first distemper of learning [is] when men study words not matter." Yet he also allowed, with credit to the value of a good library, that "the honor of the ancient authors, in fact of all authors remains undiminished" and that "things new in themselves will still be understood by reference to things already known." The library's intense concentration of things already known may overwhelm our desire to know the whole of the world. To enter those hushed rooms lined with always-partial sets of books that are still beyond any hope of total comprehension is to feel how earnestly we have piled up ideas, as if finally to write out the order of the world. For the longest time, the library has remained the place where we tried to work out what was to be done with this will to know.[13]

LEIBNIZ IN THE LIBRARY

Records of the architectural project of knowledge go back to the Egyptian libraries at Amarna and Thebes, a thousand years before the legendary library at Alexandria was assembled by the Ptolemaic kings, with its ill-fated collection of scrolls reaching into the hundreds of thousands. The Alexandrian library had its own Borgean mandate, securing a copy of every known work of the era. Libraries have always

---

12. Bacon calculated that by virtue of his method of natural and experimental history, "the investigation of Nature and all the sciences will be the work of only a few years" (*Novum Organum*, 298). Without the benefits of such a method, there was little hope, even "if all the clever minds of all ages, past and future, were to come together; if the whole human race had devoted or were to devote itself to philosophy, and if the whole earth had been or were to be nothing but academies and colleges and schools of learned men" (ibid).

13. Bacon, *Advancement of Learning*, 1.4.3; *Novum Organum*, 51, 52.

been about collecting and sheltering, ordering and owning the inscribed world. Yet the library is not just a collection of books, for though each title may seem to stand apart, protected by its bound covers, it inevitably points to other books in a web of reference that leads ever outward, mapping the world of knowledge. Thus the adage that "the library is a catalog."[14]

To step from the Alexandrian library into the early-seventeenth-century library at the University of Leiden is to find a few hundred books chained to long rows of what were, in effect, standing desks or lecterns. The chains make it seem like a room of plugged-in terminals in today's library, and the idea is not that distant. Standing before these wired books in Leiden, two or three scholars would gather in a portable seminar that could easily move from book to book in the cross-referencing of their discussion. Although the younger scholars may have felt they stood before the entire corpus of knowledge among those rows of secured books, those books, too, were indexes to other works, if only in the libraries at Oxford and Paris. To lean over one of the books and read was to enter the circulation of knowing that linked these books and libraries. Books were the source of expansive and heated conversation that stretched among writers and readers across years and geographies, languages and eras.

The library brought books together under one roof, but they then needed to be ordered in a manner that would allow people to work with the accumulated wealth of knowledge. The epistemological challenge of how to order and shelve the books certainly inspired one philosopher, who happened to find a day job as a librarian, to fantastic, if prophetic, theories of knowledge. In 1676, Gottfried Wilhelm Leibniz left his law practice in Paris to take up the librarian's tireless task for Duke Johann Friedrich of Hanover. Given Leibniz's vitality and versatility in an age before credentials, he had little trouble assuming the duties not only of head librarian for the royal collection but also of mining engineer and minor inventor for the duke.[15]

---

14. For a beautiful telling of the Alexandrian library story, including the myth of its burning, see Luciano Canfora, *The Vanished Library: A Wonder of the Ancient World*, trans. Martin Ryle (Berkeley and Los Angeles: University of California Press, 1990).

15. When not busy in the library, Leibniz worked on hydraulic presses, windmills, lamps, clocks, and Leonardo-like submarines for the duke of Hanover. Furthermore, his mathematical interests led him to propose a central statistical office for Prussia that would span military, civil, mining, forestry, and police interests: see Ian Hacking, *The Taming of Chance* (Cambridge: Cambridge University Press, 1990), 18–19. Hacking sums up Leibniz's plans: "Like so many of Leibniz's schemes, such a tabulation was futurology that has long since become routine fact."

In 1698, the library was installed in what is now known as the Leibniz-Haus, complete with private accommodations for the librarian. Could it have been while living within that wonderful library that Leibniz arrived at his famous philosophical stance—that this was the best of all possible worlds (for which he was famously skewered in Voltaire's *Candide* [1759], in which the hapless hero, when he hears Pangloss make this claim for the world, asks incredulously in response, "What can the others be like?")? Although his Panglossian optimism may have carried Leibniz—whose portraits suggest that he had certainly the best of all possible wigs, permed but unpowdered—all the way to the Broadway musical stage, my interest is in what else he learned among the books in his library.

The system for ordering books that was devised by this philosopher, lawyer, diplomat, engineer, and coinventor (along with Newton) of calculus suggests that he was not a particularly happy librarian. Like Bacon, Leibniz might be mistaken, in fact, for having wanted to do away with the intellectual need for books altogether. The library, for Leibniz, was a *magasin de science*, a storehouse of learning, a warehouse of propositions that was only as good as its ease of access to those ideas. He dreamed of "pinning down" ideas so that they might be arranged and grouped like so many butterflies in a specimen box. Or perhaps Lego provides the better metaphor; the propositions served as building blocks that could be used to build new castles of knowledge or a bridge to the future.[16]

It was not that Leibniz had lost his feeling for what books could do. He found his reading of Locke's *Essay concerning Human Understanding* so moved him that he felt compelled to write a book of his own in response. Still, this antilibrarian was dismayed by what he identified as "that horrible mass of books which keeps on growing." He felt there must be a way to pluck the pure and true ideas from the shelfloads of verbiage. Though he delighted in scientific advances, he wanted more people to be able to take advantage of this knowledge: "I even fear that after uselessly exhausting curiosity without obtaining from our investigations any considerable gain for our happiness, people may be disgusted with the sciences, and that a fatal despair may cause them to fall back into barbarism." Against the chaotic and frivolous array of ideas, he called on "persons of ability" to reset the scope of their intellectual activity: "If each one contributed only one great discovery, we should gain a good deal in a short time. A single observation or demonstration of consequence is enough to make one immortal and deserving of posterity." For those distinguished souls worried about sacrificing their claim to

16. See Markus, *Buildings and Power*, 174

immortality on behalf of this greater cause, Leibniz pointed to those famous Greek masters of geometry whose contribution was marked not by complete works but by a few lasting propositions. Modesty and discipline were called for if there was to be any hope of rendering the realm of knowledge more sensible and coherent. To write another book was of little consequence when what was needed was to ensure that people could piece together the value of what was already before them.[17]

Leibniz's contribution to this process was to propose a new kind of apparatus for managing knowledge through the design of a special sort of encyclopedia. He envisioned it beginning with the "quintessence of the best books ... extracted and joined to the best observations, not yet written, of the most expert in each profession, in order to build systems of solid knowledge for promoting man's happiness." Leibniz recommended that knowledge in this work would best be expressed in terms of probabilities, because "we can always determine what is most probable on the given premises." Through this "great method," a series of demonstrations and observations would be linked in "an exact chain" that would provide the truths "the public would like to learn." He named this device a "demonstrative Encyclopedia."[18]

No less so today than then, such bold intellectual proposals require patronage. Leibniz directed his ideas to a "great, free and curious prince," who was most likely Louis XIV. To secure support for contributors to this encyclopedia, Leibniz proposed that this prince offer prizes for those who could "disinter important knowledge hidden in the confusion of men or authors." Although the project failed to gain the patronage Leibniz sought and was not undertaken beyond the plans described here, I can't help feeling that the "demonstrative encyclopedia" showed amazing prescience. Locke was writing of "demonstrative knowledge," which went a step beyond intuitive knowledge in requiring a demonstration rather than relying on what seemed readily apparent. Locke described aspects of human understanding, whereas Leibniz imagined a device that, through such demonstrations, would extend and enhance what was already known. The encyclopedia would demonstrate, Leibniz held, "the most useful truths without needing to burden the mind with too many precepts." It would do so with an eye to calcu-

17. Gottfried Wilhelm Leibniz, *New Essays concerning Human Understanding* (ca. 1704), trans. Alfred Gideon Langley (New York: Macmillan, 1896); Gottfried Wilhelm Leibniz, "Precepts for Advancing the Sciences and Arts" (1680), in *Leibniz: Selections*, ed. Philip P. Weiner (New York: Scribner, 1951), 29–30, 32.
18. Leibniz, "Precepts," 32, 38–40.

lating the best applications of those truths: "If this Encyclopedia were made in the way I wish, we could furnish the means of finding always the consequences of fundamental truths or given facts though a manner of calculation as exact and as simple as that of Arithmetic and Algebra."[19]

Leibniz's demonstrative encyclopedia would use what was known to calculate new and needed truths on the basis of a universal culture that united humankind. This universal encyclopedia of the known world was also to be a calculating machine dedicated to demonstrating the beneficial application of ideas in philosophy and history as well as calculus and geometry. Like Leonardo with his helicopter or Babbage with his analytical engine, Leibniz worked out on paper the possibilities and form of his vision well ahead of the arrival of technology to realize those dreams. Are we now living in an era, one has to wonder, amid data mining and artificial intelligence, in which such Leibnizean mechanisms are at last destined to succeed?[20]

There was more to Leibniz's plans, however, even in his own day. In an earlier philosophical project, as a precocious lad of not yet twenty, he had developed what we might understand as the operating system or programming language—a *characteristica universalis*—for this demonstrative encyclopedia: "There must be invented, I reflected, a kind of alphabet of human thoughts, and through the connection of its letters and the analysis of words which are composed out of them, everything can be discovered and judged." After considering whether the Chinese ideogram might serve to capture the whole of a concept in a single character, he proposed assigning a "characteristic number" to each idea to enable the necessary calculations of new ideas. "Once the characteristic numbers are established for most concepts," Leibniz wrote with the admirable naïveté of youth, "mankind will then possess a new instrument which will enhance the capabilities of the mind to a far greater extent than optical instruments strengthen the eyes, and will supersede the microscope and telescope to the same extent that reason is superior to eyesight."[21]

As far-reaching and far-fetched as a calculus of ideas may seem, it falls within a long philosophical tradition dedicated to improving language's

---

19. Ibid., 40.
20. This sense of universality was global in its dimension, as Leibniz drew from his studies of China a theory of universal culture that saw an intellectual alliance forming between China and Europe: Donald F. Lach, "Leibniz and China," *Journal of the History of Ideas* (1954): 453–86.
21. Gottfried Wilhelm Leibniz, "Toward a Universal Characteristic," in Weiner, 20–24; Ian Hacking, *The Emergence of Probability* (Cambridge: Cambridge University Press, 1975), 89.

lack of precision. The "dream of a perfect language" is how Umberto Eco names this age-old quest to overcome the Babelesque confusion of tongues. A perfected language promised a completely rational source-code for programming the mind that it was bound to carry humankind into new realms of thought. Libraries and encyclopedias are but the external devices for the mental mechanism constituted by the language and mind within.[22]

Leibniz's proposed universal notation *(characteristica universalis)* was to operate within a specially devised reasoning mechanism *(calculus ratiocinator)*. The goal was not to determine the truth per se, but to weigh the probabilities on which it would be wise to base one's judgments. Because "probabilities lie at the basis of estimation and proof," he calculated, "we can consequently always estimate which event under given circumstances can be expected with the highest probability." I will return to this theme in a later chapter, but let me say here that Leibniz's plans sound a cautionary note for my project, not because of the weight he put on probabilities but because of his classic mistake in estimating how long such a project would take to complete and deliver. He figured that the work of assembling this great intellectual device would take a few of the right sort of people no more than five years to complete. After the first two years, he assumed, they would have achieved "a mastery of the doctrines most needed in practical life, namely the propositions of morals and metaphysics, according to an infallible method of calculation." He also held out hope that gradual improvements in our knowledge would result from the basic effort to arrive at this universal language, with its supporting encyclopedia: "As the science of mankind will improve, so its language will improve as well. In the meantime, it will continue to perform an admirable service by helping us retain what we know, showing us what we lack, and inventing means to fill that lack."[23]

Leibniz did not offer examples of how the demonstrative encyclopedia would work in practical (or even impractical) terms. There were no Leonardesque notebook sketches of a prototype found among the papers of this philosopher. Still, his *Demonstrationes Catholicae* from 1679, in which he could be said to have calculated a common natural theology linking Catholicism and Protestantism, might count as a suggestive instance of how the connections among divergent ideas can be demonstrated without collapsing the differences. In our own time, among the more imaginative demonstrations of Leibniz's idea is Herman

22. Umberto Eco, *The Search for the Perfect Language*, trans. James Fentress (Oxford: Blackwell, 1995), 1. Eco has a chapter on Leibniz's project.
23. Leibniz, "Toward a Universal Characteristic," 23–24, cited in Eco, ibid., 277.

Hesse's novel *The Glass Bead Game*, based on a game in which "all the insights, noble thoughts, and works of art" have been reduced to tokens that can be combined and calculated in endless new variations, which began as a way of "developing memory and ingenuity" before turning into "a kind of universal language through which the players could express values and set those in relation to one another."[24]

Leibniz's interest in stripping away the textual excess from key ideas seems all the more telling a dream in the face of today's scholarly glass-bead game. Scholars draw token citations from the abstracts of articles; they use the Internet as a demonstrative encyclopedia rendered pliable by Boolean search engines and interactive websites; and they deploy the artificial intelligence of neural networks and data mining to uncover potential hypotheses. Leibniz's prophetic vision has secured him election as patron saint of "cybernetics" by the one who coined the term, Norbert Wiener. "The *calculus ratiocinator* of Leibniz," Wiener wrote, "contains the germs of the *machina ratiocinatrix*, the reasoning machine."[25]

Philosopher-librarian Leibniz also worked out a junior version of his idea machine that turned the library into a vast encyclopedia by offering patrons a guide to the ideas that the books contained. We now call this system the subject index of the library's card catalog. The idea of cataloging a library's books was hardly new. At the great library at Alexandria, Callimachus had created a catalog that divided up the collection by genre. It was said to have run to 120 scrolls, in part because it was as much a summary as a list. Leibniz proposed that rather than simply listing titles and authors, "the index may and should indicate the places where the important propositions which concern one and the same subject are found." The catalog subsequently became the very soul of the library, with the cards being housed in their own fine oak and brass altar by author, title, and subject. In the first national implementation of a library catalog project, the revolutionary French government of 1791 created an index out of recycled playing cards in an inventory of private and monastic French libraries.[26]

24. Herman Hesse, *Magister Ludi (The Glass Bead Game)*, trans. Richard Winston and Clara Winston (New York: Bantam, 1970), 6, 21, 29.

25. Norbert Wiener took *cybernetics* from the Greek word for "steersman," and the book that launched the term is entitled *The Human Use of Human Beings: Cybernetics and Society* (Boston: Houghton Mifflin, 1950), 20. "In giving the definition of Cybernetics," Wiener wrote, "... I classed communication and control together. When I control the actions of another person, I communicate a message to him, and although the message is in the imperative mood, the technique of communication does not differ from that of a message of fact" (23–24).

26. Canfora, *Vanished Library*, 39; Leibniz, *New Essays*, 623, 625; Nicholas Baker, "Discards," in *The Size of Thoughts* (New York: Random House, 1996), 142.

Although it took nearly a quarter of a century for it to offer readers a Leibnizian subject index, the great architectural tribute to the library catalog is the British Museum's Round Reading Room, which was completed in 1857 (and has only recently closed with the moving of the British Library to its own quarters). The magnificent dome was largely devoted to housing the library's catalogs, which extended to the farthest reaches of the world defined by this library's great collection of books. The catalog was critical to managing that productive tension between excess and access, between the expanse of wonder and the call to order that mark the great library. It was central to the museum's eighteenth-century mandate to ensure that its collection was "for the Use and Benefit of the Publick." And it was too much to handle at times, judging by the range of methods the librarians came up with, including the disastrous 1841 edition of the catalog, which proved so inaccurate that it was canceled after the letter *A*. By 1881, when the museum finally added a subject index, the catalog ran to 2,500 volumes.[27]

If I seem to make too much of Leibniz and catalogs, consider for a moment Virginia Woolf's experience at the British Museum. Having been refused entry to the libraries at Oxford, she faced what she termed "the inevitable sequel" of a visit to the British Museum. She describes entering the museum's Reading Room in search of what had been written about women and fiction: "The swing-doors swung open; and there one stood under the vast dome, as if one were a thought in the huge bald forehead which is so splendidly encircled by a band of famous names. One went to the counter; one took a slip of paper; one opened a volume of the catalog, and, ... the five dots here indicate five separate minutes of stupefaction, wonder and bewilderment." Having hoped to transfer the truth to her notebook after a morning's reading, she wondered in what should now sound like a familiar refrain as she stood before that catalog, "How shall I ever find the grains of truth embedded in all this mass of paper[?]"[28]

---

27. The phrase is from the Committee of the House of Commons, April 6, 1753, recommending the purchase of the Sloane Collection, which became the core of the museum, and is cited in K. W. Humphreys, *A National Library in Theory and Practice* (London: British Museum, 1988), 7. It is worth noting that by 1985, the British Library was speaking of benefiting "information users" rather than the public (59).

28. Virginia Woolf, *A Room of One's Own* (Toronto: Macmillan, 1932), 42, 44–45, 49. Of course, her consternation concerned more than the gap that was opening before her between truth and text: "Why does Samuel Butler say, 'Wise men never say what they think of women'? Wise men never say anything else apparently."

THE ENCYCLOPEDIA

The other epistemological legacy of Leibniz's librarianship was the encyclopedia. Within decades of his death in 1716, this philosopher's dream for disinterring the "important knowledge hidden in the confusion of men or authors"—and he was hardly alone in harboring such a dream—became the commissioned work of Denis Diderot. What had originally been intended to be a modest translation of the recently published two-volume Chamber's *Cyclopaedia* was transformed in Diderot's hands into the great publishing project of the Enlightenment. Diderot envisioned his *Encyclopédie, ou dictionnaire raisonné des sicences, des arts, et des métiers* as fulfilling a double purpose: "To collect the knowledge dispersed on the surface of the earth," as he put it, "and to unfold its general system."[29]

In the words of Diderot's coeditor, Jean Le Rond d'Alembert, the encyclopedia was to be a "*reasoned dictionary*" that offered "the general principles" and "essential details" of "each science and each art," as well as "the links between subject matters." More than that, the *Encyclopédie* would realize the underlying unity to this knowledge: "The sciences and arts are mutually supporting," d'Alembert wrote in the prospectus, "and ... consequently there is a chain that binds them together ... in a truly unified system." D'Alembert saw the *Encyclopédie* as both mechanism and organism. It was at once *la belle machine de savoir ordonné* (the beautiful machine of organized knowledge) and a towering tree standing against the scruffy forest of the library, a tree from which radiated "the various branches of knowledge together under a single point of view and [would] serve to indicate their origin and their relationships to one another."[30]

The secret to realizing this unity was to find a way of classifying all knowledge, and here the encyclopedists acknowledged their great debt to Bacon and his division of knowledge into history (both civil and natural), poetry, and philosophy. That the *Encyclopédie* took 28 volumes, 17,818 articles, and 2,885 plates to cover the order of knowledge of

---

29. Leibniz, "Precepts," 32; Denis Diderot, "Encyclopédie," *Encyclopédie*, vol. 5 (1755).
30. Jean Le Rond d'Alembert, *Preliminary Discourse to the Encyclopédie of Diderot*, trans. R. N. Schwab (Chicago: University of Chicago Press, 1995), 4–5, 45–46, 160, and the entry for *dictionary* in the *Encyclopédie*. This unifying classification created its own hold on the world: Roland Barthes named the *Encyclopédie* "a huge ledger of ownership" distinguishing the Enlightenment from the "animated spirit of an adventurous knowledge" that characterized the Renaissance—"The Plates of the Encyclopedia," in *New Critical Essays* (New York: Hill & Wang, 1980), 27.

the day suggests the natural limits for encyclopedic efforts. Today's encyclopedias—or rather yesterday's, before they went online—were remarkably comparable in size, given all that we credit ourselves with now knowing.[31]

From the outset of the *Encyclopédie* project, d'Alembert, the mathematician and coeditor in the early phases, held that knowledge worked best within a closed circle of expertise, and the *Encyclopédie* was intended to represent and serve the *cité scientifique* as a Leibnizian machine of calculation. In contrast, humanist Diderot believed in pursuing far more utilitarian and productive goals with this great assembly of knowledge. In the persuasive analysis of Wilda Anderson, professor of French at Johns Hopkins University, Diderot and d'Alembert were destined to grow apart on this critical point of whether the encyclopedia should serve the ideal of a static or a dynamic conception of knowledge. As it turned out, d'Alembert washed his hands of the whole affair after the seventh volume, exasperated as much by the critiques of the work's shortcomings by such figures as Rousseau. Meanwhile, as Diderot noticed how "the proposed architectural harmony of the work," as Anderson puts it, was in reality something far less consistent and coherent, he focused his attention on how it could do a better job of serving its readership and contributors.[32]

When Diderot came to write the entry for *encyclopedia*, he envisioned this set of books to be a "living school for philosophers." Entries represented an ongoing conversation that would continue across generations. When it was working well, readers and contributors participating in this conversation had their prejudices questioned, if not overturned; they found themselves poetically and philosophically inspired by the cross-referencing. And the point of this intellectual engagement was always about taking action and making a difference with what had been learned. Anderson points out that Diderot, too, felt that the crush of books in the burgeoning library was inhibiting action, creating a crippling knowledge. As if to cheat the time and energy limits of our human capacity, he thought of the *Encyclopédie* as a mechanism of ongoing collaboration and coordination. His dream for knowledge, Anderson makes clear, was not simply to lay it all out for others but to

31. For example, what was recently the thirty-two-volume *Encyclopædia Britannica* is now available online for free. The web is also the permanent construction site for the *Stanford Encyclopedia of Philosophy*, which claims to be the first dynamic encyclopedia. It will be continually updated by the contributors, at their own discretion, and contrasting interpretations of entries will be welcomed.

32. Wilda Anderson, *Diderot's Dream* (Baltimore: Johns Hopkins University Press, 1990), 91.

show them, through such devices as cross-referencing, "how to figure it out for themselves." The *Encyclopédie* was a liberator, a springboard of efficient and strategic knowledge for catapulting the reader into action. It was a form of Leibniz's *calculus ratiocinator* without the reduction of ideas to a symbolic logic. It is another reminder, as well, that my idea of a public-knowledge project is to work through the same old dreams, desires, and dilemmas. Diderot saw that working with and through the arrangement of ideas could itself be a source of new knowledge and understanding.[33]

The French were not long in taking Diderot's point that the *Encyclopédie* did more than arrange a display-case exhibit of the world. Indeed, as its contributors dared to affirm the sovereignty of the people— "It is not the state that belongs to the prince, but the prince who belongs to the state," according to one entry—the work was censured by court and church, as well as subjected to much critique, for both trivial and substantial reasons, in pamphlet and periodical. To see it through to completion, Diderot ended up working on it in secret for a decade. In those heated intellectual times, the *Encyclopédie* was often referred to as a *machine de guerre;* Robespierre immodestly proclaimed it "the introductory chapter of the Revolution."[34]

Almost two centuries and many encyclopedia later, H. G. Wells's proposed that the world embrace a "New Encyclopedism" that would produce "a gigantic and many-sided educational renaissance." At the age of seventy, H. G. Wells engaged in a series of lectures in Britain and America promoting this idea, which could serve as yet another caution to my project. Here was a way to create "a reconditioned and more powerful Public Opinion" that would "replace our multitude of uncoordinated ganglia" (the universities and research institutes) with a new "social organ" that he named a "World Brain" or, less radically, a "World Encyclopedia." Although he was thinking of the whole of knowledge rather than the social sciences alone, he posed much the same initial question that I have asked: "What are we to do before it is too late, to make what we know and our way of thinking effective in world affairs?" He, too, was responding to an overwhelming sense of knowledge fragmentation and diffusion: "Possibly

33. Ibid., 6, 88, 91, 94, 99, 107, 111.
34. The *Encyclopédie* citation is from Lynn McDonald, *The Early Origins of the Social Sciences* (Montreal: McGill-Queen's University Press, 1993), 162; Maximilien de Robespierre, cited in Jürgen Habermas, *The Structural Transformation of the Public Sphere: An Inquiry into a Category of Bourgeois Society*, trans. Thomas Burger (Cambridge: MIT Press, 1989), 69; John Lough, "Contemporary Books and Pamphlets," in *Essays on the Encyclopédie of Diderot and d'Alembert* (Oxford: Oxford University Press, 1968), 252–338.

all the knowledge and all the directive ideas needed to establish a wise and stable settlement of the world's affairs in 1919," he told the Royal Institution of Great Britain in 1937, "existed in bits and fragments, here and there, but practically nothing had been assembled, practically nothing had been done to draw that knowledge and those ideas together into a comprehensive conception of the world." Wells was driven by "the conspicuous ineffectiveness of modern knowledge," by its "impotent diffusion" and "wildest uncoordinations," to propose a new "mechanism of knowledge."[35]

This new social organ was "really a scheme for the reorganization and reorientation of education and information throughout the world." Wells saw it as very much directed at informing the global citizen by presenting not a hasty summary but "selections, extracts, [and] quotations, very carefully assembled with the approval of outstanding authorities in each subject, carefully collated and edited and critically presented." This encyclopedia of the new age would "be alive and growing and changing continually." In his dream, anyone with intellectual aspirations was a potential contributor or critic. He envisioned a democracy of the mind, with everyone having the right to take issue with what was claimed. It would thus bring "together into close juxtaposition and under critical scrutiny many apparently conflicting systems of statement." It would also offer an index to nothing less than "*all* human knowledge, ideas and achievements" in what he described as "a complete planetary memory for all mankind," providing access to "the direct reproduction of the thing itself" through the wonders of microfilm.[36]

The first distinction I would make between my project and what Wells proposed is that I do not believe that this work would bring about the absolute and unified state of knowledge. The conflict of ideas, for Wells, was only "apparent." The World Encyclopedia would act "not merely as an assembly of fact and statement, but as an organ of adjustment and adjudication, a clearing house of misunderstandings." Leibniz, too, believed that if we just got our language of ideas properly ordered, conflicts would be resolved by careful calculation. In contrast, my interests are in making the critically diverse ways of knowing, represented by a field such as the social sciences, into a far more public resource. I want to develop our ability to juxtapose opposing analyses, to represent the differences in framework and assumption that give our thinking its richness and innovation, its contrariness and critique, its divergent ways of making sense of the world. The public-knowledge

---

35. H. G. Wells, *World Brain* (London: Methuen, 1938), xiii–xiv, 2–3, 6, 7, 8, 11, 19.
36. Ibid., 11–12, 13–14, 15, 60.

project that I envision is not devoted to resolving, except in the sense of clarifying, points of disagreement. Instead, it is aimed at affirming the potential public value of these diverse ways of analyzing and investigating matters of social concern.[37]

Although Wells recognized that his encyclopedia would not "in itself solve any single one of the vast problems that must be solved," he believed that the force of pulling together this knowledge could "hold men's minds together in something like a common interpretation of reality." This brings us to the rather sketchy area of the World Brain's political powers and governing responsibilities. Wells falls short of elaborating its exact political role, while managing to suggest that the World Brain would offer the "hope of an adequate directive control of the present destructive drift of world affairs." It would bring the whole of humankind's mental wealth "into effective reaction upon our vulgar everyday political, social and economic life," just as it "would hold the world together mentally" and "*compel* men to come to terms with one another."[38]

Ah, herein lies the danger to such encompassing visions of knowledge. Here's the political temptation in having a unified body of knowledge seemingly in one's possession. As opposed to Wells, I see the differences and conflicts in our understanding of the world as basic to our scholarly and common intellectual processes in working with ideas, values, and beliefs. Wells's sense of knowledge holding people's minds together and compelling them to act represents, for me, the danger of his encompassing vision of a world encyclopedia. Those who possess this knowledge will feel justified. As opposed to Wells, I see the differences in our approaches to knowledge—in what keeps the world apart mentally—not as something to be overcome, but as basic to our common intellectual processes in working with ideas, values, and beliefs. The public-knowledge project would protect us against this potential tyranny of reason through the diversity of understandings it would represent among the social sciences. It would provide access not only to the differences in ways of knowing but to the basis and value of those differences, which compel people to ultimately make up their own minds in the face of what is known in this plural sense of knowing. Still, I want to recognize the continuities of this encyclopedism, from Bacon and Leibniz through Diderot to Wells and on to my project. The challenge

---

37. On his *linguae characteristicae* ("an alphabet of human thoughts"), Leibniz claimed: "Most of all, it will serve to avoid those disputes in the sciences that are based on argumentation. For the [new] language will make argument and calculation the same thing": cited in Eco, *Search*, 276–77.
38. Wells, *World Brain*, xiv, 11, 16, 24–25.

remains ensuring that bringing together what we know remains a resource for people increasing rather than diminishing their possibilities. As for what has happened to Wells's version of the dream, the World Brain Expo Congress was last scheduled to meet in Hamburg in 1999.[39]

Of course, since Wells's day, the research community has only felt itself increasingly in danger of being overwhelmed by the volume of work produced, forcing greater specialization, fragmentation, and isolation among research ventures. That computers might be the answer was first suggested at the end of the Second World War by the chief scientist of the American war effort, Vannevar Bush. In his essay "As We May Think," he sought to inspire the scientists who were coming out of the "exhilarating" partnership with the armed forces, with the equally exciting prospects that lay ahead of them in civilian life. This remarkable man, an engineer, scientist, visionary, and bureaucrat, who was about to head up the new National Research and Development Corporation offered a vision in 1945 of desktop computer systems that would counter the threat of information overload. "There is a growing mountain of research. But there is increased evidence that we are being bogged down today as specialization extends. The investigator is staggered by the findings and conclusions of thousands of other workers—conclusions which he cannot find time to grasp, much less to remember, as they appear. Yet specialization becomes increasingly necessary for progress, and the effort to bridge between disciplines is correspondingly superficial."[40]

What is to be done? Where Bacon thought classification scheme, Bush thought machine. He described a "memex" machine, which would use microfilm as the medium of compressed comprehensiveness in his day to bring order to the known world: "If the human race has produced since the invention of movable type a total record, in the form of magazines, newspapers, books, tracts, advertising blurbs, correspondence, having a volume corresponding to a billion books, the whole affair, assembled and compressed, could be lugged off in a moving van."

---

39. For an interim report, see Manfred Kochen, ed., *Information for Action: From Knowledge to Wisdom* (New York: Academic, 1975). Here Wells's idea is explicitly transformed into WISE (World Information Synthesis Encyclopedia), which is treated, by a cast from Stanford, Harvard, and Yale, as an information-sciences project, as well as a social movement and "evolving social organ" (9). WISE would include not only cognitive but also emotional wisdom, through such devices as "computer aided behavior modification" and "electronic affect-mirrors" (15). I take this public-knowlege project, by comparison, to be a far more reasonable and realistic project, but I do so recognizing that it risks being lumped with the likes of WISE.

40. Vannevar Bush, "As We May Think," *Atlantic Monthly* (July 1945); reprint, Atlantic Unbound, http://www.theatlantic.com/unbound/flashbks/computer/bushf.htm.

Bush saw the flow of information extending "far beyond our present ability to make real use of the record." Although he sought mechanical relief for the problem, he was as much identifying the limits of our mental capacity to utilize or find the value of what we have produced. I find it interesting that he did not fault the excessive and unsystematic production of knowledge, only our current means of handling it. Nor did he address how to structure and relate the differences among these different forms of inquiry, or how to better organize the ideas within a given study. (Skilled readers of research often have their own tack, glancing at the abstract at the top of an article, flipping to the references to see who the authors hold with, working back to the conclusions, and then, in rare cases of real interest in the study, skimming the method.) However, Bush's mental prosthesis did seek to bring order to overflowing desktops and burgeoning bookshelves, for all the best reasons: "Presumably man's spirit should be elevated so he can better review his shady past and analyze more completely and objectively his present problems. He has built a civilization so complex that he needs to mechanize his records more fully if he is to push his experiment to its logical conclusion and not merely become bogged down part way there by overtaxing his limited memory. His excursions may be more enjoyable if he can reacquire the privilege of forgetting the manifold things he does not need to have immediately at hand, with some assurance that he can find them again if they prove important."[41]

Half a century ago, we were already awash in what was supposed to save the recently triumphant democracies. The only hope for the spirit of humankind was already seen to lie in technologies that would allow us to push the "experiment to its logical conclusion." What the conclusion amounts to is presumably a perfect knowledge of the world. It might seem that Bush's dream of electronic libraries has been realized and that those databases are already holding far, far more of what was threatening to bury the researcher of his day.

The library and encyclopedia represent our aspirations to contain and order what is known of the world. Visions of a cybernetic library-encyclopedia, such as the memex, the World Brain, and my own project, are bound to be genetically endowed with strains of Borges's Library of Babel and Leibniz's demonstrative and dynamic encyclopedia. What I am proposing takes less from Leibniz's reduction of ideas to signs and more from Diderot's incorporation of a "living school of philosophers,"

41. Ibid.

even as it might operate like a demonstrative encyclopedia through its links within the research and between the research and fields of practice. Yet this public-knowledge project is also bound to hold with the expansive architecture of the library, as a public space where people may find their way among books, catalogs, indexes, encyclopedias, and each other.

Today, the national libraries of Europe are being revitalized with new buildings in London, Paris, and Berlin, while at the same time their great collections are going digital with access coordinated through the Bibliotheca Universalis project, undertaken by the G7 nations. Among those engaged by this ultimate textual fantasy of sitting down to the whole of the written word is the great French historian of print Roger Chartier: "The opposition, long held to be insurmountable, between the closed world of any finite collection and the infinite universe of all texts ever written is thus theoretically annihilated: now the catalog of all catalogs, ideally listing the totality of written production, corresponds to electronic access to texts universally available for consultation."[42]

Although one tends to think of historians as a conservative lot, not given to such hopefulness for the future, there is clearly something immensely attractive for such a scholar to imagine that suddenly no published source falls outside the reach of his laptop. Yet what does such infinite access mean? The Library of Congress alone adds 7,000 items a day to its holdings, which now top 110 million items. The overwhelming scale of Chartier's vision is daunting. What will happen to readers, or rather *users*, of this infinite universe? Will they only grow all the more specialized in what they select, reducing the prospect of the conversation that Diderot held up as the model? What needs to develop alongside such great expansions of the public-knowledge cyberspace sector is correspondingly new ways of ordering knowledge, new ways of running the connections among texts and ideas. Meanwhile there will remain, one hopes, for Chartier, me, and others, the delights of happening across a book one remembers having long been curious about in a secondhand bookstore.[43]

---

42. Brian Lang, "Bricks and Bytes: Libraries in Flux," *Daedalus* 125, no. 4 (1996): 221–34; Chartier, "Libraries without Walls," 48. The project recalls the *Bibliotheca Universalis, sive Catalogus omnium scriptorum locupletissimus, in tribus linguis, Latina, Graeca, et Hebracia* that was compiled by Conrad Gesner in Zurich in 1545. Chartier credits Gesner's effort to create a universal guide to the entire realm of learning, ancient and modern, with detaching the notion of a world bibliotheca from the necessity of a building and thereby introducing the idea of a library without walls, which currently drives much thinking about access to information on the web (42).

Having explored more than a few centuries worth of innovative efforts to order knowledge's great house, from Hugh's scriptorium to Chartier's universal library, and having in earlier chapters reviewed the scope of public and commercial knowledge economies, I now turn to the particular and potential contribution of social-science research to the public sphere of knowing. Yet whether in looking at the history or economics of this desire to know the world better, the question remains the same: How do we care about and live by this work with knowledge, and best recognize and fulfill our obligation to those in whose name we pursue this inquiry into the ways of the world?

---

43. It is worth noting that the Librarian of Congress, James Billington, has expressed fears that "all the miscellaneous, unsorted, unverified and constantly changing information on the Internet may inundate knowledge, may move us back down the evolutionary chain from knowledge to information to raw data"; "Libraries, the Library of Congress, and the Information Age," *Daedalus* 125, no. 4 (1996): 38.

Section II
Social Science

Social-Science Ethos 5

In this section of the book, I work through the reasons, rationales, constraints, and possibilities entailed in assessing and improving the social sciences' contribution to public knowledge. This chapter addresses how this field of intellectual endeavor exists within the dynamic confluence of social contracts, academic freedoms, and epistemological theories. To set the stage for how these tensions work in social-science research, I start with the example of recent child-welfare initiatives in the United States that are designed to keep siblings together in foster-care placements. After all, our concern with knowledge is still ultimately about the consequences of what we know—in this case, the consequences for the lives of children and those who care for them.

On a practical and straightforward question of whether siblings should be placed together in foster homes, common sense dictates *yes* in response. Yet only recently have American agencies begun to implement such policies. As I write, Minnesota and Alabama require that siblings be kept together in foster homes, and California's Social Services Department is training its social workers to place siblings together. New Jersey is beginning to recruit foster parents who are willing to take siblings, and New York City and Kentucky offer extra support to foster parents with sibling placements. Inspired by common sense and by lawsuits launched by child-welfare advocates against separating siblings, revisions to the law are being made in a number of other states to allow more foster children in a single home, to enable brothers and sisters to stay together.[1]

Still, it is not easy to place more than one child in a single home at the same time. Given the expense of the incentives and training associated with such a policy, it would be reassuring to be able to point to the established benefits of this process for the children's development. This is where, as one might expect, the social sciences enter the picture. Up to

---

1. Pam Belluck, "Emphasis Shifts to Keeping Siblings Together When Using Foster Homes," *New York Times*, August 26, 1998, A18.

this point, however, only a few studies have been conducted on sibling placement, a fact that is itself a source of concern, given the scale of current policy changes. The mixed and complex results of those few studies do not appear to figure in this wave of policy reform, largely, I suspect, because they do not come down clearly on one side or the other. The limited set of studies available on this topic provides a critical example of how research fails practice by having little to offer to discussions of policies and programs. Public knowledge, not to mention the children and those who care for them, is the poorer for it. Let me show how this works.

One of the recent studies on the placement of foster children is by Maureen Smith, a psychologist at Cornell University, who compared the experience of twenty-five children placed with an older sibling to that of thirteen children who were separated from an older sibling. Smith cites three related studies, reflecting the narrow base of research on this topic by commenting that there is generally "little empirical evidence to support reasons for placing siblings together or reasons for separating siblings." One earlier study, by Martha J. Aldridge and Patricia W. Cautley, shows a split between negative and positive impacts, with sibling placement working better for boys than for girls. Another study by M. B. Thorpe and G. T. Swart, begins with the chilling notice that siblings "did reasonably well" together in World War II concentration camps, before reporting that among its contemporary sample of 115 siblings from forty-eight families, both academic and psychological advantages resulted for children who were separated from their siblings when placed in foster homes.[2]

Smith's own research found fewer emotional and behavioral problems in children placed with siblings, but the vocabulary development of children placed with their older siblings—one measure of academic development—was not as strong as that of those who had not been so placed. How is one to reconcile the apparent contradictions among these studies? How is one to work with the trade-off suggested by Smith's study alone, knowing that the positive impact on emotional and behavioral factors of sibling placement appears to be slightly stronger than the

---

2. Maureen C. Smith, "Sibling Placement in Foster Care: An Exploration of Associated Concurrent Preschool-Aged Child Functioning," *Children and Youth Services Review* 20, no. 5 (1998): 391. The cited studies include: Ilene Staff and Edith Fein, "Together or Separate: A Study of Siblings in Foster Care," *Child Welfare* 71, no. 3 (1992): 257–70; Martha J. Aldridge and Patricia Cautley, "Placing Siblings in the Same Foster Home," *Child Welfare* 55 (1976): 85–92; and M. B. Thorpe and G. T. Swart, "Risk and Protective Factors Affecting Children in Foster Care: A Pilot Study of the Role of Siblings," *Canadian Journal of Psychiatry* 37 (1992): 616–22.

academic disadvantages? However one answers these questions, simply knowing what is at risk in sibling placements, including a potential difference in academic and emotional development, constitutes a useful combination to public knowledge.

My concern, however, is that readers who manage to track down the sources are offered little help in sorting out the discrepancies among even this small set of relevant studies. And although the researchers note weaknesses that could be improved in future studies—such as standardizing teachers' evaluations of the children—they do not address how their study fits together with the earlier ones they cite, even as they come up with opposing results. Smith, for example, does not comment on what light her work casts on the differences among the other three studies. This only adds to the challenge of making sense of what is known about keeping siblings together in foster homes. Additional studies, as they further complicate the research picture, could well increase the distance between this complex body of research and the realm of public knowledge and practice. In that sense, for those who are making policy and placing and accepting the children, as well as for the children themselves, this research might as well not exist. It is not that this small body of work is deploying ideas or methods too complex for anyone but a social-science researcher to handle. As a body of knowledge, it is not working as it is intended to work, at least as long as its goal is the welfare of these children.

In a theme I will return to again, each of these studies achieves an island of understanding, each is a competent demonstration of research, and each is sufficiently independent of the others to make the connections between them a challenge to readers. The studies fall short of coming together in ways that would help more people assess why the results differ and how those differences can lead to a better understanding of the topic at stake. One study cites another, but as I analyze in chapter 9, the connections are simply too weakly strung among them. Other researchers synthesize and summarize these studies, but such efforts are limited by the autonomy and isolation of the original studies and beg the question of why the original studies did not do more to make sure of their fit with related research, a task necessary for any hope of augmenting existing knowledge.

This is not just about policy research, evaluation studies, or other forms of "applied" research directed at refining social policies. In fact, the distinction between "applied" and "basic" research is all wrong here. For neither concept is about making knowledge into a public enterprise. Applied research is like running a test on one's car that will help a mechanic zero in on a problem, whereas basic research, in this sense, concerns the work of engineers on the very design of internal combustion engines. One has to wonder, in regard to the social sciences, whether the knowledge derived from this inquiry into the social dynamics of our lives might be of value and interest to more than just the policy officials, related professionals (mechanics), or to other researchers (engineers). As it is, the current system is not working all that well for mechanics or related professionals. My belief is that carefully researched initiatives toward improving the coordination, connection, coherence, and intelligibility of the research enterprise, matched by opportunities for greater public exchange and engagement with this work, will better serve not only the public but also practitioners in related professions, as well as the researchers themselves.[3]

In terms of today's technology, such a public-knowledge initiative would entail an open and extensive website that would experiment with new forms of representing and organizing research, all with an eye to making it easier to explore the relationship among related ideas and practices, policies and programs. In the case of foster parents and children, this website would enable social workers, foster parents, advocacy groups, and the larger community to review how related studies both work together and challenge each other. Given its Leibnizian demonstrative and encyclopedic qualities, such a project would enable users to trace the line between current policies and research agendas, while also inviting them to engage in discussions of such initiatives. It would enable the public and researchers to tap into proposed and ongoing studies on the topic that may be seeking participants or other forms of input. To improve the coherence among existing and future work, researchers would be able to secure permission to explore the data gathered in any of the studies and tap into the instruments used and the research behind those data. The website would offer different starting points and different ways of moving through the material to help people gain a greater sense of what is known and what is at stake with the issue, and how it relates to ideas about childhood, siblings, families, and social welfare.

To support these efforts, the website could offer, for example, its own sidebars and footnotes on how children's emotional states are assessed

---

3. In a failed effort to entrench the distinctions between applied and basic research, Thorstein Veblen, who held that "the knowledge of things is the only end in life that justifies itself," recommended housing them in separate institutions, namely, the university and the professional school: *Higher Learning in America* (New York: Hill & Wang, 1957), 8.

and on the implications of, for example, assessing "receptive vocabulary" as a measure of academic achievement. Links could be provided, as well, to more conceptual pieces on changing ideas of state and family. Visitors could pose questions or initiate discussions connected to any point in the site. This careful coordination of related resources would be as useful to those engaged in mapping out future research strategies as it would be to those directly affected by foster-placement policies. Participants in the website would be likely, through their questions and suggestions, to offer additional links to related work, such as Pam Belluck's *New York Times* article, which I cited earlier in this chapter.

Belluck's piece offers a range of opinion on the issue of sibling placement, as well as examples of current programs and a vivid portrayal of how Chicago's Hull House worked with a very difficult set of four siblings who did not get along very well, and what it took to bring peace and progress to their lives together. "I guess they really love each other," concluded Mary Hardwick, the skilled foster parent who was finally able to establish a measure of harmony among them. "They just don't know how to express it. But all of them together is better. I wouldn't want to be split from my sisters and brothers." This type of information needs to stand with the research, adding to what I would call its public quality.

That quality depends on ease of access, first of all in finding a way into this knowledge and then in appreciating the relationship among the known parts of this phenomenon. Links are needed from parts to whole, research to practice, practice to program, program to policy, and policy to other social issues. These links will add up not to a single irrevocable conclusion but to the many things that can be understood, that need to be weighed, and that can inform decisions. The intention is to give the public, as well as related professionals such as social workers, a feeling of being party to what the research has established and of having a say in setting a research agenda that is working to illuminate the larger world of activity and reflection.

This contribution to public knowledge is really about establishing a dynamic and responsive research archive, with the information being layered and linked to facilitate different levels of public engagement in a dialogue about how knowledge works inside and outside the academy. Research in the social sciences would gradually become far more driven and shaped by this coordinated information site serving researchers, professionals, and public alike. To encourage a greater exchange between research and public may alarms some social scientists. What will come of a consumer-driven market model of research? Although I can readily imagine the reaction of abhorrence and apprehension over what such a public-knowledge project would do to the social sciences, the time has come to realize that this academic discipline operates within the scope of a social contract, one that does not necessarily compromise academic traditions of research and scholarship.[4]

THE SOCIAL CONTRACT

The concept of a social contract is one way of framing what the social sciences owe to the public. The educational and research enterprise of the social sciences largely exists, after all, through a political act of will renewed annually through a myriad of government and private budgetary processes. The closer one gets to that noisy political arena of government funding agencies, now given to talk about social investment and returns, the more sense the legal and commercial language of contracts makes. There may have been a time when economists, faced with politicians demanding, "What have economists contributed to the gross national product?" could glibly reply, "We invented it." Now, it seems clear that something more than academic wordplay is required. In Canada, for example, the social sciences and humanities have recently been put on notice by the principal federal granting agency. "The new rule will be 'get public or perish,'" in the words of Marc Renaud, head of the Social Sciences and Humanities Research Council and sociologist at the University of Montreal, for "people have a duty to explain what they are doing": "There is a lack of connection between the builders of knowledge and the consumers of research. That bridge has to be built."[5]

One also finds this social-contract theme taken up by other sciences, if not always willingly. Among the reluctant is medical educator John

---

4. My proposal for a public-knowledge project can be taken as a variation on Joseph Ben-David's recommendations, in "How to Organize Research in the Social Sciences," *Daedalus* (spring 1973), that more time and effort need to be devoted to the diagnosis of a given sociological problem and to the design of the research, as well as to setting up "archives of information" that include data banks for coordinating research efforts: "I am suggesting that we devote many more resources to creating a system whereby the results of well conceived research and data collection can be continuously fed back into ongoing research" (45–46). He does this, however, not in the name of improved public service but out of a professionalism he sees as distinct from "an external morality, such as that dictated by a political view" (49).

5. Marc Renaud cited a Jennifer Lewington "Research Boss Takes Aim at Ivory Tower," *Toronto Globe and Mail*, July 7, 1998, A6. The legal dimensions of accountability, recently refreshed within the scope of presidential politics, are apparent in a 1974 U.S. Supreme Court decision that held that "the public has a right to every man's evidence." The case "turned back President Nixon's efforts to withhold the White House tapes": Stephen Gillers, "Clinton Is No Ordinary Witness," *New York Times*, July 28, 1998, A19. For the promises relating to federal funding of the social sciences, see National Science Foundation, http://www.nsf.gov/sbe/sbeovrvw.htm.

Colloton, who regrets having to trade a sense of "covenant" for one of contract in academic medicine: "The societal trust underlying our long-standing covenant is rapidly giving way to a clarion call for accountability and shared decision-making on many fronts—both in the public and private sectors." Colloton sees no choice for medicine but to "respond to [the public's] doubts and changing expectations," which means that medicine "must now redefine and expand its commitment to society." The Association of American Medical Colleges (AAMC) has established a "Working Group on Fulfilling the Social Contract," which concluded not long ago that "upholding the social contract requires assuming accountability for equitable distribution of a social good (health) throughout society." On a similar note, Jane Lubchenco, a zoologist at the University of Oregon, took up this contractual theme in her 1997 presidential address to the American Association of the Advancement of Science. Lubchenco calls for science to enter into a new social contract for a "Century of the Environment," which will meet an "urgent need for knowledge to understand and manage the biosphere." The terms of the contract she proposes between the sciences and society resonate with those I would pose for the social sciences. She calls on the sciences to "(1) address the most urgent needs of society, in proportion to their importance; (2) communicate their knowledge and under-standing widely in order to inform the decisions of individuals and institutions; and (3) exercise good judgment, wisdom, and humility."[6]

In the social sciences, this interest in revitalizing the field by reconnecting it with public interests dates back to at least the 1930s with Robert Lynd's *Knowledge for What?* Lynd saw the social sciences as helping people understand and shape the institutions that influence their lives, by exploring "what kinds of order actually do exist in the whole range of the behavior of human beings." The social sciences were "human tools of knowledge" that he saw as handicapped by their "failure … to think through and to integrate their several responsibilities for the common problem of relating the analysis of parts to analysis of the whole." The point of this integration for this advocate-sociologist was

---

6. John W. Colloton, "Academic Medicine's Changing Covenant with Society," *Academic Medicine* 64, no.2 (1989): 55–60; Layton McCurdy, Leslie D. Goode, et al., "Fulfilling the Social Contract between Medical Schools and the Public," *Academic Medicine* 72, no. 12 (December 1997): 1065. It is interesting to note that the AAMC took a largely public-relations approach, complete with focus groups, to renewing the contract, producing "messages and tools to communicate" that "expand understanding and rebuild public trust" (1069). This seems an easier and more likely route than actually reforming the practices of the organization. Jane Lubchenco, "Entering the Century of the Environment: A New Social Contract for Science," *Science*, January 23, 1998, 495.

to devise programs of action that spoke to the question of "what techniques of information and what rituals for the strengthening of community feeling do we know or can we discover that might be deliberately employed to strengthen democratic action?" For my part, I would switch Lynd's larger question to "Knowledge for whom?" to make it clear that decisions about these concrete programs are to be made by a larger public who can consult this knowledge and can judge for itself.[7]

Two decades later, C. Wright Mills managed to occasionally command the wider public of best-seller books in his belief that "it [is] now the social scientist's foremost political and intellectual task—for here the two coincide—to make clear the elements of contemporary uneasiness and indifference." Such research could make "reason democratically relevant to human affairs in a free society, and so realize the classic values that underlie the promise of our studies." As social critic and public intellectual, Mills sought to advance the democratic rule of reason.[8]

Then at the end of the 1980s, Alan Wolfe, currently a Boston College sociologist, cast sociology as "the theater of moral debate in modern society" and social scientists as "the most common guideposts for moral obligation in a secular, nonliterary age." What is needed now more than ever, he claimed, is sociology's moral guidance in restoring the lost qualities of a civil society, to help "modern liberal democracies ... do a better job of managing their discontents." Wolfe worried about the ability of social scientists to deliver on their promise of "a distinctive way of thinking about obligations to others," without giving much thought to how to improve their public participation, were they to recover their sense of moral and civic purpose. He spoke of what sociology has to offer modern liberal democrats in their efforts to construct a civil society, which still leaves the question of how sociology can improve its participation, as an intellectual force and a resource, in that civil and constructive process.[9]

When it comes to those probing the future of the social sciences, the concern is no less to reach a broader public, through "new social ideas

---

7. Robert Lynd, *Knowledge for What? The Place of Social Science in American Culture* (Princeton: Princeton University Press, 1939), 125, 15, 219. Lynd also made this plea for the contribution of public knowledge to democracy: "What kind of culture would it be in which information came through without suppression, bias, or curtailment to every citizen and in forms conducive to effective learning?" (219).

8. C. Wright Mills, *The Sociological Imagination* (New York: Oxford University Press, 1959), 13, 194.

9. Alan Wolfe, *Whose Keeper? Social Science and Moral Obligation* (Berkeley and Los Angeles: University of California Press, 1989), 7, 190, 208, 261.

aimed to shape social knowledge into publicly engaged knowledges," according to the prescient Steven Seidman. Those who are refashioning sociology for the postmodern era of the twenty-first century—Seidman names Robert Bellah, Zygmunt Bauman, Dorothy Smith, and Immanuel Wallerstein—apparently understand that "to play a role in renewal, sociology must reorient its conceptual center around public life rather than narrow, specialty area disciplinary problems."[10]

This reoriented conceptual center (and renewed social contract) for sociology will require experimenting with new ways of engaging public life and public knowledge. Returning to my earlier example of the research on siblings in foster homes, the researchers had every reason to believe that their work addressed an important aspect of "public life," but that still didn't qualify their work as "publicly engaged knowledge," at least as I would interpret it. To call on the social sciences to reorient their scholarly interests toward public life and public philosophies— a call that has been heard repeatedly over the course of the twentieth century—requires a concomitant concern with how to increase the general intelligibility of the resulting knowledge for public and professional alike.

If nothing else, this concept of a social contract encourages a clarification of expectations for both the research community and the public. The public will need to appreciate, for example, that the social sciences cannot help anyone understand why a specific child might take his father's gun (and why that gun isn't properly locked up) and then use it with devastating effects. Research may, however, be able to help people understand how such a tragedy fits within the changing state of violence and how it reflects inadequacies in recent changes to the gun laws. This is small consolation in the face of tragedy, when pictures of funerals cover the papers. It may even seem heartless to think that there could be some public value to making available statistics on youth violence, the impact of "waiting-period" and "shall-issue" gun laws, recent polls on changes in those laws, and recent work on the factors associated with adolescent angst and anomie, including research on and perhaps links to school and nonschool programs that try to address those conditions. None of this will dictate or compel what-should-be-done.

---

10. Steven Seidman, *Contested Knowledge: Social Theory in the Postmodern Era*, 2d ed. (Oxford: Blackwell, 1998), 301, 310. See Robert Bellah et al., *Habits of the Heart: Individualism and Commitment in American Life* (Berkeley and Los Angeles: University of California Press, 1985); Zygmunt Bauman, *Intimations of Postmodernity* (New York: Routledge, 1992); Dorothy E. Smith, *The Conceptual Practices of Power: A Feminist Sociology of Knowledge* (Boston: Northeastern University Press, 1990); and Immanuel Wallerstein, *The Modern World System* (New York: Academic, 1974).

And the evidence that has been assembled, such as the relation between the legalization of concealed weapons and the reduction of mass shootings, hardly forms a basis for consensus on action. As it is, public-interest groups, insurance companies, the NRA, and the lawyers of victims' families have their researchers scour the social-science literature for support. The public-knowledge project I advocate would expand access to the intellectual resources assembled by the social sciences, enabling more of this work to figure in the discussion, the sense-making, the responses, and the proposals.[11]

Then there is the press, which, in the face of these incidents, calls on experts for a few quotable lines or sound bites to be interspersed within the write-up or broadcast of the event in a blend of news and commentary. This has become a journalistic habit that, I am afraid, does not do either public or scholar much good. For example, following the 1998 Springfield, Oregon, school shooting that left four students dead, a *New York Times* reporter spoke to Dr. Alvin Pousaint of the Judge Baker Children's Center at the Harvard Medical Center. Pousaint was quoted as observing that "a lot of violent movies blur the lines between the good guys and the bad guys and make a hero of anyone who fights, or mix violence with humor." He also advised parents and teachers to take children's remarks about revenge seriously: "A lot of deaths could be prevented if we responded to the clues people give in advance." I know that when suddenly called on by the media to comment on a current event I have said inadequate and banal things that hardly reflect years of careful research. It is not something we "experts" do particularly well. It is not what the knowledge we carefully strive to assemble lends itself to, which is why I think we need to find another way of making what the social sciences have to offer more readily available. Even if our efforts did little to change sound-bite journalism, our comments could at least lead the interested to something more than dead-end information.[12]

---

11. John R. Lott Jr., *More Guns, Less Crime: Understanding Crime and Gun-Control Laws* (Chicago: University of Chicago Press, 1998). The Amazon.com review of this book, by Ted Frank (December 27, 1999), notes that "Lott takes the time to refute each argument; it's almost touching the way he footnotes each time he telephones an attacker [of his claims] who eventually hangs up on him without substantiating any of [the attacker's] claims."

12. Tamar Lewin, "More Victims and Much Less Sense in the String of Shootings at Schools," *New York Times*, May 22, 1998, A12. This goes some distance to disprove political scientist Austin Ranney's warning of some years ago on behalf of academics: "If all we can offer is common sense or a passion for social justice, then we have no special claim to and will not receive any special attention paid to any other citizens enjoying these admirable but widely diffused assets": "The Study of Policy Content: A Framework for Choice," in *Political Science and Public Policy*, ed. Austin Ranney (Chicago: Markham, 1968), 17.

That brings me to the question of what would a renewed social contract do to the "academic ethic" so critical to the scholarly pursuit of knowledge? I would make my case that greater public engagement need not undermine the traditions and standards of scholarship by taking up the challenge posed by Edward Shils's relatively conservative essay, "The Academic Ethic," which he published in 1982 after working with the International Council of the Future of the University. Shils, a Distinguished Service Professor at the University of Chicago—whose motto is *Cresat scientia, vita excolatur* (Let knowledge grow that life be enriched)—certainly reveres the clerical calling of academic life: "The academic cannot 'let himself go,'" given his "commitment to the life of scientific and scholarly knowledge." There is to be no 1960s-style professorial activism for Shils. The academic faith is such that one commits oneself "to the observance of the norms of disinterested scrutiny of evidence and logical reasoning."[13]

This was Max Weber's original hope, as if a value-free social science was the best form of public service. The impossibility, as well as undesirability, of this vision has been repeatedly attacked since, perhaps most notably by Alvin Gouldner. For me, the implausibility of disinterest is not an issue. Social scientists can and will go on pursuing standards of objectivity and openly stating values, while knowing that there is always more to be said about those inevitable biases, much as I discussed with the 1930s sociology of race relations in chapter 2. Greater public engagement with this knowledge would seem to help this reflective process along. Interested knowledge still has much to offer in the thinking through of issues and in understanding what is known of our lives together. All we risked is that people will see that scholars hold to different possibilities for objectivity.[14]

A second apparent barrier between Shils's academic ethic and my push for public knowledge is his placement of the "acquisition and

---

13. Edward Shils, "The Academic Ethic," in *The Calling of Education: The Academic Ethic and Other Essays on Higher Education*, ed. Steven Grosby (Chicago: University of Chicago Press, 1997), 109, 116. Shils worked with the Committee on Social Thought at the University of Chicago, made famous not long ago as a bastion of conservative thinking by Allan Bloom's best-selling rant against the decline of learning in today's universities, *The Closing of the American Mind: How Higher Education Has Failed Democracy and Impoverished the Souls of Today's Students* (New York: Simon & Schuster, 1987). Bloom's book makes Shils's essay seem a reasonable case for the university's necessary autonomy in its devotion to instruction and scholarship.

14. "Like Berkeley's argument for solipsism, Weber's brief for a value-free sociology is a tight one and, some say, logically unassailable. Yet it is also absurd. For both arguments appeal to reason but ignore experience": Alvin W. Gouldner, "Anti-Minotaur: The Myth of a Value-Free Sociology," in *For Sociology: Renewal and Critique in Sociology Today* (New York: Basic Books, 1973), 3.

transmission of knowledge" at the center of his academic ethic and his setting the "application" of knowledge outside the scope of the university's concerns, for such contract- and mission-oriented research, he holds, can only corrupt. Of course, the vulnerability of research and researchers is always going to be a problem. We may well be haunted, for example, by the horrendous instance of the tobacco industry's sustained sponsorship of health-related research. But such instances of abuse and cover-up, whether conducted by university or industry, only emphasize the value of creating greater public openness around research processes. As for Shils's emphasis on acquisition and transmission, the acquisition of knowledge achieves its value through its transmission to others, and in the social sciences, extending the transmission of knowledge to the broader public, not as a form of application but as a source of knowledge and understanding, only extends its viability and value.[15]

For his part, Shils sees the universities' debt to society as standing apart from their commitment to knowledge: "On the one side, they are responsible for the maintenance and advancement of knowledge and on the other they are responsible for performing important functions for their societies." Similarly, he limits the obligations of teaching to the education of a certain segment of each new generation, namely, those who can spend a few years on campus before heading into the job market with some smattering of knowledge and truth. Shils does *not* see the teaching role as initiating a lifelong interest in knowledge among the public. Yet such an approach would seem to expand the reach of the academic ethic, moving it from the monastic to the pastoral, to sustain Shils's clerical conceit. Although research is all about the pursuit of knowledge, what brings the academic into the realm of the ethical is how it touches on people's lives and their relationships, as in the obligations, in this case, between the scholar and the public.[16]

The extended public regard paid by social-science research need not compromise Shils's sense of the scholar's "obligation to investigate whatever he regards as important intellectually and practically" or the scholar's obligation to refuse "to accept the domination of current popular, political and academic prejudices regarding what is permissible to investigate." What will distinguish social scientists' public contribution is how their work will illuminate, critique, and exemplify those prejudices while engaging the public in discussing how this work is "intellectually and practically" important. Such public engagement is bound to complicate matters; talking about the work becomes more of

---

15. Shils, "Academic Ethic," 10, 31.
16. Ibid., 89, 91.

the work. In some cases this engagement might balance the academic prejudices of peer reviews and granting agencies, and in others it might simply add to the general educational value of the academic trade. One would also hope that the demonstration of greater public value in social-science research through this public-knowledge project should engender greater tolerance for more daring and speculative, more decidedly impractical, research and scholarship.[17]

Shils, on the other hand, would limit the responsibilities of scholarly transmission to publishing research results "in such a way that colleagues can study and assess them." The "obligation to knowledge," which consists in pursuing one's intellectual interests, entails seeking "'open' publication" of the results. Why not, I ask, expand that publication beyond the quotation marks of a so-called openness, especially with social-science research that bears so closely on how we live? And yet, after setting the scholar off from the world, toward the end of his essay on the academic ethic, he proposes that "the proper audience" for research is the wider public, using the examples of textbooks and popular surveys, as well as *Scientific American*, all of which have certainly expanded the audience for research. Shils and I also turn out to be of one mind on the importance of sharing knowledge on a public scale, although I still see it as more than a means of garnering wider support for, and drawing new generations into, the intellectual quest. Shils rightly fears that the public will expect scholars to have a straightforward answer to every difficult problem. As I have already noted, working with this expectation is one of the many educational responsibilities and potential gains of the social sciences going public.[18]

When it comes to what keeps social scientists writing for no one other than their colleagues, they tend to blame the university's tenure and promotion committees. These committees find it easiest to count and assess discrete units of empirical research that have been peer reviewed and published in a scholarly journal. This has the effect of not only narrowing the audience to scholars but of encouraging "the piecemeal accumulation of original empirical evidence without a corresponding emphasis on theory development and projects designed to accumulate, assess, and integrate previous research," as John Adair, a psychologist at

---

17. Ibid., 50.
18. Ibid., 51, 93–94. In an earlier piece, on "the calling of sociology," Shils recalls a time when "sociologists thought it was part of their task to share their knowledge with the public." This sense has been lost as more sophisticated research methods have "made for [a] self-enclosure" that largely excludes the public. Statistics is one culprit of a "self-confinement" that "is the intention of some and the fate of many sociologists": "The Calling of Sociology," in *The Calling of Sociology and Other Essays on the Pursuit of Learning* (Chicago: University of Chicago Press, 1980), 83.

the University of Manitoba, notes. The fragmentation within the research is not just an artifact of press coverage or public perception. It is built into the way social scientists go about their research "totally entrenched in their cubicles of insight," as William Wresch has nicely put it.[19]

This theme of fragmentation has also been taken up by political scientist David Ricci of Hebrew University in Jerusalem, when he describes how increases in social-science research activity are remarkably detached from any sense of what needs to be known: "One tends to develop research projects which break ground that others have not tilled before, to stake out small areas of inquiry that other scholars have not yet invaded and conquered for their own. There is, therefore, a propensity constantly to refashion the scope of political science into smaller and smaller realms of expertise, so that some scholars can quickly stand forth as patently competent with regard to subjects that other scholars have overlooked." As if that were not enough, this deliberate diffusion leads scholars' colleagues, when called on to sit in judgment on their work, to simply count the number of publications rather than read them, given that each colleague has a narrow area of expertise.[20]

Ricci tells a dismal tale of knowledge dissipated in *The Tragedy of Political Science*. The tragedy comes of the split in the field's commitment between the pursuit of academic professionalism and the promotion of democratic politics and processes. Individual works of scholarship may demonstrate a surpassing professional competence, he points out, but these autonomous, self-contained works tend to add up to a relatively inchoate body of research, with "findings and teachings that do not foster democracy." This is the failure of a discipline that has been "charged with surveying the province of public affairs and institutions, with the resultant knowledge transmitted to citizens in such a way as to encourage civility, tolerance, moderation, patriotism, an appreciation of rights and obligations, and, not the least, a willingness to support wise government policy."[21]

Against such an ambitious and admirable program of public service, Ricci finds "vocational incoherence" exemplified by political

---

19. John G. Adair, "Research Needs in the Social Sciences," in *The Human Sciences: Their Contribution to Society and Future Research Needs*, ed. Baha Abu-Laban and Brenda Gail Rule (Edmonton: University of Alberta Press, 1988), 164; William Wresch, *Disconnected: Haves and Have-Nots in the Information Age* (New Brunswick, N.J.: Rutgers University Press, 1992), 90; James Rule: "The fact that our disciplines now enjoy a relatively secure claim on university appointments surely insulates us to some degree from the need to justify our 'contributions' to the broader public": *Theory and Progress in Social Science* (Cambridge: Cambridge University Press, 1997), 41.

20. David M. Ricci, *The Tragedy of Political Science: Politics, Scholarship, Democracy* (New Haven: Yale University Press, 1988), 222.

21. Ibid., 25, 7.

scientists' failure to come up with a common definition of what their field is about. He compares this to the discipline's promise at the close of the nineteenth century, when political science was poised to meet public "demand for a new breed of men who, apparently able to partly pierce the veil of uncertainty that shrouded interdependence [of complex societies], would be available for consultation at critical moments in the lives of individuals or society." Ricci is no less dismayed by a field doomed to "strive without success to produce the reliable knowledge that might enable us to somehow change political behavior for the better."[22]

Although I obviously share Ricci's concern with research's isolation and fragmentation, I am not nearly as dismayed by this failure to agree upon what counts as political science. After all, it was just such an earlier unity of purpose that distinguished the questionable contribution of political science to America's cold-war efforts. The field's current diversity can only enrich the range of meaning and action, if the how and why of these differences, as well as the issues and values at stake, can be made readily apparent. The coherence that might enable a greater public presence for the social sciences depends on a better understanding of how research programs operate in relation to each other, with the differences among programs helping to establish the sense that can be made of things. This approach to knowledge is intended to serve a society that is, after all, no less divided on such critical points as what is fairly called political and scientific.[23]

Against these tendencies toward diffusion and fragmentation, a renewed social contract for the social sciences would depend on researchers finding new ways of connecting their work to what it challenges, complements, redirects, and responds to, both in other research studies and in the forums of policy and practice. The current system of

---

22. Ibid., 209, 49–50, 296.
23. According to Ira Katznelson, during the cold war the discipline rallied around the shared assumption that America and democracy "needed political science to secure its liberal regime against internal and external enemies," including "the dangers of mass politics": "The Subtle Politics of Developing Emergency: Political Science as Liberal Guardianship," in *The Cold War and the University: Toward an Intellectual History of the Postwar Years*, ed. Noam Chomsky et al. (New York: New Press, 1997), 235. This was cold-war intelligence work by nonsurreptitious means, funded by the Ford Foundation and other foundations in their effort "to provide assistance ... in designing research so as to be useful to government and business": L. Gary Cowan et al., *Report of the Committee on African Studies* (New York: Ford Foundation, 1958), 1—cited in Laura Nader, "The Phantom Factor: Impact of the Cold War on Anthropology," in Chomsky et al., *Cold War and the University*, 118. The Defense Department's Advanced Research Projects Agency was developing social-science databases on nations and cultures even before it became famous for developing what became the Internet.

scholarly referencing (to which I've devoted chapter 9) needs to be replaced by a system that does far better at connecting and relating ideas across research fields as well as across arenas of social practice. Fortunately, research programs are now developing that are based on close cooperation among researchers, related professionals, and communities, connecting the knowledge of scholarship and experience in fields such as education. What I wish to see is whether such programs can become part of a larger public-knowledge project that introduces the results of this more integrated approach to knowledge into the larger public sphere. This call for a renewed social contract can also be understood as an appeal to the social sciences to find their place within a public philosophy that is critical to democracy.[24]

PUBLIC PHILOSOPHY

John Dewey is the most obvious philosopher of public knowledge in the American context. His contributions to the philosophy of pragmatism had a profound influence on social scientists in the first half of the twentieth century, Robert Lynd not the least of them. He directly addressed what the social sciences owe to the public in two sets of lectures. The first were given in 1926 to Kenyon College in Gambier, Ohio, and published under the title *The Public and Its Problems*. In his view, the problems largely involved how to transform the Great Society, as he repeatedly referred to America, into the Great Community. It takes a community, he believed, to ensure a democracy, and that community must be very much a work of public knowledge: "In a word, that expansion and reinforcement of personal understanding and judgement by the cumulative and transmitted intellectual wealth of the community which may render nugatory the indictment of democracy drawn on the basis of the ignorance, bias and levity of the masses, can be fulfilled only in relations of personal intercourse in the local community," Dewey felt no less strongly that democracy requires the public to participate in ideas that matter, rather than sit in the bleachers watching those ideas played out in political arenas.[25]

---

24. Gary L. Anderson and Kathryn Herr, "The New Paradigm Wars: Is There Room for Rigorous Practitioner Knowledge in Schools and Universities?" *Educational Researcher* 28, no. 5 (June–July 1999).

25. In a 1928 symposium at the University of Virginia, Dewey proposed that philosophy itself was a social science: "Philosophy," in *Research in the Social Sciences: Its Fundamental Methods and Objectives*, ed. Wilson Gee (New York: Macmillan, 1929), 241–65. On his influence on social science, see Smith, *Crucible*, 36–43; John Dewey, *The Public and Its Problems* (New York: Holt, 1926), 180.

Dewey wanted the social sciences to serve people in that play of ideas. He called for "a genuine social science [that] would manifest its reality in the daily press, while learned books and articles supply and polish tools of inquiry." He spoke of inquiry directed at furnishing "knowledge as a precondition of public judgement." He was prepared for the argument that this knowledge would have little impact: "For it is argued the mass of the reading public is not interested in learning and assimilating the result of accurate investigation." Yet the problem of the "secluded library alcoves" frequented by "a few intellectuals" was for Dewey a matter of how ideas are presented—a "question of art." Dewey saw the press as a channel to the public with which he was willing to experiment in his own version of a public-knowledge venture: "A newspaper which was only a daily edition of a quarterly journal of sociology or political sciences would undoubtedly possess a limited circulation and a narrow influence. Even at that, however, the mere existence and accessibility of such material would have some regulative effect." Through the use of existing technologies, he sought to blend journalism and research in the name of the public good: "The highest and most difficult kind of inquiry and a subtle, delicate, vivid, and responsive art of communication must take possession of the physical machinery of transmission and circulation and breathe life into it." This statement could stand as the public-knowledge manifesto in perhaps its first iteration.[26]

Yet Dewey was not above calling this machinery to account for its service to democracy: "When the machine age has thus perfected its machinery it will be a means of life and not its despotic master. Democracy will come into its own, for democracy is the name of a life of free and enriching communion. It had its seer in Walt Whitman. It will have its consummation when free social inquiry is indissolubly wedded to the art of full and moving communication." The question remains of how we are to bring these machines and poets together, if not by continuing to experiment with this "life with free and enriching communication." What Dewey refers to as "intellectual instrumentalities for the formation of an organized public" need to be judged on how well they extend the reach of democracy as a way of life with the support of this new machine age, because for most people living in most places, there is no going back to the town-hall meetings of Dewey's yesteryear. The participation that he saw as so critical will need to take other forms.[27]

26. Dewey, *Public and Its Problems*, 180, 183, 184.
27. Ibid., 84, 142.

Dewey carried these themes forward, with a focus on a public philosophy of knowledge, in a second set of lectures, this time at the University of Edinburgh in 1929. In addressing his theme of the "quest for certainty" at a time when a good deal of certainty was about to collapse, he held that we are sadly deluded if we imagine ourselves to be in pursuit of a self-contained and unified body of knowledge that can stand apart from the world it describes. The quest for such certainty reflects an ailment that has much to do with how we respond to this frustrated human capacity for knowledge: "Man has never had such a varied body of knowledge in his possession before, and probably never before has he been so uncertain and so perplexed as to what his knowledge means, what it points to in action and consequences." Dewey was concerned, as I am, with righting this situation, and his attempts to do so suggest that knowledge that is such a source of uncertainty and confusion may not be knowledge at all.[28]

To begin with, Dewey held that knowledge could be assessed by how it functions within the larger, practical world, and he took exception to those who believed that knowledge exists at a remove from the world: "Independence from any specified application is readily taken to be equivalent to independence from application as such; it is as if specialists, engaged in perfecting tools and having no concern with their use and so interested in the operation of perfecting them that they carry results beyond any existing possibilities of use, were to argue that they are dealing with an independent realm having no connection with tools or utilities." Now, I want to be careful with this tool metaphor lest the instrumentality of knowledge be taken too literally, as if knowledge was a tool to fix what's broken. I defend in this book, in a way that Dewey did not in these lectures, the usefulness of knowledge as a device for also finding one's bearings, for taking the measure of things—that is, the usefulness of knowledge as a tool for helping one make greater sense of the world. That greater sense can lead, as per Dewey, to knowledge as a source of action, whether in public policy or in one's personal life. The measure of knowledge in this public sense lies in what it does for people, how it works for them.[29]

Having given up on the certainty of a fixed and steadfast knowledge unaffected by the world, we are to pursue a "diversification of discoveries and the opening up of new points of view and new methods." For

---

28. John Dewey, "The Quest for Certainty," in *The Later Works, 1929*, ed. Jo Ann Boydston, vol. 41 (Carbondale: Southern Illinois University Press, 1988), 248.
29. Ibid., 123.

Dewey, the progress of knowledge is not about integrating what we know into a singular whole, a unified theory, but about creating a greater and more effective engagement with the world: "The value of hypothetical ideas ... is not determined by their internal elaboration and consistency, but by the consequences they effect in existence as that is perceptively experienced." What the social sciences offer to the critical determination of those consequences testing is a refinement of methods that help us to see how ideas work themselves out in the world.[30]

Clearly, the reader can see why I am drawn to Dewey's public philosophy of knowledge. I realize that social scientists rarely judge the quality of knowledge drawn from research by how it works on the world or how it works on people's understanding. More often, knowledge claims are grounded in research methods and traditional epistemological concerns of reliability and validity. My focus on what the social sciences can do for public knowledge, however, is all about increasing the public consequences of this knowledge, which, *pace* Dewey, only strengthen its claim as knowledge. This approach is all about increasing the democratic force of knowledge in the hands of people, rather than, in that other sense of the instrumentality of knowledge, simply adding to the power that experts exercise over the public on its behalf.[31]

An emphasis on the instrumental nature of knowledge can easily be seen to serve political regimes other than democracies, as indeed it has done.[32] Dewey was not above entering the fray between those who sought to cut off social science from its social reform roots in favor of scientific objectivity, and those who would bring science into the service of specific moral and political agendas. Research, for Dewey, was to be directed by "the fundamentally moral nature of the social problem." He wanted methods in the social sciences that would do away with the pretense of objectivity and embrace both the "choice of values" and the "personal responsibility for judgement and action." Dewey's philosophy of knowledge had everything to do with rigorously testing what could be

---

30. Ibid., 132.

31. George Lundberg, *Can Science Save Us?* (New York: Longman, Green, 1947), 26–27: "If social scientists possessed an equally demonstrable relevant body of knowledge and technique ... then knowledge would be equally above the reach of political upheaval. The services of real social scientists would be as indispensable to Fascists, as to Communists and Democrats."

32. Dewey, "The Quest for Certainty," 108, 238, 64. It is interesting to compare Dewey's stance to the striking point made by Amartya Sen, Nobel Prize economist, who holds that famines are brought about not by shortages of food but by inadequacies and inequities in the channels of distribution and "the entitlements of different sections of a society": "The Ethical Dimension," *Scientific American* (January 1999): 19.

known of the human condition, which set the social sciences apart as an intellectual enterprise.[33]

The political side of the case for these public concerns with knowledge is made all the more forcefully by Virginia Polytech sociologist Steve Fuller, whose theory of "social epistemology" is concerned with improving how the pursuit of knowledge is organized. He holds that "the key issue in regulating knowledge production is not how to accumulate more but how to redistribute it more equitably." He makes the democratic politics of such a stance apparent by counterposing an "Authoritarian Theory of Knowledge," which would reject the goal of improved distribution because "the rationality of thinking for oneself diminishes as society's knowledge gathering activities expand to the point of requiring a division of cognitive labor into autonomous expertises." Thus we have the irony that as civilization advances, it may seem to make less sense to think for oneself when we have specialists to do it for us. Within this authoritarian "cognitive economy," one defers to experts, for there alone lies the hope for increasing a "society's store of knowledge." Yet if we are to reject this loss of individual autonomy and rationality, how are we to find the advantage of social-science research?[34]

The devil in such deference to expertise lies in degree. On the one hand, people may totally defer to the experts in a given area of social service by turning over responsibilities for research, policy, implementation, administration, and evaluation, as the biblical Pharaoh turned to Joseph based on the young convict's unsurpassed skills at dream reading. On the other hand, people may say to the experts, "Thank you very much for the impressive range of social-science research, as no one else could have pulled off such systematic and rigorous work. Now that we have your results, we invite you to join in the public debate over how we should act on what we know, perhaps responding to a follow-up call for your research assistance in evaluating the resulting action." Fuller's point is well taken, that making a body of research public in an intelligible and coherent way is terribly inefficient compared with simply producing more research. Inefficiencies will be especially great at the outset, as both public and researchers participate in designing better ways to organize and present the results of scholarly inquiry.

Democracies demand those sorts of inefficiencies. Everyone in a democracy needs to understand what, under an authoritarian regime, only the few need to grasp. The "irrationality" of all this participation

---

33. John Dewey, *Liberalism and Social Action* (New York: Capricorn, ca. 1935), 47–48.
34. Steve Fuller, *Social Epistemology* (Bloomington: Indiana University Press, 1988), 29, 278, 279. Dewey, too, emphasizes equity of distribution as a proper concern.

and access is the price of increasing people's self-determination and autonomy. Democracy thrives within the cognitive redundancy of so many people seeking to understand for themselves, taking the time to challenge and chew over the risks and prospects they face. My hope is that increasingly accessible forms of social-science research will support informed dissent against the rationalized efficiency arguments promoted by those holding to authoritarian theories of knowledge. This will require people to find their own way among social-science studies, discovering how these studies relate to each other, as well as to policies and pro-grams, even if these studies' critiques are in deadly opposition to each other. How this equitable distribution of knowledge might best be afforded will inevitably be the subject of much debate, much trial and error, if not always in the spirit of Dewey. Improving the public exchange will draw energy and resources away from the research itself, yet it still seems to me to be a welcome intellectual advance over whatever con-tribution yet another study might make within an increasingly fragmentary universe of knowledge.

Yet as things now stand, the social sciences remain riddled with cog-nitive inefficiencies. This is what comes of a professional ethos given to the fervent production of research not so much for its own sake but as a crude productivity model for the scholarly profession. It will take considerable commitment and resources to transform the sheer multi-plication of published fragments into a more reliable source of public knowledge. But here we are in the midst of a whole new range of tech-nologies, and we have only begun to explore how they can help manage, order, and offer greater access to knowledge. The private sector is already using this new machinery to enhance its intellectual and infor-mational assets, both for internal use and to improve what it can offer its clients. The public sector deserves no less, yet as the social sciences fail to take advantage of these new technologies to improve their contribu-tion to public knowledge, they face the prospect of becoming even less of a political force, thereby undermining their public support. Improv-ing this public contribution is bound to assist social scientists, not only in securing public support but also (as they will always be the most intensely interested audience of their own work) in making the connec-tions, finding the coherence, relating the oppositions, and doing a better job of communicating these ideas. Such efforts would help more people understand more of what is known about the world around us in ways that challenge the too readily assumed scope and consequences of that knowledge.

Limited Impact 6

Police commissioners do not often thank social-science professors for their help in fighting crime. It was noteworthy, then, when a few years back then-Commissioner William J. Bratton of New York City commended James Q. Wilson, political scientist and professor emeritus at UCLA, for his theory of broken windows (one window left broken leads to the breaking of others). Bratton felt that this homiletic call for greater vigilance led to policing strategies that have dramatically reduced crime in New York and other American cities in recent times. Wilson has often written for the *New York Times*, as well as the *Atlantic, Public Interest*, and other magazines. When the *Times* did a feature on him, it was headlined "A Thinker Attuned to Doing," and named him among "the most influential thinkers in the country" and one of the "most important political scientists of the past 40 years." Given my concern with the gap between research and public knowledge, Wilson's adept stepping across the line between academic and public life is worth considering and celebrating. Yet I also want to make clear why Wilson's contribution, though he is a thoughtful essayist on social policies and practices, does not define for me what is needed to improve the impact and value of the social sciences.[1]

In 1982, Wilson and George Kelling published an essay in the *Atlantic* proposing that if officials took action against the basic signs of urban decay, such as broken windows, they would send out an influential message to the community about the restoration of law and order. They cited how people felt safer when police began to walk the beat in Newark again, and how this sense of "public order" appeared to provide a barrier against crime. Actually, putting officers back on the street did *not* initially reduce crime in those communities—nor did Wilson and Kelling expect it to; it only made people *feel* more secure. The reductions in crime rates followed some years later and have continued to fall since 1992 on a

---

1. Richard Bernstein, "A Thinker Attuned to Doing," *New York Times*, August 22, 1998, A15.

national scale, making it difficult to pinpoint causes. The drop has been attributed to the strength of the economy and employment levels, an aging population, reductions in crack cocaine use, huge increases in the number of people in prison, tighter gun controls, and sponsorship of community-support programs. But still, Commissioner Bratton and others seem happy to credit Wilson's research-based theory for its contribution.[2]

The method of scholarly influence is the interesting point here—from social experiment (in Newark) to social-science research (conducted by George Kelling) to public statement (in the *Atlantic* by Wilson and Kelling) to public action (by police departments) to social change (reflected in crime rates). The exception in this sequence is how these two social scientists reached out to a wider readership through the *Atlantic*. Although Wilson tends to dismiss his broken-window piece as but one of many such essays that he has written, its impact is just the sort of return that the public should expect on occasion from its investment in scholarship. The broken-window essay also makes apparent how the lessons learned from this field can be mobilized by metaphors and analogies that capture people's imagination. Yet Wilson's status as a public intellectual speaks equally well to one of the current limits of the social sciences' impact, as few researchers can fill such public shoes and as the research itself figures relatively little in the public intellectual's writing for the popular media.[3]

Any efforts to reduce the gap between social-science research and public practices, which is a source of frustration to both researchers and public, will need to draw on those cases where research does have a public impact. The instances of direct and indirect, achieved and frustrated impact that I review in this chapter reflect a general assumption that research effectiveness is all about its determination of policies

2. James Q. Wilson and George L. Kelling, "Broken Windows," *Atlantic* (March 1982), http://www.theatlantic.com/election/connection/crime/windows.htm; Fox Butterfield, "Crime Fell 7 Percent in '98, Continuing a 7-Year Trend," *New York Times*, May 17, 1999, A12; Sylvia Nasa and Kirsten B. Mitchell, "Booming Job Market Draws Young Black Men in Fold," *New York Times*, May 23, 1999, A1.

3. Wilson: "I'm glad that ['Broken Windows' has] had some influence. It was important that the police pay attention to the orderliness as well as to crime. But 'Broken Windows' is the title of one essay I wrote among many. I don't see it as a great literary moment in my life": cited in Bernstein, "Thinker Attuned to Doing." To take another more recent instance of how effective certain newsstand publications are for academic impact, the *American Prospect* has been credited for shaping President Clinton's 1992 election strategy in health care, welfare, and urban issues, and he used the magazine's contributors in drawing up his list for appointments in these areas: Eric Alterman, "Tiny Circulations, Big Ideas: 'General Interest' Journals and the Shaping of Public Policy," *Chronicle of Higher Education*, June 5, 1998, B6.

and programs. Whether this impact is the whole of the social-science project is not so much my concern here as is what we can learn from this record about the potential for research to make a greater contribution to public understanding of, and participation in, these social arenas. Yet I also want to consider the cautious reserve of those who insist that the social sciences need to stand off carefully from this public domain if they are to be of any use at all.

RESEARCH EFFECTS

If ever there was a sweeping claim made for social science's impact on the world, it is found in John Maynard Keynes's colorful statement from the 1930s about the reach of ideas: "The ideas of economists and political philosophers, both when they are right and when they are wrong, are more powerful than is commonly understood. Indeed the world is ruled by little else. Practical men, who believe themselves to be quite exempt from any intellectual influence, are usually the slaves of some defunct economist. Madmen in authority, who hear voices in the air, are distilling the frenzy from some academic scribbler of a few years back.... It is ideas not vested interests which are dangerous for good or evil." I certainly agree with Keynes's ascription of influence and its dangers, so much so that I seek to make more of such scribbling and defunctness readily apparent to a wider public, for what better way could there be to set practical souls free and undermine authoritative madmen held captive by such ideas.[4]

When one looks to the more specific instance of the "major advances" in twentieth-century social science, as Karl Deutsch, Andrei Markovits, and John Platt have done, one finds a stream of ideas that, much as Keynes warned, now sit comfortably within the public domain. The list of sixty-two major advances from 1900 to 1965 that these Harvard social scientists compiled includes attitude surveys, opinion polling, and cost–benefit analysis, all of which are good examples of the social sciences' considerable political impact not only as a source of knowledge but as a way of thinking. They also mention computer simulations of economic systems, now child's play with the introduction of Simcity—a popular game for the home computer. This intellectual hit parade also includes Mohandas K. Gandhi and his large-scale nonviolent political action, as well as Vladimir Lenin and Mao Tse-tung for their political theories. The

---

4. John Maynard Keynes, *The General Theory of Employment, Interest, and Money* (London: Macmillan, 1936), 383–84.

social sciences, then, are not without impact. My issue is with ensuring, amid that impact, that people have a chance to engage and challenge this form of inquiry, this way of determining what there is to be known, that passes as social science.[5]

It might be better then to review particular instances of social-science research's influence on the world, as a source of understanding and theory, rhetoric and metaphor, facts and figures. For example, William Foote Whyte, a Cornell University sociologist, points to the profound effect of research on the economic recovery of postwar Japan through a "creative misunderstanding," which took place when the country adopted the "participative management" praised by American academics. The Japanese assumed that this approach must have been working well in American factories, but of course it wasn't being used at all and wouldn't be until the Japanese had proved that they could make the practice far exceed the expectations of the theory. The theory, in effect, was launched out of the blue, only to bound back showering industrial improvement along the way.[6]

Research can also demonstrate a lack of impact, apparent in a case such as psychiatry's historical assumption of responsibility for the study of, and intervention in, suicide. The field would appear to have had little impact on suicide levels, which have doubled in children, for example, over the last twenty years. It is certainly little consolation to imagine that those levels might have only been worse for want of that research. And finally, research can have a decidedly negative impact on the lives of people. In too may cases since its very origins in the nineteenth century, well-respected research in the social sciences has supported treating women as a form of flawed male, African Americans as less than wholly developed human beings, and gays as suffering mental illness. Sometimes, the most powerful and effective scholarship is necessarily directed at correcting earlier, egregious sins within research practices that have

---

5. Karl W. Deutsch, Andrei S. Markovits, and John Platt, "Major Advances in the Social Sciences since 1900: An Analysis of the Conditions and Effects of Creativity," in *Advances in the Social Sciences, 1900–1980: What, Who, Where, How?* ed. Karl W. Deutsch, Andrei S. Markovits, and John Platt (Lanham, Md.: University Press of America, 1982).

6. William Foote Whyte, "On the Uses of Social Science Research," *American Sociological Review* 51 (1986): 555–63; Robert Cole, *Work, Mobility, and Participation* (Berkeley and Los Angeles: University of California Press, 1980). On the tendency of research on policy—a major area of research impact—to be more often "rhetorical-discursive" than "quantitative-empirical" in nature: see Janet A. Schneider, Nancy J. Stevens, and Louis G. Torantzky, "Policy Research and Analysis: An Empirical Profile, 1975–1980," *Policy Sciences* 15 (1982).

simply amplified contemporary prejudices with their scientifically crafted distortions of reason and data.[7]

Certainly, one of the challenges of this public-knowledge project will be tracking the impact of social-science research on people's thinking. We need to be prepared to catch no more than a glimpse, largely by inference, of its effects. While it is easy to place a figure on what people invest in knowledge, from newspaper subscriptions to consultants' contracts, when it comes to how particular forms of knowledge influence people's thinking and action, there are only cries and whispers. This has not deterred enterprising researchers from inventing such handy devices as the Research Utilization (RU) Index and the Information Utilization (IU) Scale, which rank the degree to which ideas have been attended to and taken up in such areas as policy making and professional practices.[8]

In my own field of education, complaints about the ineffectiveness of research are common, and not just from disgruntled parents or teachers. In 1971, the Rand Corporation reported that "research has found nothing that consistently and unambiguously makes a difference in student outcomes.... Research has not discovered any educational practice that offers a high probability of success." This report suggests that not a classroom anywhere had benefited from the countless studies that had been conducted on learning and teaching. But, of course, we might argue, after Keynes, that teachers are constantly putting ideas to work that they have picked up here or there from research and developed on their own. That no one teaching method has proven universally effective is as it should

---

7. D. W. Light, "Treating Suicide: The Illusions of a Professional Movement," *International Social Science* 20 (1972); Dinitia smith, "Evolving Answers to the Why of Suicide," *New York Times,* July 31, 1999, A15. Among the early identifications and correctives of this tendency to treat white men as the norm, see Stephen Jay Gould, *The Mismeasure of Man* (New York: Norton, 1981); and Barbara Ehrenreich and Deirdre English, *For Her Own Good: 150 Years of the Experts' Advice to Women* (Garden City, N.Y.: Anchor, 1978).

8. Fritz Machlup, the Princeton economist who first set out the scope of a knowledge economy in the 1960s, insists that the benefit of knowledge is not to be measured, whether within the whole economy or in specific programs: "Uses, Value, and Benefits of Knowledge," *Knowledge: Creation, Diffusion, Utilization* 1, no. 1 (September 1979): 77, 79–80. For the RU Index, see D. Pelz and J. A. Horsely, "Measuring Utilization of Nursing Research," in *Utilizing Evaluation: Concepts and Measurement Techniques,* ed James A. Ciarlo (Beverly Hills: Sage, 1981). For the IU Scale, see J. K. Larsen, *Information Utilization and Non-utilization* (Palo Alto, Calif.: American Institutes for Research in the Behavioral Sciences, 1982), with reviews of the measurement question in William N. Dunn, "Measuring Knowledge Use," *Knowledge: Creation, Diffusion, Utilization* 5, no. 1 (September 1983); and in Tim Booth, "Researching Policy Research: Issues of Utilization in Decision Making," *Knowledge: Creation, Diffusion, Utilization* 12, no. 1 (September 1990).

be with an extremely complex social phenomenon driven by multi-layered agendas operating among the students, teachers, administrators, community, and elected officials. (Think of the myriad factors that come into play during a morning's reading lesson among thirty children and a teacher.) Going public with more of the available research, it needs to be recognized, is only very rarely going to turn up that special something "that consistently and unambiguously makes a difference in student outcomes." But it is going to offer insights into the processes and programs, the ideas and theories, in ways that can be a source of meaning and perhaps of change.[9]

It might seem that if research is going to have an impact, it will come with "applied research"—evaluation, program, and policy studies—as opposed to "basic research." As I have already suggested with this distinction, and what earlier examples in this chapter make clear, is that the basic ideas and theories of the social sciences are as important to public knowledge as the more practical findings. What is thought of as basic research in education, for example, can be shown to have made a difference in the larger world. The basic research of an early giant in educational psychology, Edward Thorndike, who was a student of William James at Harvard before joining Teachers College at Columbia University, was on the limits of learning transfer across subject areas, which he managed to turn against the claim of the then-current argument that teaching of Latin and Greek was the perfect tool for sharpening students' minds. The brain is not a muscle that could be strengthened by the dumbbells of dead languages, Thorndike's research established. His work contributed to the "relevance" argument of the modern curriculum.

Research also had an impact on the very architecture of schools, as University of Chicago psychologist J. W. Getzels argues in the essay that introduced me to the Thorndike example. Getzels holds that when educational psychologists stopped treating learners in their research studies as empty vessels and began regarding them as solvers of open-ended problems, the architectural design of classrooms changed in the 1970s from being rectangular boxes to wall-less open spaces. Now that we are back to boxy classrooms, it may be that the current emphasis in policy and research on test scores, carefully set out in columns and rows, has led to students' being similarly arranged at their desks. Could the current talk of "learning communities" among researchers and educators represent the metaphorical point of resistance to this accountability-by-

---

9. Harvey A. Averch et al., *How Effective Is Schooling? A Critical Review and Synthesis of Research Findings* (Santa Monica, Calif.: Rand Corporation, 1971), iv.

column-and-row tendency? What is "basic" about this research into learning and its impact is how it articulates very different ideas of what it means to learn, in ways that demonstrate just how knowledge and action work on each other.[10]

Certainly, the greatest political impact of basic educational research is found in the U.S. Supreme Court ruling on *Brown v. Board of Education* in 1954. The ruling set aside previous court decisions upholding segregation by drawing, at least in part, on psychological research submitted by the NAACP as evidence that the doctrine of separate-but-equal was damaging to African Americans. Among the more interesting objections raised by those who defended segregation was that social-science research did not constitute a legitimate form of evidence to place before the Court. The Court accepted the research, which still raised concerns among some who supported the ruling because the move suggested that damages had to be firmly established (by such means as research) before rights could be asserted.

The research by the psychologist Kenneth Clark on the consequences of American racial attitudes for children changed, through this court decision, the meaning of equality in America. If the school desegregation that followed produced only modest gains in African American student achievement, it is another reminder of how the struggle for justice is made up of small steps. The social sciences are particularly good at ascertaining incremental gains and losses, possibilities and risks, in ways that I think should be a greater part of public thinking about the larger issues of what should be done. There is just such research emerging now on the value of affirmative action in education. On the other hand, continuing research on racial differences in IQ continues to be used to bolster arguments, most notoriously in Richard Herrnstein and Charles Murray's *The Bell Curve,* that oppose the basic principles of that hard-won equality. If we have slowly learned, especially since the Great Society initiatives of the 1960s, that school reform in itself is not going to end poverty or racism, we should be all the more concerned with carefully calculating how risks are reduced and possibilities increased, if only by degrees. And that's why social-science research needs to be part

---

10. J. W. Getzels, "Paradigm and Practice: On the Impact of Basic Research in Education," in *Knowledge for Policy: Improving Education through Research,* ed. Don S. Anderson and Bruce J. Biddle (London: Falmer, 1991), 104–9. On learning community, see, for example, Lauren B. Resnick and Megan William Hall, "Learning Organizations for Sustainable Education Reform," *Daedalus* 127, no. 4 (fall 1998): "School-based learning communities can produce improvements in student achievement when they develop individual teaching capacity and when they facilitate a common learning culture in a school as a whole" (111).

of what people talk about, part of the check and balance, when they are considering what can be done in the long, slow struggle for a greater measure of justice. We need to remember, as well, that those who do research, as much as those who do policy, are guided in their work by conceptions of the good that need to be treated as an always open question in an open society.[11]

In 1962, the American Sociological Associatiion (ASA) took the unusual step of dedicating a section of its annual convention to "the uses of sociology." The reason for this, the then-president of the ASA observed, was that "doubt is often raised as to whether the rapidly mountain stream of empirical studies and the increasing number of publications on social theory have contributed to anything the educated citizen would find worthwhile." That doubt is no less present today. This ASA conference theme led to *The Uses of Sociology,* a collection of essays dedicated to Robert Lynd's *Knowledge for What?* (1939), whose call for sociology's greater public service to democracy I discussed earlier. Nearly thirty years after Lynd's book, some forty sociologists made their case in *The Uses of Sociology* for just how socially useful sociology could be in the areas of health, education, foreign policy, justice, social welfare, and public administration, among others.[12]

Sociology's usefulness, according to the book's editors, Paul Lazarsfeld, William Sewell, and Harold Wilensky, is to be found in its service to a *client.* The useful sociologist can translate a client's problem into a research design and then, with research results in hand, translate the obtained knowledge back into an action plan for the client. This professional model of "client" and "translation" is best supported, according to the editors, by "a third force, a middleman to mediate between

11. Irving L. Horowitz and J. E. Katz, "Brown v. Board of Education," in Anderson and Biddle, *Knowledge for Policy.* On the use of IQ, see Richard J. Herrnstein and Charles Murray, *The Bell Curve: Intelligence and Class Structure in American Life* (New York: Free Press, 1994) and Joe L. Kincheloe, Shirley R. Steinberg, and Aaron Gresson, *Measured Lies: The Bell Curve Examined* (New York: St. Martin's, 1996). For a strong example of research on affirmative action, see William G. Bowen and Derek Bok, *The Shape of the River: Long-Term Consequences of Considering Race in College and University Admissions* (Princeton, N.J.: Princeton University Press, 1998). On the calibration of hope, Edmund W. Gordon, the first research director of the Head Start program, has recently stated: "Back in the 60s, there was desegregation, there was the War on Poverty, there was Head Start—and most us really thought that we were going to do it. I must say that I no longer believe that. I think that schools can be more powerful, but I don't think they can reverse all the ill effects of a starkly disadvantaged status in society." Cited in James Traub, "What Schools Can Do," *New York Times Magazine,* January 16, 2000, 68.

12. Paul F. Lazarsfeld, William H. Sewell, and Harold L. Wilensky, eds., preface to *The Uses of Sociology* (New York: Basic Books, 1967); Robert S. Lynd, *Knowledge for What? The Place of Social Science in American Culture* (Princeton, N.J.: Princeton University Press, 1939).

client and sociologist." Today there is much client-contract research, as well as many information brokers hired to translate and summarize studies. From my standpoint, this particular professionalized framing of social-science usefulness only serves to reduce the sociologist's overall debt to public knowledge. A model of consultants informing clients through mediators is too narrowly conceived for, if not actually contrary to, the notion of public service and the openness it entails.[13]

Still, this commitment to a client is a step beyond the more typical internal loop of sociologists doing sociology for sociologists. Judith Kramer, at Brooklyn College, one of the few women in *The Uses of Sociology*, feels it necessary to remind her colleagues that "as long as sociologists talk only to each other, they incur little social risk; the price of their professional security, however, is the failure to fulfill the social promise of the sociological imagination." If this seems too obvious to mention (given that it is the theme of my book), there are others in the collection, such as Roger Angell at the University of Michigan, who speak of the sociology that is "an end in itself" (as opposed to "applied research," which is "a means to some other end"). As I have stated, the ideas as well as the data (both for basic and applied research) all hold a potential intellectual interest for the public, and for practitioners, that we have hardly begun to test. Thus, I believe that this public-knowledge model of the social sciences has room for Harvard professor Nathan Glazer's brief that "sociology's functions are primarily those of complicating and undermining received opinions on social life." Such knowledge can enable people to test their assumptions, check suspicions, or find the consolation of a sensible explanation.[14]

When it comes to research that has no other aspiration than to be useful, the stand out should be the evaluation study. An evaluation is typically commissioned to assess the effectiveness of a specific program on its own terms. There is little that is theoretical or abstract about this pursuit of knowledge. But here, too, the record of effectiveness is rocky. Such studies often lack reliability and consistency, and lead to various interpretations of what the program has achieved. Just how bad it can get is glibly suggested by Gary Walker of Public/Private Ventures, who observed at a recent Brookings Institution conference titled "Learning What Works" that a decade of research on national service programs, at

13. Lazarsfeld, Sewell, and Wilensky, introduction to *Uses of Sociology*, xxviii.
14. Judith R. Kramer, "Resistance to Sociological Data: A Case Study"; Robert C. Angell, "The Ethical Problems of Applied Research"; and Nathan Glazer, "The Ideological Uses of Sociology," in Lazarsfeld, Sewell, and Wilensky, *Uses of Sociology*, pp. 788, 725, and 76 respectively.

a cost of perhaps $13 million, has not answered what he sees as the question most likely to be asked by conservative critics: Does national service promote volunteerism? Evaluation studies can seem to operate more as a safeguard against substantial program abuse—offering demonstrable accountability and risk management—than as a means of understanding and working with the process and its consequences. This, too, speaks to the challenge of a public-knowledge project to improve the connections within the research, between underlying theory and program evaluation, and with public interests across the political spectrum.[15]

Nowhere is the effect of evaluation studies more profoundly ambivalent than with the most famous of American initiatives for children, Head Start, which was at the forefront of the War of Poverty when it was launched in 1965. Head Start appears to have been little affected by its many hundreds of evaluation studies, although such research appears to have influenced other early childhood policies in Washington. One of the earliest evaluation studies of Head Start, conducted by the Westinghouse Learning Corporation in the late 1960s, found little evidence to support the program ("a head-start into oblivion," critics then claimed). Yet the Westinghouse study also made it clear, in all of the controversy surrounding its methods and interpretations, just how integrated research and politics really are when it comes to matters that matter.[16]

Since then, the Head Start program has worked with 15 million children with funding to the tune of $31 billion up to 1997. More recent and more sophisticated assessments of its effectiveness have established a positive impact on children's academic performance, which continues substantially longer in white children's school life than black children's, while its immunization program contributes to better health for both. It is well to remember that when it comes to what drives support for such programs and policies, evaluation research is but one source of understanding, of inspiration and insight, in what is equally an educational and a political program.[17]

---

15. M. C. Alkin, R. Daillak, and P. White, "Does Evaluation Make a Difference?" in Anderson and Biddle, *Knowledge for Policy*; Gary Walker, *Learning What Works: Evaluating Complex Social Interventions. Report on the Symposium,* October 22, 1997 (Washington: Brookings Institution, 1997).

16. David K. Cohen and Michael S. Garet, "Reforming Educational Policy and Applied Social Research," in Anderson and Biddle, *Knowledge for Policy*; Tim Booth, "Researching Policy Research: Issues of Utilization in Decision Making," *Knowledge: Creation, Diffusion, Utilization* 12, no. 1 (September 1980).

17. Lynn A. Karoly, Peter W. Greenwood, Susan S. Everingham, Jill Houbé, M. Rebecca Kilburn, C. Peter Rydell, Matthew Sanders, and James Chiesa, *Investing in Our Children: What We Know and Don't Know about* the *Costs and Benefits of Early Childhood Interventions* (Santa Monica, Calif.: Rand Corporation, 1998). For a summary of

Nor is it to be forgotten that the very formation of the Head Start program itself was a powerful instance of research's influence, having been initiated during the Johnson administration under the direction of the Cornell psychologist Urie Bronfenbrenner, who applied his ecological theory of child development to the design of this far-reaching program. The mid-1960s was a time of particular governmental optimism, with Daniel Patrick Moynihan, for example, positively glowing over a "professionalization of reform" representing a "technique that offers a profound promise of social sanity and stability in the time to come." Moynihan, former Harvard professor of government turned senator from New York, did not doubt that the emerging wealth of information was being effectively utilized by a rising class of professionals to the benefit of both economy and social policy. He himself helped to link social-science researchers to political actors, and he was not alone in this academic faith, as the government of the day welcomed social scientists, especially economists, into its ranks.[18]

In 1970, however, Moynihan admitted in the pages of *Psychology Today* that he'd been terribly wrong in thinking that economic growth would foster a government surplus for social programs, with a growing middle class bringing "more and more energetic persons to the calling of social change" and an "exponential increase in knowledge" giving "method and direction to such change." His faith in "a fairly self-correcting and self-improving society," despite the continuing growth in knowledge, had come to an end. The social sciences seemed unable to switch from putting forward the case for change to implementing proposed changes through the programs of the Great Society and the War on Poverty. The response to this foundering, according to the acerbic Moynihan, who did little to hide his frustration and disappointment, was that "the silent majority of social scientists" had since sought out "research topics no one seems too much interested in just at the moment," as well as increasingly obscure ways of stating the obvious. And in the meantime, Nathan Glazer has observed, reflecting his own disillusionment with the era as well as with

positive findings on Head Start, see the National Head Start Association's "Research Bites," http://www.nhsa.org/research/bites.htm; and for a braoder view of program limits and possibilities, Traub, "What Schools Can Do." Barry White, of the U.S. Office of Management and Budget, confirms that research on the ineffectiveness of the politically popular Elementary and Secondary Education Act of 1965 was used in the 1980s "to change the program, not eliminate it or cut it back": "Education Research and US Federal Educational Policy," in *Knowledge Bases for Education Policies* (Paris: OECD, 1996), 65.

18. Daniel Patrick Moynihan, "The Professionalization of Reform," *Public Interest* 1 (1965): 8; Nathan Glazer, *The Limits of Social Policy* (Cambridge: Harvard University Press, 1998), 10.

the impact of the social sciences, "one could hear from young delinquents the very explanations and excuses that social psychologists and sociologists themselves were making for behavior that damaged society—and themselves." Something was clearly wrong with the system.[19]

In 1972, Ida Merriam, the assistant commissioner of research for the Social Security Administration frankly warned researchers, in the *Journal of Social Policy*, of "a growing recognition that much of the federally supported extra-mural research, particularly in the social sciences, has added little or nothing to either basic knowledge or to practical decision-making." This strained link between research and policy appears, in the words of Martin Rein, an MIT professor of social policy, to be "neither consensual, graceful or self-evident." At best, Rein noted, research could "sharpen the areas of disagreement; make the issues more uncertain, complex and technical," as if to balance their strictly political treatment. Policy officials tended to work, in his estimation, from "fragmentary evidence" drawn from "unrepresentative programs."[20]

Then there is the exploitation of research's potential impact by advocacy groups to drive foreign policy. Aryreh Neier, whom the *New York Times Magazine* calls the dean of American human rights activists and who is currently president of the Open Society Institute, describes the technique of "shaming" that was developed by Human Rights Watch and used with the Reagan administration. The process was intended to expose Washington hypocrisy, in all its furor about fighting the evil empire in the name of civil liberties, by "producing thick, amply documented reports [on human rights violations among Reagan-supported regimes].... Our emphasis was on providing the *evidentiary* bases for the claims we were making." As a result Congress started to set human rights standards in 1981 that the Reagan administration had to certify were in place to keep foreign aid flowing. Lives were saved, as Vice President George Bush was dispatched to put an end to the death squads in El Salvador. The Human Rights Watch strategy was a success of the moment, one that apparently no longer works on Capitol Hill, according to journalist David Rieff. He calls on today's human rights movement, much as I am calling on the social sciences, once again to "take its case to the public, not just rely on its influence and its certainty that it does an enormous amount of good in the world."[21]

19. Daniel Patrick Moynihan, "Eliteland," *Psychology Today*, September 1970, 35, 66, 68; Glazer, *Limits of Social Policy*, 15.
20. Ida Merriam, cited in Martin Rein, *Social Science and Public Policy* (Harmondsworth, England: Penguin, 1976), 97, 12.
21. Aryreh Neier cited in David Rieff, "The Precarious Triumph of Human Rights," *New York Times Magazine,* August 8, 1999, 38.

It has to be said that in the normal course of things the weight of research is only felt on policy as a result of what Harvard education professor Carol Weiss describes as "knowledge creep," a term that nicely captures the slow trickle and seep of ideas as they find their way into policy deliberations (that is, if it isn't being used to describe the researcher). Weiss found that policy wonks possess only a vague awareness of what the research community is up to in their area, although they are prepared to affirm the general importance of the social sciences to their work. She describes how research can provide a background sensibility on, for example, whether an issue is amenable to policy action, pointing to how the California court "scaled down its expectations" for prisoner rehabilitation as a result of various evaluation studies. Nonetheless, Weiss remains concerned that research continues to reach officials in a haphazard manner, through channels she does not hesitate to call "slow, wasteful, and sloppy."[22]

More recently, in the face of continuing frustration over the research–policy connections, Weiss has proposed that the public be regarded by researchers as an "evaluation user" with the goal of promoting a civil society of people active in "communal and associational life." She lends her support to what is, in effect, a public-knowledge project by suggesting, for example, that "it would be interesting to seek empirical confirmation of the idea that civil society informed through the results of evaluation would be more likely to support program improvement." She also feels a forum is needed "where program managers, planners, and policy makers can interact with evaluators, researchers, and academic experts to discuss their questions, offer their own experience and learn about the state of knowledge in the field."[23]

---

22. Carol Hirschon Weiss, "Knowledge Creep and Decision Accretion," in Anderson and Biddle, Knowledge for Policy, 183–92; Carol Hirschon Weiss, "Research and Policy Making: A Limited Partnership," in Heller, Use and Abuse, 217, 219, 230, 233. Cheol Oh proposes greater consultation among researchers and policy makers on the design and measures used: Linking Social Science Information to Policy-Making (Greenwich, Conn.: Jai Press, 1996), 142. In analyzing 120 research projects directed at policy in the Netherlands, Mark Van De Vall and Cheryl Bolas found that a greater impact was created by using survey results as opposed to explanatory social experiments; providing lesser rather than greater amounts of information; keeping technical terms down, using summaries, and placing statistical tables in appendixes; and presenting controversial results: "Using Social Policy Research for Reducing Social Problems: An Empirical Analysis of Structure and Function," Journal of Applied Behavioral Science 18, no. 1 (1982): 59, 62.

23. Carol Hirschon Weiss, "Have We Learned Anything New about the Use of Evaluation?" American Journal of Education 19, no. 1 (1998): 23, 28, 29, 31. Weiss does cite studies that show the influence of evaluation research on policy but still holds that such instances are "by no means commonplace or easy" (24).

The sense that the public and professional value of research needs to be increased is no less present among government insiders, such as Walter Williams, who was originally a policy analyst in the Johnson administration's Office of Economic Opportunity. Williams has come to wonder "whether more and more policy information, analysis, and analysts enhance public decision making or overwhelm the democratic process with numbers and arguments of questionable validity that are beyond the capacity of both the governors and the governed to interpret." My sense is that the research community would do well to attend to Williams's point by working with, and on, that public capacity to interpret, which is related, of course, to Weiss's concern with improving channels of communication. After that, we can begin to sort out whether there is too much information with too little credibility.[24]

Finally, we can look abroad to the Organization for Economic Cooperation and Development (OECD), which in 1995 held a conference in the Netherlands on improving the impact of educational research on policy makers and practitioners. The OECD devotes a good deal of its energies to gathering and collating data from member nations on policy issues, giving the organization a serious stake in the topic of research effectiveness. The prevailing sense among the member nations at the conference was clearly that, although all policies "are justified publicly by reference to research of some sort," as one official put it, the process is not very effective, with programs being supported by questionable studies or flying in the face of reliable studies. While the current research and development investment in education amounts to only a quarter of a percentage point of total educational expenditures—a level, one OECD official noted, far lower than "in any respectable branch of private industry"—what research resources are available could do a far better job of supporting the policy process.[25]

What is especially encouraging is that the government officials attending the OECD conference were not especially concerned that research provide a single set of answers to policy questions. They knew they would be best served by a "pluralistic" approach to the research, enabling them to consider a variety of approaches and findings. One participant also insisted that the public was more interested than policy officials in this research. And while some noted that sharing this research with the public risked arming potential critics, even the reluctant

---

24. Walter Williams, *Honest Numbers and Democracy: Social Policy Analysis in the White House, Congress, and the Federal Agencies* (Washington: Georgetown University Press, 1998), x.
25. Tom Alexander, "Information Needs: OECD Perspective," in *Knowledge Bases for Education Policies*, 15; White, "Education Research," 63.

recognized that it could "give structure to public debate." The problem with the research, however, at least according to Ray Rist, an educational researcher at George Washington University, is his colleagues' failure to attune their work to the culture, the language, and the processes of policy makers. "There is no broad-based and sustained effort within the contemporary social science communities," Rist writes in his contribution to the OECD conference, "to address the information needs of policy-makers from the point of view of policy-makers."[26]

While I share the concern for improving the intelligibility and impact of research for policy officials, I don't think it is enough, as significant as it would be, to simply improve the link between research and policy. While an increase in research-based policies certainly offers advantages, it needs to be matched by a corresponding improvement to research's contribution to the public process of policy formation. For only at that point does research begin to strengthen the democratic basis of policymaking. When policy analysts David Cohen and Michael Garet speak of research's pursuit of greater "political authority," in policy contexts, for example, I prefer to think of greater *political engagement*. The point of improved coordination and coherence within the research enterprise is to enable the public, equipped with this knowledge, to have a greater impact on political process. If we are not talking about improving research's contribution to public participation in policymaking and other political processes, then we risk slipping into the social engineering model of research dictating policy. What's needed is a meeting place, a commons or public space, for policy makers, researchers, and the public that would be designed to improve how this knowledge works with what people know and need to know, as well as with what they don't yet know they need to know.[27]

26. Claude Thélot, "Problems and Issues for Governments in the Interaction between Users and Producers of Knowledge," in *Knowledge Bases for Education Policies,* 38. Some years ago, James Coleman argued that pluralistic policy research is able "to weaken central authority vis-à-vis outside interests": "The Nature of Society and the Nature of Social Research," *Knowledge: Creation, Diffusion, Utilization* 1, no. 3 (March 1980): 147; Ray Rist, "Information Needs in the Policy Arena: Linking Educational Research to the Policy Cycle," in *Knowledge Bases for Education Policies,* 38, 151.

27. Cohen and Garet, "Reforming Educational Policy." Viviane M. J. Robinson, with the School of Education at the University of Auckland, argues that researchers should reduce the "research-practice gap" by working far more closely with practitioners in thinking through the problem at hand, rather than simply confronting the beliefs and values "of those who control the targeted practices": "Methodology and the Research-Practice Gap," *Educational Researcher* 27, no. 1 (January–February 1998). For a review of the need to design and build new sorts of national systems for educational research, see Susan S. Klein and Margaret K. Gwaltney, "Charting the Education Dissemination System," *Knowledge: Creation, Diffusion, Utilization* 12, no. 3 (March 1991). See also Michael Huberman, "Steps toward an Integrated Model of Research Utilization," *Knowledge: Creation, Diffusion, Utilization* 8, no. 4 (June 1987).

My argument for greater openness and sharing of research is aimed not so much at improving its impact on policies and programs, as at improving its value as a public resource for understanding and working through the possibilities and risks of the issue at hand. Research is itself a tool for working with the values at play in a given community, giving shape to both progressive and conservative tendencies, and as such should be an open part of the public domain and its political processes. Social scientists need to think more about how their work serves the public, policy makers, and practitioners, and how it helps bring them together around an understanding of what is at stake in the issues that confront us. This is a decidedly new role for research, and as such it calls for testing the means and benefits of increasing public engagement in this realm of knowledge. It also calls for confronting a variation on the academic ethic question I addressed in the previous chapter and that is the belief among some researchers that such public engagement can only have the opposite effect that I imagine, reducing the value, especially the scientific value, of the social sciences.

KEEPING A SAFE DISTANCE

For all of the enthusiasm that Ray Rist and I may share for drawing researchers, policy officials, practitioners, and public closer together, there are other social scientists who are equally worried about undue public influence and proximity. Stanford economist Henry Levin, for example, worries about the coercive influence of public interests on the social sciences. Research attuned to policy, he warns, is bound to diminish the scientific value of the work and is thus ultimately self-defeating. Levin is happy to get involved in public projects. Witness his initiation of the highly successful Accelerated Schools Project. But when it comes to the public place of research, he favors a certain tension and distance between policy makers and researchers that may seem to reduce the potential for research's policy influence. The distance that Levin seeks to maintain, however, does not preclude greater efforts on the part of researchers to make their autonomous work intelligible to a wider public. Nor does his stance preclude making the tensions between research and policy apparent, as if to say, "Here, this is what is gained by keeping apart; this is why we need to have a distinct voice in understanding the larger order of things."[28]

---

28. Henry Levin, "Why Isn't Educational Research More Useful?" in Anderson and Biddle, *Knowledge for Policy.* Similarly, Richard Shavelson and David Berliner argue that the possibility of research aimed at engineering better classrooms is largely a

I would draw a second instance of this apparent distancing from Edgar Z. Friedenberg, with whom I studied some years ago. This sociologist of education would deliver biting portraits of the school's daily assault on human dignity without feeling compelled to give in to optimistic prognoses for improving the situation. His goal was not to be helpful or constructive in that programmatic sense. At the end of his *The Vanishing Adolescent*, with its indictment of the school's contribution to student alienation, he supposes that "what is needed is no program of technical-training-cum-indoctrination, but the patient development of the kind of character and mind that conceives itself too clearly to consent to its own betrayal."[29]

On being challenged that this was not much to go on for getting down to the work of such character development, he would look a little surprised and take his stance as a scientist who was working very hard at simply comprehending a critical human process. Yet it is obvious that the moral fiber of Friedenberg's work lies in its powerful testimony to the qualities of youth lost to schooling. He was able to stand off from the schooling process and, because of that distance, to name it with remarkable focus so that his readers experienced both the outrage and the abiding compassion he felt for those whose lives in school amounted to less as a result of the experience that was supposed to bring them more.

For all of the standing off from policy and practice, Friedenberg has managed, through the power and grace of his analysis, to demonstrate the public service of this critical witnessing of the young in school. His work can leave one feeling that if only educators could see the young in this way, they would have taken the first step toward changing the schools. After all, educators are in a far better position to work on reforms than Friedenberg, who as it turns out, did not go to school as a child.

This bearing of witness has long proved a powerful source of public knowledge. It is, at some level, fundamental to our senses of justice and history. Yet a witness needs to be heard, so that his or her testimony can become part of a web of meaning, connecting, in the case of the social sciences, the practitioners, activists, policy makers, and public. Even among those deeply concerned with the intellectual autonomy of the social sciences, the knowledge at issue is still driven by this need to inquire, bear witness, and testify, as if to affirm that *this* we have within

---

category mistake because most research is focused on "the socially mediated and individually constructed" nature of learning that eludes policy efforts: "Erosion of the Education Research Infrastructure: A Reply to Finn," in Anderson and Biddle, *Knowledge for Policy*, 80–81.

29. Edgar Z. Friedenberg, *The Vanishing Adolescent* (New York: Dell, 1959), 218.

our power to know. Social scientists' work includes understanding just how their ideas stand up as knowledge within the larger world, and how that standing could be advanced so as to improve that world.

AGAINST THE LIMITS

When Robert Donmoyer, an education professor at Ohio State University, was editor of *Educational Researcher*, he introduced the theme of "talking truth to power" as a way of addressing research's policy impact. It led him to take extraordinary editorial action with two articles that took contrary stances in analyzing America's standing in international studies of student achievement. He wrote to both authors, asking them to modify their not-give-an-inch attitudes. "As long as the research community tells the policy community contradictory things," Donmoyer explained to the authors, "the research community cannot expect to have much influence in decision making." It was a strange request for an academic editor to make, and it was not clear whether he wanted the authors to approximate a united front, or demonstrate how their differences in approach were helpful to situating achievement tests within the larger political context of education. But neither happened in this case, and the articles simply ended up at loggerheads. As I discussed earlier, policy officials may be better prepared for pluralistic findings than researchers give them credit for. What can support this research plurality is for studies to address the basis for the differences as if they, too, like the rest of us, were talking values to power, values that divide systems of knowledge just as they divide political systems.[30]

When the late Berkeley political scientist Aaron Wildavsky first used the slightly arrogant theme of speaking truth to power some years ago, he proposed that researchers not go it alone but that citizens be included in the policy process as potential policy analysts. Wildavsky argued that

---

30. Robert Donmoyer, "Revisiting the 'Talking "Truth" to Power' Problem," *Educational Researcher* 26, no. 3 (1997): 2. The two articles are Lawrence C. Stedman, "International Achievement Differences: An Assessment of a New Perspective," *Educational Researcher* 26, no. 3 (1997): 4–15; and G. W. Bracey, "On Comparing the Incomparable: A Response to Baker and Stedman," *Educational Researcher* 26, no. 3 (1997): 19–26. Comparisons are often made between the role of research in educational reform and in the medical profession. Educational psychologist Thomas Good takes this a step further: "It is difficult to imagine that President Clinton would call for radical changes (without data) in medical procedures, electrical codes for homes or standards for the sale of meat and vegetables; however, in sharp contrast, it appears by inference that the education of our children does not require careful supervision, professional standards, or research evidence": "Educational Researchers Comment on the Educational Summit and Other Policy Proclamations from 1983–1996," *Educational Researcher* 25, no. 8 (1997): 2–4.

this could only enhance the public's moral development around public and civil interests, as well as develop their "willingness to share" and their "ability to take independent action," in the spirit of Kant's hopes for public enlightenment. He recommended that citizens specialize in different policy areas, which would allow them to stay on top of the research. Wildavsky made it the task of policy analysis "to create incentives (a structure or pattern of relationships) that generate information the people affected can use—not, to be sure, to control the decisions affecting their lives (for that would destroy the autonomy of others), but to bargain over outcomes intelligently." This proposal approaches the sort of democratic engagement with public knowledge that I seek for the social sciences.[31]

When it comes to what researchers need to do at this point to increase the power of their truths, it is worth comparing the responses of leading figures in a field, such as educational research, to what I am proposing with the public-knowledge project. A few years ago, the American Educational Research Association (AERA) gathered a panel of three of its former presidents and asked them point blank, "What should researchers do?" All three rightly understood the question to be about research relevance and professional effectiveness, and each tackled it in the blustery way of the grand old men of the profession while drawing surprisingly on technical innovations they saw as pointing the way forward.[32]

Having served as president of AERA in the early 1980s, William Cooley now directs a program in educational policy at the University of Pittsburgh. His response to the question of what researchers should do is to tell them to stop researching. Cooley comes out against the flood. He thinks people have had enough of research in the traditional sense. University faculty should opt for direct and local involvement in school reform. This, he holds, is bound to have a far greater impact than the endless journal-filling of the current research process. To bring his point

---

31. Aaron Wildavsky, *Speaking Truth to Power: The Art and Craft of Policy Analysis* (Boston: Little, Brown, 1976), 252, 255, 265.
32. William W. Cooley, N. L. Gage, and Michael Scriven, "The 'Vision Thing': Educational Research and AERA in the Twenty-first Century, Part I: Competing Visions of What Educational Researchers Should Do," *Educational Researcher* 26, no. 4 (1997): 18–21. The perennial nature of the question they faced has been affirmed by more recent presidential addresses to the AERA, which have taken blunt titles like "Why Do Educational Research?" It remains among the goals of this association not only to "ensure the continued funding for research" but also to "communicate the findings of high-quality research in ways that influence policy and practice": Penelope L. Peterson, "Why Do Educational Research? Rethinking Our Roles and Identities, Our Texts and Contexts," *Educational Researcher* 27, no. 3 (1998): 9.

home, he offers the instance of his own work, which is devoted to building a large database covering Pennsylvania's schools. "Now as issues arise," he declares with obvious pride, "I can work up data in ways that can shed light on such concerns as school finance reform, vouchers, student assessment, and accountability." Cooley's model of assembling local resources pertinent to policy issues is certainly one way of bringing greater knowledge to bear on these issues. There is a real service element to Cooley's approach, which I admire. Yet I would still want to explore whether this information can be made part of a public resource, whether it can be connected to other related databases for comparisons of similar data, and whether it can draw in related research so that people are working with the diversity of inquiries and understandings that have been assembled on these topics.[33]

The second of the former AERA presidents, having served in the early 1960s, is N. L. Gage, an educational psychologist at Stanford. His opening gambit is to deny the charge of professional ineffectiveness. He points to a period two decades ago when "a lot of prestigious journalists and behavioral scientists were alleging that educational research had yielded no knowledge that was generalizable and therefore useful in improving education, schooling, teaching, and educational outcomes." He disagreed with the judgment then and he disagrees now. The reason is that he believes a reliable path to knowledge has been found with the development of "meta-analysis" techniques. The term meta-analysis was coined in 1976 by Gene V. Glass, a professor of education at Arizona University. It refers to a statistical procedure that can be applied to sets of quantitative studies that are focused on assessing the same phenomenon. The studies themselves may offer contradictory findings and may use very different measures; they may also report no statistically significant difference resulting from the treatment or situation under scrutiny. Yet rather than simply count the number of studies on each side of the question or dismiss the whole set, meta-analysis statistically combines the "effect size" of the treatment in each study, no matter how slight or whether it is a negative or a positive. It then determines the significance of the combined force of the studies.[34]

This procedure is clearly designed to work against both research fragmentation and flooding by channeling related studies into single measures of effect. Meta-analysis has been used, for example, to reassess

33. Cooley, Gage, and Scriven, "The 'Vision Thing,'" 18.
34. Cooley, Gage, and Scriven, "The 'Vision Thing,'" 20; Gene V. Glass, "Primary, Secondary and Meta-Analysis of Research," *Educational Researcher* 5, no. 10 (1976).

some five hundred studies in juvenile delinquency that had originally been judged by the National Academy of Sciences to indicate that social programs offer little hope of dealing effectively with delinquency. The meta-analysis of the studies suggested, by contrast, that the programs reduced delinquency by 10 percent. Further analysis by this technique pointed out that programs directed at changing delinquents' behavior were successful in 20 to 30 percent of the cases and that the least successful programs were get-tough programs directed at deterrence. In another study, meta-analysis techniques determined that patients did benefit from different forms of psychotherapy, although one therapy was no better than another; this after expert reviews had concluded that most therapies were worthless.[35]

Yet from where I stand, meta-analysis is a way of compensating for a serious lack of coordination in research design among projects tackling the same topic. Defenders of the process appear resigned to the fact that research is likely to go on and on as it always has, "without thought to how it will fit together in the end," as Gene Glass and his team of meta-analysts put it. They hold that the "limited 'reliability'" gained by ensuring comparable data among studies "would probably be more than off-set by the creativity that would be stanched by uniformity." I am not so sure about either the limited gains or the loss of creativity. What is this ethos of disregard in research, which can pay so little mind to how studies work together in the end to create a coherent, comprehensible picture, given the level of professionalism on which social scientists pride themselves.[36]

Two recent studies of how well meta-analysis works suggest other reasons for concern about this method of recovering the otherwise squandered value of research. On reviewing the results of 302 meta-analyses in the social sciences, one study by Charles Mann found an unusually high tendency for them to yield a positive effect for the factor or practice under study. Only 6 of the meta-analyses found a negative effect, and fewer than 30 came up with no significant effect.[37]

---

35. Charles Mann, "Can Meta-Analysis Make Policy?" *Science* (November 1994): 960–61.
36. Gene V. Glass, Barry McGaw, and Mary Lee Smith, *Meta-Analysis in Social Research* (Beverly Hills, Calif.: Sage, 1981), 20, 230.
37. Mann, "Can Meta-Analysis Make Policy?" 962. In Michael J. Dunkin's review of synthesizing research, he found nine types of errors that can creep into this work, and provided an instance in which all nine were present, from the initial selection of the research to the conclusions drawn. The real problem, Dunkin notes, is that, as with the research synthesized, no one can "go to the trouble of a detailed scrutiny required to check the validity" of the studies: "Types of Errors in Synthesizing Research in Education," *Review of Educational Research* 66, no. 2 (1996): 95.

A second study of meta-analysis, this time in medical research, concluded that it is at best a stopgap measure that should be used only until more comprehensive and coordinated research studies can be conducted on the topic. Finally, a rather sensational example of the shortcomings of meta-analysis is the widely reported findings of a global and ongoing decline in men's sperm count, which has more recently been exposed as the thoroughly misleading result of a flawed meta-analysis that was used in 1992 to combine the results of sixty-one studies.[38]

Meta-analysis may currently be the best statistical method for reconciling results among otherwise isolated studies. It certainly addresses a multitude of sins stemming from professional autonomy and academic freedom, compensating for the assumption that research must run wild and untrammeled or die. But perhaps our dependence on this method can be reduced by improving levels of coordination in the very design and initiation of research projects by making the process, at every stage, far more of a public venture directed by an interest in finding ways to improve research's public value.

Finally, third on this panel of AERA past presidents was Michael Scriven, who served in the 1970s and now directs an educational evaluation center. Scriven not only accepts the general charge of research ineffectiveness, he also assumes responsibility for placing the profession's wake-up call. "The association as a group almost entirely failed to discharge its principal duty to the society that supports it," Scriven bluntly states. Without letting up, he chastises his colleagues over their snobbish disdain for the educational achievements of commercially successful programs offered by the likes of Behavioral Research Labs and Evelyn Wood Speed Reading. Yet Scriven is not without hope for the research profession. He recommends turning to "the applied science of expertise (and its epistemology) that has grown out of the field of artificial intelligence work."[39]

The building of better decision-support machines may seem to approach the public-knowledge project I am proposing. Yet I would worry that Scriven's applied expertise could foster a technocracy of

---

38. By comparing the results of subsequent medical studies conducted with the comprehensibility and the coordination that the metastudy attempts to simulate statistically, it was found that the results from twelve large randomized, controlled trials were "not predicted accurately 35 percent of the time by the meta-analyses published previously on the same topics": Jacques LeLorier et al., "Discrepancies between Meta-Analyses and Subsequent Large Randomized, Controlled Trials," *New England Journal of Medicine* 337 (1997); Lorenz Rhomberg and Sophia Hernandez Dias, "The Sperm-Count Debate," *Risk in Perspective*, November 1997.
39. Cooley, Gage, and Scriven, "The 'Vision Thing,'" 21.

professionalism with its specter of a less-than-democratic form of social engineering. At any rate, it would seem of little benefit to public knowledge. When truth talks to power, the temptation is for power to then employ truth, in mind and machine, paying truth to manage and thereby strengthen power. The political question that needs facing, then, is how to support a greater distribution, rather than concentration, of power and knowledge in the inevitable development of increasingly comprehensive databases, meta-studies, and artificial intelligences.[40]

These former AERA presidents strike me as missing something basic, as educators, in their commitment to professional over public interests. Their visions for research lack a concern for the educational value of this knowledge and for the democratic element of increasing public participation in the important public work of education. Their approaches could well serve as targets of Ivan Illich's impassioned denunciation in the 1970s of the "Age of Disabling Professions" and the tyranny of expertise: "The Age of Professions will be remembered as the time when politics withered, when voters, guided by professors, entrusted to technocrats the power to legislate needs, renounced the authority to decide who needs what and suffered monopolistic oligarchies to determine the means by which these needs shall be met."[41]

The public impact of social-science research is bound to be limited by a range of factors that include gaps in its coverage of critical topics, unexplained contradictions among its studies, and the distance researchers keep from public processes. As social-science research is increasingly published on the new and very public medium of the web, researchers need to explore just how this technology could be used to increase the engagement of this intellectual project with public interests. Scholars have always taken advantage of available technologies to increase the value and reach of the knowledge they have to offer, whether by using footnotes, printing presses, or hyperlinks. Once again, the research community is in the midst of experimenting with the latest broadcasting system, although not yet with sufficient attention, I would hold, to how it can expand and shape the part played by knowledge in the larger world. To improve the public value of the social sciences

---

40. Robert Lane warned nearly four decades ago that the growth of a "knowledgeable society" not only would shrink "the domain of ideology" but also would cause politics to decline through both the compelling force of knowing and the "preformulation of policy" by professionals and their associations: "The Decline of Politics and Ideology in a Knowledgeable Society," *American Sociology Review* 31 (1966): 661–62.

41. Illich offers little latitude toward this priesthood that would "not only recommend what is good, but ordain what is right": Ivan Illich, "Disabling Professions," in *Disabling Professions*, ed. Ivan Illich et al. (New York: Marion Boyars, 1977), 12, 17.

beyond the newsstand appearance of public intellectuals such as James Q. Wilson and the sporadic success of press releases on research studies, I am proposing that the research community create a public space for sharing its inquiries into the human condition with public and practitioner. It is a matter of contributing metaphor and metadata to the broader articulation of our humanity, even as that contribution is bound to be shaped in turn by this greater exchange. Impact, after all, is about action and reaction.

Chance of Knowledge 7

If social-science research can be said to be about one thing, it is about chance, the chance associated with risks and possibilities. Chance rules the social sciences. If the social sciences are going to improve the public value of this research, it will be by working with and on the public's understanding of chance. When a recent research study claimed that Asian-American parents possess "significantly higher" educational expectations for their children than Latino and European-American parents, this was because the *chance* that the difference in parents' expectations is mere coincidence had been calculated to be less than 1 in 20, otherwise represented statistically as $p < .05$. (Had the chance of coincidence been greater than 1 in 20, then the difference would have been dismissed as lacking statistical significance.) This difference is worth taking into account, chances are, when working with communities on improving educational test scores. Chance plays no less a part in research that does not use statistical analysis to arrive at its conclusions. By interviewing a student teacher over the course of her teacher-education program, a researcher finds just how it is that a prospective teacher with an extensive knowledge of a subject area is still *likely* to need a good deal of

---

1. The first example is drawn from Lynn Okagaki and Peter A. Frensch, "Parenting and Children's School Achievement: A Multiethnic Perspective," *American Educational Research Journal* 35, no. 1 (spring 1998): 134–35. The study controlled for the influence of the children's grades on the parents and for the parents' perceptions of the children's ability. Other significant differences, such as the one between the Asian-American parents' minimum expectations and those of Latino and European-American parents, had 1 chance in 10,000 of being coincidental ($p < .0001$). Gerd Gigerenzer, Zeno Swijtink, Theodore Porter, Lorraine Daston, John Beatty, and Lorenz Krüger caution that "the question whether a significance level is a meaningful measure for discrepancy, or whether any other meaningful measure can be developed, remains unsettled": *The Empire of Chance: How Probability Changed Science and Everyday Life* (Cambridge: Cambridge University Press, 1989), 95. The second example is from Diane Holt-Reynolds, "Good Readers, Good Teachers? Subject Matter Expertise as a Challenge in Learning to Teach," *Harvard Educational Review* 69, no. 1 (spring 1999): 39.

help transforming that expertise into lessons for her students. This is the order of knowledge offered by the social sciences.[1]

Whether by numbers or narrative, social-science research is a method for constraining the inevitable play of chance in assuming that what we have learned can stand as knowledge—knowledge we can build on, further test, or apply elsewhere. The resulting knowledge is then neither definitive nor assured. It is probable, and probabilities can help us to appreciate risks and possibilities, as well as to track differences and imbalances. Of course, the social sciences are hardly alone in playing with chance. Chance frames our modern understanding. And as the public is already living out this form of knowing, it falls to social scientists to use their careful work with probabilities to help the public understand and expand such important measures as the proportions of fairness and equity in the world.

Although there is not now, nor ever likely to be, a common or unified theory of probability, this broad concept of how one can reasonably work with chance comes as close as any idea can, as I suggested above, to capturing what is common to the vast range of social-science research. In combination with the computer, probability has also become a model for how we think and how the brain functions. Probability is a mental prosthetic, a calculating mechanism built to extend the reach of reason. In a world otherwise short on certainties and absolutes, that which can be established as probable, with whatever measure of precision, offers our best intellectual refuge against the unknown.[2]

The concept of probability that we live by began to assume its particularly modern form during the seventeenth century. At the time, it had to be rescued from the intellectual contempt in which it was held. This is evident in John Locke's *Essay Concerning Human Understanding*, published in 1690, when he posits that "probability is nothing but the appearance" of a demonstrated proof linking two ideas, and as such it can "supply the defect of our knowledge and ... guide us where that fails." What is probable, he maintains, is first "a conformity of anything with our own knowledge, observation, experience, and, secondly the testimony of others." While Locke did point to the importance of "observation" in the study of probability, he also held to its classical tradition by which a claim was probably true to the degree it was supported by venerable and ancient authorities.[3]

---

2. Both the mental model of probability and the computer emerged in the 1960s. See Gigerenzer et al., *Empire of Chance*, 203–11, who write of psychology's "dream of the mechanization of knowledge"(210).

3. John Locke, *Essay Concerning Human Understanding*, vol. 2 (1690; reprint, New York: Dover, 1959), 363, 365.

Today, we are far more likely to see probability as a permanent feature of knowledge, an essential element of what we know. We may be inconsistent in our reasoning, weak in our inferring, and unreliable in our weighing of evidence, as the psychological literature has repeatedly demonstrated, but many people are also aware that knowledge is a matter of probability rather than certainty, a matter of the relationship between claim (hypothesis, supposition) and evidence (data, testimony, authority) whether in the courtroom, laboratory, government office, or daily life. "You be the judge," is the epistemic maxim of this democratic spirit. Rather than covering a defect, probability offers the surest of paths today to greater understanding. As the play of chance disrupts our best efforts to understand the world, so a careful working of chance wins back some measure of reassurance over what can be known today, at least according to the social sciences.

Although this chapter concerns the modern calculation of probability, the social sciences have not been so foolish as to give up on the far older tradition of probability, that of citing authorities to establish the likelihood that such and such is as we claim it to be. Citations shift the burden of proof and truth to the cited. This, too, is a matter of researchers' earnest efforts at bringing chance to bear. They are not ones to let any form of probability, ancient or recent, go untried in bracing their earnest claims against the unknown. So for all of the mathematical wizardry and methodological brilliance brought to the science of probability, scholars have known enough not to let go of its oldest and still reassuring form. This we know, because others (Aristotle et al.) have held it so.

Not only does probability speak to what is common across the social sciences' diverse projects, but, as a modern intellectual force, it lies at the very heart of what is meant by "knowledge" today in the most common sense. Probability forms a strong link between social-science research and public knowledge. This way of extending our knowledge of the world began to take shape some three centuries ago, when a few mathematically and philosophically inclined Europeans wondered just how much chance could be squeezed out of people's playing the odds, hedging their bets, looking to past instances, asking what's normal, and generally calculating the risks and possibilities they faced.

The calculation of probabilities may have been initially pursued as an intriguing intellectual puzzle, but it was still undertaken with the Enlightenment's highest intent and purpose—promoting the rule of reason. The study of probability held out the promise of greater knowledge by virtue of its precision and degree of certainty, but it was also concerned with establishing what was reasonably fair and equitable. Proportion and ratio are critical to probability, with their attending concepts of distribution and allotment. Think of the blindfolded figure of justice, holding aloft her scales as if nature's most basic force would help us find out the just. Those scales speak to that elusive and ultimate ratio of one to one, which we approach by careful calculations of likely balance.

It should be no surprise to learn, then, that the study of probability in human affairs began as a search for moral certainty and developed into what in the nineteenth century was called a "moral science." Here was an intellectual source of uplift for an impoverished humankind, just as religious faith was faltering. Here was a method, in fact a myriad of methods, for achieving a divine form of justice on earth and for undermining the power of chance and injustice to drain life of meaning.[4]

Probability stands as the epistemological engine of the modern state. It gives shape, scope, and substance to the very idea of the nation. It informs the nation's policies and programs. It educates the professions and constitutes an intellectual enterprise in this knowledge economy. Although random sampling only found a place in statistical thinking at the beginning of this century and attitude measures took hold as a way of gauging military morale during the Second World War, now people turn to the results of polls on the front page of their daily papers, as well as to economic indicators, recovery and remission rates in health, and every form of statistic in sports. One now finds that opinion-poll error factors are the stuff of newspaper cartoons, probabilities determine where candy bars are placed on grocery shelves, and presentation-quality graphics programs for statistics are standard issue on laptops.[5]

In this unlikely way, probability underwrites a good part of what counts as knowledge in the modern world. What went into making probability a way of knowing needs to be present in thinking about improving the links between the social sciences and public knowledge. I suspect that between this chapter and the next, between what the social sciences can offer of chance and risk, lies the better part of what can be asked and offered of the body of social-science research as a public good.

---

4. As a nineteenth-century example, consider social reformer and economist Beatrice Webb's comment in her diary of 1884 that "social questions are the vital questions of today: they take the place of religion": cited in Gertrude Himmelfarb, *Poverty and Compassion: The Moral Imagination of the Late Victorians* (New York: Knopf, 1991), 4.
5. One recent Canadian cartoon: "But the polls clearly show that people don't want tax cuts," the liberal says, holding up the newspaper while the conservative reading over his shoulder recites, "Accurate to 3 percentage points 19 out of 20 times ... I'll be damned." In final frame, the conservative adds, "OK, so it's the twentieth time," with his supportive wife quipping, "I love statistics": Michael Eddenden, "Between Polls," *Toronto Globe and Mail,* May 25, 1999, A13.

DEVELOPING PROBABILITIES

Ian Hacking does a wonderful job of portraying probability's "philosophical success story," beginning with its origins in European intellectual life around 1660. A University of Toronto professor who works at the Institute for the History and Philosophy of Science and Technology, Hacking allows for probability's earlier cameo appearances in, among other places, the great fourth-century Indian epic *Mahábarata* and the medieval scholasticism of Thomas Aquinas. But the modern version that we live and breathe got its start in the late seventeenth century as mathematically talented philosophers, lawyers, and scientists applied probability to a breathtaking spectrum of questions. They took to riding the wave of reason into the realm of the probable, pushing logic and mathematics into specifying how best to determine the truth in a criminal trial or predict the odds in a game of chance. Probability first took hold in this dual sense: Is there a reason to believe? Can the chances be calculated? Probability began to seem the most promising way of thinking about what could be known.[6]

No one pushed this idea in more directions in those early days than French mathematician and man-of-letters Blaise Pascal. Pascal's life as a young man was marked by scientific breakthroughs in inventing a barometer, hydraulic press, syringe, and calculator (later improved by Leibniz). But his letters in 1654, when he was thirty-one, to the jurist and mathematician Pierre de Fermat, which dealt with predicting outcomes for *balla*, a game of chance, gave rise to probability theory. Even in that first instance, probability was about achieving a "fair distribution," "in justice," in the sense of apportionment, as the two men focused on how the stakes should be distributed when a game was interrupted and one player was ahead.[7]

Pascal is best known for his unfinished and posthumously published defense of Christianity with its attack on Jesuits, Jews, and others, known as the *Pensées*. Here he applied probability to the most profound of questions at that time, if not now—namely, whether God existed. His quest to *prove* God's existence has always struck me as the paradigmatic

---

6. Ian Hacking, *The Emergence of Probability* (Cambridge: Cambridge University Press, 1975), 3–5. Hacking notes of probability's current ubiquity: "No public decision, no risk analysis, no environmental impact, no military strategy can be conducted without a decision theory couched in terms of probabilities. By covering opinion with a veneer of objectivity, we replace judgement by computation."

7. See Peter L. Bernstein, *Against the Gods: The Remarkable Story of Risk* (New York: Wiley, 1996), 63–68; and Alain Desrosières, *The Politics of Large Numbers*, trans. Camille Naish (Cambridge: Harvard University Press, 1998), 48.

research project, the primal or ur-quest for certain knowledge. It can seem as if all that we have since labored to prove, using increasingly intricate research methods, has been a profane variation on this sacred drive for the Great Assurance, the Absolute Certainty. Yet Pascal's posing of the Question seems a little irreverent for a seventeenth-century Catholic. He frames it as a "wager" between "God is" and "He is not," in a way that reflects on the character of our own continuing pursuit of knowledge: "You have two things to lose: the true and the good; and two things to stake: your reason and your will, your knowledge and your happiness; and your nature has two things to avoid: error and wretchedness."[8]

Pascal, it should be noted, is using probability not to prove that God exists, but only to establish that it makes sense to believe in God, as the odds-on favorite way of life. This in itself sets a radical new framework for what can be hoped of knowledge. Pascal demonstrates why we should side with God by asking how one could possibly risk the potential rewards of a heavenly eternity for the immediate pleasures of one's present life. After all, as he reminds both epistemologists and atheists, "every gambler takes a certain risk for an uncertain gain, and yet he is taking a certain finite risk for an uncertain finite gain without sinning against reason." Here stands the faith of social science in a phrase, as research, too, is directed at helping people live "without sinning against reason." Reason calls for following the odds-on favorite, the most probable course. If we cannot know the truth of God, or of justice for that matter, we can compare probabilities. "This is conclusive," Pascal writes of the certainty of probability, "and if men are capable of any truth, this is it."[9]

To say that what we *can* know is what is *probable* or *likely* was intellectually unsettling in the seventeenth century, and to a certain degree it still is. Yet, this probable knowing was not the whole of life for Pascal, as his famous line reminds us: "The heart has its reasons of which reason knows nothing." After a midnight revelation in 1654, he abandoned his mathematical interests in favor of a religious devotion that consumed

---

8. Blaise Pascal, *Pensées*, trans. A. J. Krailsheimer (Harmondsworth, England: Penguin, 1966), 150–52. Pascal also asks, "But is it probable that probability brings certainty?" (230). Half a century later, demographic theology took form, as in John Arbuthnot's 1710 memoir, *An Argument for Divine Providence Taken from the Contant Regularity Observed in the Birth of Both Sexes*: see Gigerenzer et al., *Empire of Chance*, 23. Neil LaBute offers today's version of the wager in the screenplay for the film *Friends and Neighbors* (1998), as a character states: "I mean, if there ends up being a God or something like that whole eternity thing out there, like, then, yeah, probably so [we'll have to pay for our behavior]. I dunno. We'll see. But until then, we're on my time, O.K.? The interim's mine.": cited in John Lahr, "A Touch of Bad," *New Yorker*, July 5, 1999, 46.

9. Pascal, *Pensées*, 150–52.

the final eight years of his life at the Port-Royal monastery. In 1662, the year of Pascal's death, his religious brethren at Port-Royal published *Logic, or The Art of Thinking,* a work that was still being taught at Oxford and Edinburgh well into the nineteenth century. *Logic* concludes with four chapters on probability that include discussions of statistical inference and numerical calculation, as well as providing guidance on judging miracles, human authorities, and historical events. It ends with a lesson on how to calculate the odds in games of chance.[10]

For Pascal and his colleagues, the study of probability was not set against the willful ignorance of religious belief. This tentativeness is part of a Christian tradition found in Paul's caution, in 1 Cor. 8:2, that "if anyone imagines that he knows something, he does not yet know as he ought to know" (RSV). In the Enlightenment, probability was a way of knowing the world that encompassed both science and spirit. There are other sources of certitude in our lives, such as blinding faith or overwhelming love, which can carry us beyond reason. But more often we grab at what is likely and probable, realizing as child and adult that what is feared is the *unknown.* Whether in the Bible's admonition that to save a life is to save the entire world, or Pascal's protection of the winner's interests in an interrupted game of *balla,* ratios extend the force of reason on the world. They give us another reason to believe, if only in what we know. Through their correspondence, Pascal and Fermat established that probability was not a bluff in the face of uncertainty. It was the working of reason itself and, as such, was intellectually liberating. This calculation of frequencies and distributions added enormously to the reasoning powers of a science based, after Bacon, on experimentation. It wrought conclusions from the data, compiling and ordering the results in a comprehensible form.[11]

If Pascal and Fermat were its great mathematicians, then Leibniz was probability's first philosopher, according to Hacking. Leibniz chose to apply the idea of probability to the justice system, another of the great playing fields of human judgment. The reader may recall from chapter 4 that Leibniz had served as a lawyer among his many roles, and clearly probability was a factor in weighing the evidence in a trial. The evidence brought before a court is presented to support suppositions about a crime committed. At one extreme, the jury is instructed in a criminal case to convict only when the evidence leaves jurors without a "shadow" of a doubt; at the other—in American civil cases, for example—they need

10. Hacking, *Emergence of Probability,* 73–76.
11. Gigerenzer et al., *Empire of Chance,* 6, 37.

find only a preponderance of the evidence leaning one way or the other to reach a verdict. In the language of Leibniz's day, probability formed part of "natural jurisprudence" and, as such, offered a degree of "moral certainty" not otherwise available to those making a judgment in such a situation. But Leibniz realized that probability also spoke to a "degree of possibility." This was the source of Leibniz's famous optimism that this simply had to be the best of all possible worlds. After all, that we have *this* world, and not one of various *other* possible worlds, serves as proof that the world we have is the best (i.e., most probable) of all possible worlds. We can think of this idea as the survival of the probable-est.[12]

On the somewhat more practical side of Leibniz's labors—earning him a second title from Hacking as "the philosophical godfather to Prussian official statistics"—in 1700 he offered the Prussians a fifty-six-category statistical evaluation of the nation (which included the number of marriageable women, able-bodied men who could bear arms, etc.). Leibniz's proposal, which Hacking names an instance of "futurology that has long since become routine fact," was the start of the prodigious compilation of "moral" statistics that took place in Prussia, certainly, but also in France and eventually throughout the rest of Europe. Leibniz joined with others in advising state officials how it was in their interests to command data and compile statistics that would prove a powerful instrument for monitoring and guiding the state.[13]

Records of births and deaths had long been gathered in parishes and local government offices, but now state officials sought to compile these data to better monitor and manage national resources, from pork production to ethnic purity. These officials gathered as much information as possible so that they might have the "law of large numbers" on their side (which holds that increases in the size of sample improve the reliability of observed regularities). What was named "Statistik" in Germany and "political arithmetic" in England produced a steady stream of numbers that specified the very dimensions of the nation. The resulting

---

12. Hacking, *Emergence of Probability*, 57, 163, 127, 137. Hacking refers to "Leibniz's infuriating ability to get the right answer by an unjustifiable inference from the wrong data" (120).

13. Hacking, *The Taming of Chance* (Cambridge: Cambridge University Press, 1990), 18–19. Hacking also offers the earlier instance of census-taking in Ireland, which was "completely surveyed for land, buildings, people and cattle ... in order to facilitate the rape of that nation by the English in 1679" (17). By 1769, Prussia was regularly compiling completely separate tables on Jewish families as a way of monitoring the health of the state. These data later fueled anti-Semitism, leading Richard Boeckh, director of the Berlin statistical office, to complain in 1880 of "the abuse and demoralization of statistics through the anti-Semitism agitation" (23, 193, 197). In 1860, the German government was publishing 410 periodicals devoted to statistics (Hacking, *Emergence of Probability*, 33).

statistics bound an otherwise disparate people together, aligning them within columns of numbers like an army ready to march against enemies from other lands. They made a nation more readily comprehensible, just as they made it more readily governable by bureaucrat and politician, with such knowledge proving its own road to power. Statistics became a necessary point of education for the aspiring bureaucrat.[14]

For the public in the eighteenth century, it was another matter. In France's *ancien regime,* Alain Desrosières points out, in his recent political history of statistics, demographic numbers were buried within the country's secretive political culture, whereas in England even a national census was successfully resisted by those who treated it as a threat to English liberty. In the absence of public access to this information in both countries, a grassroots tradition of social inquiry developed among scholars, jurists, travelers, and professionals. The Royal Society of Medicine in France, for example, conducted a survey in 1776 on health and illness among the nation's inhabitants. These private societies were necessarily working with partial surveys and less-than-comprehensive data, and had to resort to estimates and other "algebraist's" artifices that advanced the art of statistical calculation.[15]

By the end of the eighteenth century, the French mathematician the Marquis de Laplace could assert that "the most important questions of life ... are indeed for the most part only problems of probability." Given that "nearly all our knowledge is problematical," he reckoned, mathematical and moral hope could be found in accurate assessments of risk and advantage. The early days of the French Revolution had that effect on people. With the calendar turned back to zero, the world must have seemed ready to be recalculated anew. Laplace was among those sharing a hope in starting over through this probable path to reason and knowledge. Among the aspects of civil life to which this pro-

---

14. Paul Lazerfeld, "Notes on the History of Quantification in Sociology," in *On Social Research and Its Language* (Chicago: University of Chicago Press, 1993), 281. In addition, Theodore Porter notes that bureaucrats, who otherwise "lack[ed] the mandate of a popular election or divine right," found the power of numbers especially compelling: "Measurement was not simply a link to theory, but a technology for managing events and an ethic that structured and gave meaning to scientific practice." He also cites Weber's conclusion that "bureaucratic administration means fundamentally domination through knowledge": *Trust in Numbers: The Pursuit of Objectivity in Science and Public Life* (Princeton: Princeton University Press, 1995), 8, 72, 194. Hacking, *Taming of Chance,* 104: "Thanks to superstition, laziness, equivocation, [and] befuddlement with tables of numbers, the law of large numbers ... became for the next generation or two, a synthetic *a priori* truth."
15. Desrosières, *Politics of Large Numbers,* 22, 28–32, 60–67. *Les annales d'hygiène publique et de médecine légale* was founded in 1829 for statistical and nonstatistical surveys of poverty, alcoholism, illness, prostitution, and delinquency (82): "Statistics in its oldest, eighteenth-century sense, was a description of the state, by and for itself " (147).

tégé of the encyclopedist and mathematician Jean d'Alembert applied his mathematical skills was the reduction of the chances that the newly established citizen juries would wrongly convict an accused, by stipulating that at least nine of the twelve votes should be required to decide a defendant's fate.[16]

It began to seem possible that probability's resulting knowledge and insight could serve as a guide for social action. In the 1830s, physicians who were intent on improving their operating techniques on gallstones and other surgical procedures started consulting the mortality statistics that resulted from their work. Despite the resistance of some, who expressed a fear that doctors would cure numbers and not diseases, it was gradually becoming apparent that within those accumulating numbers lay the knowledge for managing the risks of modern living. Here was reason to gather and publish data on everything; here was the vast statistical landfill of the modern state, on which would be built towering concepts of the healthy and the pathological, the normal and the deviant, drawn from murder, suicide, divorce, or any of the numerous other measures. The numbers defined the scope of social reality and concern; crime rates were first calculated in 1830, whereas unemployment figured in the tables only after 1900. (The politics of these categories and classifications should serve as a reminder that these formations and their consequences need to be discussed openly within the scope of a public-knowledge project.)[17]

Around 1830, the Belgian mathematician and astronomer Adolphe Quételet created a statistical portrait of the "average man," principally a male Caucasian at the gentle peak of the bell curve. It brought deceptive coherence to the welter of facts and figures that had been collected. Quételet rather sardonically held out the fiscal benefits offered by such calculations, which would afford a "kind of budget for the scaffold, the galleys and the prisons, [which could be] achieved by the French nation with greater regularity, without doubt, than the financial budget." Given the consistency of the numbers, he also dared to posit that crime was a quality of the community rather than an individual failing. The Enlightenment assumption of a common human nature governed by a universal reason was being eroded by the calculation of distributed sensibilities

---

16. Pierre Simon, Marquis de Laplace, *A Philosophical Essay on Probabilities*, trans. Frederick William Truscott and Frederick Lincoln Emory (New York: Dover, 1952), 1, 3. Gigerenzer et al. note how, with Laplace, probability assumes a far more prescriptive than descriptive role, as a "a tool rather than a model of enlightenment": *Empire of Chance*, 18.

17. Hacking, *Emergence of Probability*, 112; Hacking, *Taming of Chance*, 87, 89; Gigerenzer et al., *Empire of Chance*, 46; Porter, *Trust in Numbers*, 37, 43.

and differentiated aptitudes and capacities. This idea was propounded on an international and comparative scale by nation and race through the congresses Quételet initiated, as well as by the International Statistical Institute, introduced in 1885 (which ratified classifications for occupations and diseases).[18]

The French philosopher credited with initiating the field of sociology, Auguste Comte, was among those who sought to steer this new discipline clear of statistics. He worried that reducing people's experiences to mere numbers, with little attention to cause and effect, only added to life's incoherence. And he felt that the idea of the "norm" confused what was average with what was ideal, as we might worry whether our children possess above-average intelligence while also wondering whether their behavior is normal. Yet the study of statistics and its norms thrived, along with other forms of what came to be referred to as "moral analysis" or the "science of morality," which was directed at improving the human lot.[19]

It was Francis Galton, explorer, meteorologist, physical anthropologist, and cousin of Darwin, who demonstrated just how far this statistical morality could be taken. By the final decades of the nineteenth century, Galton was publishing papers on the "regression toward mediocrity in hereditary stature," which described why succeeding generations did not keep getting taller (a process that we now term "regression toward the mean"). It was a small step for Galton to then move from the language of regressive mediocrity to the benefits of selective breeding and eugenics. He was keen to apply his statistical understanding of heredity to "the cultivation of race" and the study of "conditions under which men of a high type are produced," which is how he described eugenics on introducing the term in 1883. This knowledge, in which Quételet's normal distribution became a "law of deviation," offered for Galton a vision of the way forward for humankind. This may have been why he held that probability "reigns with serenity and in complete effacement amidst the wildest confusion." Still, he was ready

18. Adolfe Quételet cited in Hacking, *Taming of Chance*, 105, 110; Gigerenzer et al., *Empire of Chance*, 47. The constraining curve that we know now as the bell curve, or a "normal distribution," was then known as the "law of errors" (governing observations, for example) or the "law of possibility": Desrosières, *Politics of Large Numbers*, 75, 78, 155. We return to the "average-man" issue today with the current Human Genome Project, which would decode and sequence the DNA of different species. A special effort to determine the human genome will be achieved, in one instance, by working with five individuals—three men and two women—drawn from "the major ethnic groups": Nicholas Wade, "The Genome's Combative Entrepreneur," *New York Times*, May 18, 1999, D2.

19. Hacking, *Taming Chance*, 168.

to concede that laws drawn from statistics "may never be exactly correct in any one case, but at the same time they will always be approximately true and always serviceable for explanation."[20]

This worrisome harnessing of the power of probability for shaping the world in its "serviceable" approximations was given a further boost in 1892 by Karl Pearson, professor of applied mathematics at University College in London. Pearson is best known for developing the correlation coefficient, which measures the strength of association among qualities, whether in human beings or other entities. The Pearson coefficient, which, in effect, links probabilities (between the tight and tidy limits of −1 and +1), gets at the heart of what modern social science has to offer. We find our way through the world in the relation of probabilities, with, at best, a partial sense of cause and effect: "*A* is not the sole cause of *B* but it contributes to the production of *B*; there may be other, many or few, causes at work, some of which we do not know and may never know.... Henceforward the philosophical view of the universe was to be that of a correlated system of variates, approaching but by no means reaching perfect correlation, i.e., absolute causality." In this new universe, Pearson carefully delineated at another point, "we can but describe experience; we never reach an 'explanation,' connoting necessity." Knowledge, then, was dangerously supple rather than absolute, for to describe experience, in this case, was to describe human possibilities.[21]

By the time Pearson had become the Galton Professor of Eugenics, running the Galton Laboratory at University College and speaking to the Men's and Women's Club about birth control—with all of this work intended, in his words, "to alter the relative fertility of the good and bad stocks"—eugenics was on its way to becoming a social movement that would be championed by scientists, supported in the press, and taught in colleges. It went on to do particularly well in the United States between the world wars, prompting "family planning" booths at state fairs and sterilization and miscegenation laws in state legislatures (which were to serve as a model for later social policies in Nazi Germany).[22]

20. Francis Galton, "Regression toward Mediocrity in Hereditary Stature," *Journal of the Anthropological Institute* 15 (1886); Francis Galton, *Inquiries into Human Faculty and Its Development* (London: Dent, 1883), 24, 44; Hacking, *Taming of Chance*, 2, 180.
21. Karl Pearson, *The Grammar of Science* (1892), cited in Hacking, *Taming of Chance*, 188; and in Desrosières, *Politics of Large Numbers*, 100–101.
22. Stefan Kühl, *The Nazi Connection: Eugenics, American Racism, and German National Socialism* (New York: Oxford University Press, 1994). While on this topic of good and evil uses of knowledge, it should be noted that the Nazis were the first to make public the link between cancer and smoking; See Robert N. Proctor, *The Nazi War on Cancer* (New York: Oxford University Press, 1999). For the Pearson quotation, and his efforts

The eugenics movement certainly represents the danger of wide-spread public engagement with the social sciences. Going public with powerful ideas and methods, as Galton and Pearson did, can test and tempt people's values. It is the strength of a democracy that gives these ideas a hearing and if that enables them to gather a following, it also allows the ideas to be debated in an open and informed manner. Public knowledge is at the heart of this issue, and if sterilization laws were enforced largely in secret, the miscegenation laws and color bars were not. Democracy's dependence on public vigilance needs to be supported not only by a free press but a critical and open social science capable of informing and calling people on the moral import and consequences of such knowledge.

The Pearson coefficient continues to find countless scientific applications, proving useful in identifying, for example, the persistence and extent of racism and other injustices. Probability was to become, as Pearson had it, "the grammar of science." It is now also the grammar of our lives. People are everywhere guided by coefficients in their understanding and action. "Stats" are an indisputable part of public knowledge.

There were some so impressed by the power of probability as to imagine that everything can be explained by statistics. This form of "statistical fatalism" or doctrine of necessity took hold in the nineteenth century. It presupposed that what statistical regularities and normal curves of distribution demonstrated, above all, was that our lives were ruled by causal laws. Given an intelligence "sufficiently vast ... [and] nothing would be uncertain," as Laplace put it, "and the future, as the past, would be present to its eyes." What could be shown to be probable needed only further calculations to make it predictable, from a nation's murder rate to certain children's ending up in prison. Why should there be a limit, determinists asked, to what can be statistically calculated or predicted? With increased scientific precision, chance would eventually be eliminated, and life would then be a matter of controlled responses. One can feel the temptation of thinking that everything must have an identifiable cause, especially as such knowledge speaks to the near-elimination of risk in the course of our lives.[23]

This statistical determinism, however, was successfully undermined by those who realized that chance was here to stay as one of life's con-

to exclude Jewish immigration to Britain, see Elazar Barkan, The Retreat of Scientific Racism: Changing Concepts of Race in Britain and the United States between the Wars (Cambridge: Cambridge University Press, 1992), 151–57.

23. Laplace, *Philosophical Essay on Probabilities,* 4.

stants. The constancy of chance was proposed at the close of the nineteenth century by Charles S. Peirce, a philosopher who found himself in the employ of the United States Coast and Geodetic Survey. Peirce held that to attribute something to chance did not have to mean that the real cause had yet to be named; chance was a condition of existence, reflected in "the diversity and irregularity of the universe." A few decades later, physicists discovered this principle at work in the limits to what can be determined or predicted at the atomic level. Chance cannot be eliminated no matter how precise the calculation of factors, for the very gathering of additional information changes the situation being examined. We would do well to understand how to work with the play of chance and probabilities, as has happened with recent developments in chaos theory.[24]

In these efforts, we should not lose sight of why probability first attracted Pascal and Fermat's attention. It was not about whether chance was an inimical part of reality or a compensating projection of the mind, but about how far one could go in calculating what was fair and equitable. What we seek to wrest from chance, through the careful weighing of the evidence is a greater understanding of—and a reasonable sense of how to improve—the ways in which we live. The social sciences' quest for knowledge needs to be judged, then, on a public scale, with an eye to how well it furthers our common understanding of what is just. This means continuing to develop research programs, along with categories and divisions of experience and humanity, that will help people work against continuing inequities. But it also means developing and evaluating the ways in which the research forms part of the public discourse of belief and values about what should be done.

Prevailing ideas of the probable, then, have grown out of games of chance, wagers on God, legal decisions, astronomical measurements, and quantum mechanics. This way of thinking about knowledge got its

24. Charles S. Peirce, "The Doctrine of Necessity Examined," in *The Essential Writings*, ed. Edward C. Moore (Amherst, N.Y.: Prometheus, 1998), 187; Hacking, *Taming of Chance*, 1 (see also 11–15). The physicist Werner Heisenberg's famous "uncertainty principle" stated that, in his words, "One could not fix both quantities [the position and velocity of atomic particles] simultaneously and with an arbitrarily high accuracy." Heisenberg goes on to say that "These uncetainties ... may be called subjective in so far as they refer to our incomplete knowledge of the world"—*Physics and Philosophy: The Revolution in Modern Science* (New York: Harper & Row, 1958), 42, 53–4. On chaos theory, as physicist David Ruelle, of the Institut des Hautes Etudes Scientifiques, explains: "Certain dynamical situations do not produce equilibrium, but rather a chaotic, unpredictable time evolution." Ruelle sees the dynamics of chaos at work in social settings—"Legislators and government officials are thus faced with the possibility that their decisions, intended to produce a better equilibrium, will in fact lead to wild and unpredictable fluctuations, with possible disastrous effects"—even as he sets such events outside the scope of what his chaos theory is currently capable of analyzing—*Chance and Chaos* (Princeton: Princeton University Press, 1991), 85.

start no less from the weighing of evidence than from the calculation of ratios. Working in probabilities does not mean giving oneself up to the numbers, any more than it means becoming a slave to "rational choice" models that plot human behavior as a maximizing of advantage. John Maynard Keynes put a nice spin on what we have made of probability when he said it is "concerned with the *degrees* of rational belief." Keynes put the emphasis on "degrees" in a way that I find hovers nicely between what can be precisely measured and what is more of a quality that can assure and guide us without a number attached to it.[25]

In one sense, the social sciences represent a public investment in increasing the degree of rational belief, knowing that it is increased only by degrees rather than fully achieved. How does one increase the chance that the "best" students go to the "best" colleges? Carefully build a scholastic aptitude test (SAT) by conducting some sixty calculations on each multiple-choice test item to ensure its ability to discriminate among test takers. Of course such precision will only go so far. It will not forestall disputes over the basic fairness of the tests nor prevent the recent legal threat of the U.S. Education Department's Office of Civil Rights against colleges using SAT scores as the primary basis of admission.[26]

How does one assess the fair treatment of female athletes in colleges? Compare which male athletes are getting what, whether by scholarship, level of coaching salaries, or equipment budgets. Comparisons of such measures, down to the percentage point and the dollar, now represent in a legal sense what we mean by fair. Is a coach's salary really a measure of the quality of an athlete's experience? Such is the social science challenge, the call for ingenuity, in establishing a public basis for assessing the fairness of policies and practices.[27]

---

25. John Maynard Keynes, *The Theory of Probability* (London: Macmillan, 1921), 20. Desrosières notes that Keynes was not above modifying figures to suit his convictions and that if by chance they did suit him he was said to exclaim something like, "Heavens, you found the right figure!" *Politics of Large Numbers*, 316.

26. The Educational Testing Service, after going to such lengths to achieve a fair measure, nevertheless recommends that its tests be used for college admission in conjunction with an applicant's grade point average and teacher recommendations. This is consistent with the civil-rights "principle of disparate impact," which calls for alternative forms of assessment when an instrument shows that gender or race results in significantly lower scores, which is the case with SATs: Steven A. Holmes, "Conservatives Say Pamphlet on Testing Goes Too Far," *New York Times,* June 12, 1999, A10; Patrick Healy, "Civil Rights Office Questions Legality of Colleges' Use of Standardized Test," *Chronicle of Higher Education,* May 28, 1999, A28.

27. The 1996 Equity in Athletic Disclosures Act enables the Office for Civil Rights of the U.S. Department of Justice to monitor whether educational institutions receiving federal funds award athletic scholarships to women in the same proportion as to men, within a single percentage point: Welch Suggs, "More Women Participate in Intercollegiate Athletics," *Chronicle of Higher Education,* May 21, 1999, A45.

The SATs and gender equity research are both attempts to establish fair measures against historical trends that have been other than fair. The research should only be a starting point, however, in what needs to be a public process of deciding how policies and programs speak to a just world. The research, I am arguing, should be designed and presented in ways that support this greater public deliberation. My concern remains that far too often social-science research represents a surplus of intellectual capacity that has yet to fully realize its intellectual value within this culture. Certainly, the private arm of the social sciences is heavily employed in public-relations, polling, and marketing divisions, keeping us well equipped in consumer goods and smiling politicians. But the public sector, given to detailed investigations of social issues, appears to be a vastly underutilized public resource, though fully charged and developed, judging by research productivity. Social-science research has a capacity for precision that could do more for the public's understanding of the play of chance, the risks and possibilities at stake, in finding a way forward on matters of common and global interest.

PROBABILITY PROFILING

I conclude this consideration of chance with a problem posed by probability that has become the scene of recent civil-rights legal battles. It stems from the police use of "racial profiling" to question members of racial minorities on suspicion of criminal activity. Investigations into this practice have recently resulted in an out-of-court settlement between the Civil Rights Division of the federal Department of Justice and the State of New Jersey. The New Jersey State Police had been stopping and searching three times as many black or Hispanic drivers as white ones on the New Jersey Turnpike. The resulting car searches had turned up contraband in 13.5 percent of the minority drivers compared to 10 percent among white drivers, a difference that the federal government charged did not warrant the race-based surveillance. A similar situation had been documented in Maryland a number of years earlier.[28]

The typical justification for racial profiling, offered in this case by New York City police commissioner Howard Safir, is that the police are simply relying on "the demographics of known violent crime suspects as reported by crime victims." This defense was used when four New York City policemen shot to death an unarmed and innocent African immi-

---

28. Jerry Gray, "U.S. Threatens Race Profile Suit and New Jersey Seeks Settlement," *New York Times,* April 30, 1999, A1, A30; Steven Holmes, "Both a Victim of Racial Profiling—and a Practitioner," *New York Times,* April 25, 1999, WR7; Brent Staples, "Why 'Racial Profiling' Will Be Tough to Fight," *New York Times,* May 24, 1999, A30.

grant, Amadou Diallo, on February 4, 1999. Racial profiling has also been used by U.S. customs officers, and dozens of lawsuits across the country are currently related to the practice. Something is seriously amiss with this use of probability.[29]

This disturbing pattern of police action obviously draws on social-science ideas of demographics and probabilities. As things now stand, 10 percent of young black males are incarcerated, compared to the overall adult rate of less than 1 percent. In certain police precincts, 71 percent of the suspects are identified by their victims as black men. But taking race as a risk category in itself can make it *the* factor in a criminal profile, given the long-standing racist tendencies in this society, and this will have an impact on incarceration and reporting rates. When it comes to what can be done, Randall Kennedy, a law professor at Harvard, has argued that in the face of racial profiling and "for preventive reasons, policy makers ought to insist that officers have not only a reason but also an extraordinary reason for using racial distinctions in policing."[30]

This brings us back to the social sciences' role in the prevention of crime, as well as to the risks associated with public knowledge. The public's interests lie in eliminating risks (recall the determinist's dream), and this is where the trouble begins (as we saw with eugenics). But there are limits to this management of risk. What we are seeing now, after many years of the American courts refusing to take issue with profiling, is an open weighing of human rights and risk management, of morality and science in the courts and press. Studies of racial profiling by police officers have established the degree to which this practice represents a statistical reinforcement of prejudices, giving them the thinnest veneer of legitimacy.[31]

29. Fox Butterfield, "Crime Fell 7 Percent in '98, Continuing a 7-Year Trend," *New York Times,* May 17, 1999, A12; Sylvia Nasa and Kirsten B. Mitchell, "Booming Job Market Draws Young Black Men into Fold," *New York Times,* May 23, 1999, A1.
30. Steven R. Donziger, ed., *The Real War on Crime: The Report of the National Criminal Justice Commission* (New York: HarperPerennial, 1996), 35; Holmes, "Both a Victim," WK7; Randall Kennedy, "Race, the Police, and 'Reasonable Suspicion,'" *Perspectives on Crime and Justice: 1997–1998 Lecture Series* (National Institute of Justice, 1998), 33. In response to a question at this lecture, Kennedy went on to say, "I understand the logic of [profiling]; it is not irrational—it is reasonable in certain contexts. But over the long haul, it is going to be counterproductive. So we are going to bend over backwards, if necessary, to treat all people in the same way in our law enforcement policy and in reality" (45).
31. Randall Kennedy, *Race, Crime, and the Law* (New York: Pantheon, 1997), 148–49. Kennedy treats profiling as an imbalanced application of risk: "Just as race can signal a heightened risk that a black person will die younger, earn less money, reside farther away from employment opportunities, experience more unpleasant encounters with police, and possess less education than a white person, so, too, race can signal a heightened risk that a black person will commit or has committed certain criminal offenses" (145).

Here a statistical and historical understanding of prejudice needs to accompany changes in policy, not because that will end the prejudice (any more than a new policy will, as Kennedy acknowledges) but because making such knowledge public is the obligation of a democracy. This use of profiling by some police officers establishes, once again, that a little public knowledge can go a long way and that, with a critical topic like race, it can be in decidedly the wrong direction. In light of the New Jersey and the Diallo cases, President Clinton ordered federal law-enforcement agencies to record the race and ethnicity of the people they question, as a check on this tendency to misuse the commonplace concept of probabilities with race and crime. Although ordering law-enforcement officers to collect social-science data discrimination is an extraordinary measure, it provides an excellent instance of increased professional and public engagement for a public approach to knowledge.[32]

With knowledge always in this partial state, we must work against chance to improve the proportions and probabilities of a just world. The social sciences need to help with this constant refinement, revision, and adjustment of our knowing. This is not about speaking truth to power; it is not about redressing public ignorance. It is about the social sciences assuming greater responsibility for the state of public knowledge. "It may help," the social scientist should offer, "if we share what we know about probability in this situation. This is, after all, my line of work. The reason I seek public funding for it is because I believe it can shed further light on such situations as profiling. Let me fill in a bit more of the relevant demographics in an effort to right troubling historical tendencies by which African American are poorly served by the justice system."

Profiling also came up in response to the tragic 1999 school shooting in Littleton, Colorado. As one commentator put it, "What many schools really seem to want is a metal detector for personality." Who were these potential killers, people wanted to know, and how might we have stopped them before the killing? Of course, this desire for a me(n)tal detector is wishing against chance. It not only asks the social sciences for what knowledge cannot determine, it jeopardizes people's rights in the process, an already long-standing temptation for schools. The problem is no less present when the profiles name personality traits rather than race as the issue. One proposed set of characteristics to be watched for in combination included a fascination with violence, easy access to weapons, and a flawed character. However, this approach is

---

32. Steven Holmes, "Clinton Orders Investigations of Possible Racial Profiling," *New York Times,* June 10, 1999, A20.

playing the wrong end of chance, for it works backward, by grabbing hold of what appears to be common to the murders and then seeking to apply this knowledge to the hundreds of students who pour into any given high school on any given day. A fascination with violence and access to weapons define the nation, whereas this sense of flawed character really only defines the criminal after the crime.[33]

Probability can provide a way of comparing how well different programs and policies address issues of violence among large populations. The lessons that probability still has to teach, within the scope of this public-knowledge project, are in large part about the frustrating limits of this slight knowledge. When my grandfather wrote the story of his life as a physician, he chose an epigraph from Maimonides in which the twelfth-century Jewish philosopher and physician allowed that there might have been better doctors in the city, but that "I know my limitations far better than I know the limitations of others." Probability is about knowing the limits to what we can know and thus the limits to our very claims on knowledge. It is as if to say that, in wanting to do something that might help others, one can at least know the chance it has of making a difference, even as one also knows that this is all that we have to go on.[34]

Whether by statistics or ethnography, surveys or interviews, model building or historical analysis, the methods developed by the social sciences over the course of the twentieth century offer a form of reasoning about public and private lives. My proposal—which is for social scientists to test new forms of representing and connecting knowledge using new technologies of public access—is directed at improving the contribution that these standardized and vulnerable methods of working with what is probable make to public reasoning and public knowledge. This increased public participation could, in turn, add to the quality of social-science research. The language of chance is a ready part of everyday life and reason. It turns up in the newspaper; it finds its way into the novel. Cormac McCarthy's *Cities of the Plain* concludes with a mythical figure speaking of how "we stand in this great democracy of the possible" knowing that only "the probability of the actual is absolute."[35]

Such are the fictions by which we find our way. Such are the hopes and certainties with which we work. What chance would steal from meaning,

33. Timothy Egan, "The Trouble with Looking for Signs of Trouble," *New York Times*, April 25, 1999, WK1, 18.
34. A. I. Willinsky, *A Doctor's Memoirs* (Toronto: Macmillan, 1960).
35. Cormac McCarthy, *Cities of the Plain* (New York: Knopf, 1998), 284–85.

we have calculated to regain. The social sciences have developed the probability of the actual into a powerful source of understanding. This highly developed capacity for working with the nuances and subtleties of probability will not produce a unified or singular knowledge of the world. Rather, it creates many different ways of testing ideas against the limits of knowing, of describing the proportions and ratios by which we live, in the hope of improving life on this planet. This improvement will require that the social sciences help people realize the spirit of the original inquiry into probability, the spirit of seeking both just and fair proportions, as well as greater understanding and knowledge of the risks and possibilities presented by this chancy world.

Risk of Knowing 8

My earlier book on public knowledge, *Technologies of Knowing* (1999) opened with a discussion of the exasperation that women felt at the time in the face of conflicting advice on breast cancer. Some physicians and cancer organizations recommended, and some opposed, mammograms before the age of fifty. A similar difference of opinion voiced over the value of breast self-examinations. The research on these methods of detection offered equivocal results as to their effectiveness in saving lives. Clearly a more coordinated approach was needed to help people make sense of the discrepancies in the findings and I explored some of those possibilities in *Technologies of Knowing.* Although questions remain concerning the efficacy of mammograms and self-examination, the good news is that the death rate from breast cancer declined 5.6 percent from 1990 through 1993. The reduction has been attributed to improved detection and treatment, which is to credit, at least in part, the role of public knowledge in fighting the disease. Despite continuing uncertainties over early dection methods in this instance, increases in public awareness do contribute to greater vigilance and research support.

What brings me back to this topic now is a recent shift in the American health community's public-education campaign on breast cancer toward what I consider a far more responsible stand on public knowledge. The National Cancer Institute and the American Cancer Society have dropped their earlier shock tactic of organizing their campaign around a single statistic—1 in 8—which describes the chances a woman faces of getting breast cancer in her lifetime.[1]

Now, the ratio itself—1 in 8—is deadly accurate. What became an issue is how the figure was used in these public-education campaigns. As Dr. Barbara Weber, director of the Breast Cancer Program at the University of Pennsylvania, makes clear in addressing the unforeseen

---

1. The information and quotations on breast cancer are from Denise Grady, "In Breast Cancer Data, Hope, Fear, and Confusion," *New York Times,* January 26, 1999, D1.

consequences of focusing on this are ratio, "It's a double-edged sword. It has heightened women's awareness, and it's probably responsible for getting them to have mammograms and breast examinations. It may have helped get money for research. But the downside is that many people are overly frightened, and overestimate their risk."

Women have a right to be frightened. They are not overestimating their risk, at least as the risk is defined by that ratio; they are staring it in the face. Some may have given up on the disease, while others may have ignored other important aspects of their health. More women than appears necessary have had mastectomies as a preventative measure. Still others have refused, out of a concern for breast cancer, estrogen treatments that are known to reduce the chances of heart disease, which remains by far the largest killer of women.[2]

This response is not about a limited grasp of the publicized risk. Rather, the women suffered from the limits to the knowledge they were offered. The 1-in-8 ratio represents a small portion of what is known about this risk. Yet it was made to appear as a fixed ratio, unrelated to the particular circumstances of women's lives. The problem is not that "most people aren't used to dealing with numbers like that," as one epidemiologist who studies such risk ratios put it. Women were dealing with the numbers. What they weren't given a chance to deal with was the *rest* of what the health community knew about the risk of breast cancer. Recall the inspiration that Stephen Jay Gould drew, as I related at the beginning of the book, from his insight into the nature of the medical calculations pertaining to his cancer. For, in the case of breast cancer, it turns out that if one calculates the probabilities by decade instead of over a lifetime, the ratios drop considerably. The risk for any given decade is never greater than 1 in 34, and that rate is for women in their seventies. For women in their thirties, the risk is 1 in 250. The influence of age and period of calculation demonstrate how there is more to understanding the risk than a single ratio.

The shift away from promoting this single ratio is greatly supported by the National Cancer Institute's distribution of a Breast Cancer Risk Assessment tool that allows women to calculate on a computer the risk they face, based on age and a number of other factors. The tool gives the risk not only over a lifetime but also for the next five years and in comparison to women of the same age who have no additional risk factors. Although it offers explanations of how these calculations are

---

2. One recent study found that 74 percent of women who had had bilateral prophylactic mastectomy felt it reduced emotional concerns about developing the disease: Denise Grady, "Study Says Few Women Rue Preventive Breast Operation," *New York Times*, May 17, 1999, A14.

arrived at, women are encouraged to discuss their results with their doctor. The difference between the original single-ratio breast cancer campaign and the current distribution of the means for calculating the risk captures where I want to go with the social sciences' support of public knowledge. To the charge that women are looking for simple answers, Dr. Susan Love, a breast surgeon, counters that from her experience it's "the media that require 'the answers' and that women are perfectly able to make the best decision possible based on inadequate information. They do this every day. And women understand that the answers may change with further data."[3]

One caution to this new approach comes from Dr. Alexandra Heerdt, a breast surgeon who directs a program at Memorial Sloan-Kettering Cancer Center in New York, which monitors women at high risk. Heerdt reports that a major benefit of working with these women is the peace of mind it affords them, which comes of knowing that "someone else is bearing the burden with them." This is a telling reminder that expanding the social sciences' contribution to public knowledge adds its own weight to living, its own need, in some cases, for additional professional, compassionate support. Is it better, then, for people not to know more about the risks they face? I think not.

The principle here is that whatever the burden or level of interest in knowing, people have a right to know what is known (however conditional and contingent that knowing is). This discussion of breast cancer detection represents an instance of the public's underlying right to know what has been learned on its behalf. Giving women the tools to calculate the risk brings home this aspect of what the social sciences make of knowledge. In this chapter I argue for the wisdom of thinking about this knowledge within a framework of risk and possibility, a framework that seeks to ascertain what is at risk in a given situation and what are the possibilities.[4]

The elements of risk and possibility, as variations on the theme of probability and chance, have long been woven into the fabric of our thinking, and especially so in the second half of the twentieth century with the emergence of what some term a "risk society." The move from a calculation of probabilities to the analysis of risk escalates what is at

3. National Cancer Institute, http://cancertrials.nci.nih.gov; Susan Love, "Wondering about a Wonder Drug," *New York Times*, August 3, 1999, A19.
4. Still, some make too much of risk. Financier Peter L. Bernstein, for example, claims that "mastering risk," as he puts it, "is the revolutionary idea that defines the boundary between modern times and the past," because it enables the "human passion for games and wagering [to be channeled] into economic growth, improved quality of life and technological progress"; *Against the Gods: The Remarkable Story of Risk* (New York: Wiley, 1996), 1.

stake in knowing. To speak of risk becomes a way of focusing our attention. Events are probable. Species are endangered. People are at risk. There is no question that risk seems a decidedly negative take on knowledge. Risk analysis is all about danger and death. Those who assure us that, on a per-mile basis, the risk of dying in an airplane is far lower than in a car are hardly harbingers of good news for those driving out to airports. Risk may well be no more than bad news made worse by increasingly precise probabilities, against which we are asked, after Pascal, to wage body and soul.

Yet rather than restricting the assessment of "risk" to serious environmental and health threats, I would encourage the social sciences to offer a broader guide to the risks and possibilities posed by the social dynamics of our lives. It could only add to the public intelligibility of this knowledge. The enormous research apparatus of the social sciences is given, in one sense, to carefully ascertaining what is risked each day through the circumstances of poverty, race, gender, and other factors. We can ask, then, what a child risks in speaking a language at school other than the one her teacher speaks. Educators can consider the possibilities of treating bilingualism as an educational advantage for the benefit of classrooms and the community, rather than as a disability on the child's part and a handicap for the teacher. Similarly, affirmative action can be seen in terms of risks and possibilities for students, universities, and workplaces. Social scientists certainly bring their own politics to the estimation of these risks, but presumably the probabilities ascertained, whether by statistical calculation or close observation, would clarify the play of values and consequences in these risks.

I find it easy enough, for example, to cast my own educational research into the risk-management model. In trying to help teachers in their efforts to move beyond what I see as damaging educational practices and programs, I have studied ways of reducing the risks that students learning to write will discourage artfully disciplined self-expression, that Juliet's strength and valor will be lost to a class reading *Romeo and Juliet*, that young women will fail to find computers a useful addition to their schooling, that teachers will not build on the emerging sense of a Pacific community among students in Vietnam and California, and so on. To place research in this light calls for not only identifying the risks but also for finding ways of effectively addressing them.

This range of risks and possibilities can be carefully analyzed and interpreted from different perspectives. They can be compared, discussed, and acted upon as part of a public discourse. The democratic right to know includes having access to this work on the risks and possibilities entailed in how we live, in how our communities operate and are governed, in how the world works. This expanded sense of risk could bring an important focus to the pursuit of knowledge for both researchers and public. It could further the integration of different orders of knowledge in the social sciences by bringing an understanding of the risks of poverty, for example, demonstrated by significant differences in disease, accident, and suicide mortality rates, to an analysis of how social services operate within a public-housing project. Risk is at once a general metaphor for grasping what lies within the scope of people's lives and a recognized point of political leverage and legislative action.[5]

ASSURANCE, INC.

In thinking about how risk has long been part of the very public knowledge from which the social sciences draw their spirit of inquiry, one needs to consider both the private and public arms of what is, in effect, a risk industry. The private arm of that industry takes the form of the insurance business, whereas its public arm has developed into the social-welfare programs of modern governments. Both have much to teach us about how the social sciences can do more for public knowledge

At the turn of the seventeenth century, the emerging London insurance industry had taken on sufficient economic force that the English Parliament felt compelled to regulate it, with some goading from Francis Bacon. (Yet this meddling in insurance should *not* be taken as evidence of Bacon's authorship of *The [Uninsured] Merchant of Venice* as a theatrical warning against those who dare do business without it.) It was not long before the Royal Exchange Assurance Corporation and the London Assurance Corporation were writing policies for *whatever* the well-to-do did not wish to risk, whether to fire or cuckoldry [6]

Until 1762, when the mathematician James Dodson introduced the use of mortality tables for setting life insurance premiums for policies underwritten by his Equitable Society for the Assurance of Lives, the assessment of risk had been largely a matter of the personal judgment of individual cases. The actuarial table promised a more reliable return for

---

5. John D. Graham, Bei-Hung Chang, and John S. Evans, "Poorer Is Riskier," *Risk Analysis* 12, no. 3 (1992): 222–37.

6. Among the interesting historical tidbits from this era, it appears that those who underwrote maritime shipping in the seventeenth century were especially given to doing business in Edward Lloyd's coffeehouse, where the most reliable information on the shipping trade was to be found. This led to the publication of *Lloyd's List* and then eventually to a merger of interests among the coffee-patron underwriters, who formed the notable Lloyd's of London in 1771. See Bernstein, *Against the Gods,* 88–96.

the company at a fairer policy price for the purchaser, if not also a greater assurance that the money would be there when it was needed.[7]

Certainly, underwriters still counted on their intuitive feel for the risk at hand to set premium rates, and probability statistics played almost no part in maritime and fire insurance. Yet this well-established insurance industry attested to the value of the knowledge of risk and the epistemological value of probability. The calculating philosophers who staffed the actuarial offices of the insurance companies used what was known in order to conquer what was out of reach, arriving at an estimable risk that could be underwritten by a premium.[8]

Today, the insurance industry continues in its underrated epistemic leadership, this time for the very Information Age. Forget the mind-numbing visits by insurance agents sent by head offices, where huge roomfuls of heads-down actuaries, like rows of cabbages, calculate mortality rates. Today, risk management is all about data mining, and in the case of insurance the great gold mine is the friendly police department, now open for information business. In *Policing the Risk Society*, Richard Ericson and Kevin Haggerty, sociologists at the University of British Columbia, describe how the police "collaborate with insurance companies in joint investigations, routinely act for insurers as brokers of insurance-formatted knowledge of crimes and accidents, and serve insurance companies by producing and distributing information on how to reduce loss and prevent accidents." The police are part of a larger system dedicated to producing "risk-profiles" of populations "for the purpose of economic exchange, life-course management, and identity management." The police patrol with a keyboard instead of a nightstick, in a memorable image from Ericson and Haggerty, which enables the "typing" or "profiling" of populations.[9]

Next time a police officer is standing in your front yard, patiently recording the details of the stolen bicycle that neither she nor you hold

---

7. See Gerd Gigerenzer, Zeno Swijtink, Theodore Porter, Lorraine Daston, John Beatty, and Lorenz Krüger, *The Empire of Chance: How Probability Changed Science and Everyday Life* (Cambridge: Cambridge University Press, 1989), 24, 26. Hacking notes that the idea of using mortality rates in calculating the cost of annuities had apparently emerged briefly in the Dutch republic in the 1670s: Ian Hacking, *The Taming of Chance* (Cambridge: Cambridge University Press, 1990), 40.
8. When Lloyd's suffered its great crash in the 1980s, losing close to $20 billion in five years, among the contributing factors to this debacle was its continuing to write insurance on asbestos risks into the 1960s, despite research that had established the risk decades earlier, as well as on vulnerable environmental pollution: Adam Raphael, "Lessons of Lloyd's: The Limits of Insurance," in *The Politics of Risk Society,* ed. Jane Franklin (London: Polity, 1998).
9. Richard V. Ericson and Kevin D. Haggerty, *Policing the Risk Society* (Toronto: University of Toronto Press, 1997), 108.

out the slightest hope of recovering, appreciate that what counts here are the data. The information extracted from the data will keep us in bicycles, police, and insurance. "Policing and the society in which it takes place," Ericson and Haggerty explain, "are best understood in terms of a model of risk communication." In the words of one officer, "information is increasingly seen as a resource. We are trying to establish information as an asset." Thus, state and commerce conspire to manage destinies at a distance, with the resulting information protecting insurance-company clients and shareholders. It is enough to cause one to wonder if knowledge workers, from police to professors, are really paid to traffic in the articulation of risk, as all this talk forms a system of management.[10]

Insurance, or better yet "assurance," as it was originally known, represents a model of knowledge devoted to managing risk and offering peace of mind at a price that those who can afford it are more than willing to pay. Among the interesting epistemological features of this insurance model is how little concerned it is with the reasons why things happen. As French sociologist François Ewald puts it, "The idea of cause is replaced by the idea of distributive sharing of a collective burden, to which each member's contribution can be fixed according to a rule." To be fair, this concept of the economic utility of risk has also led to iusurance-industry sponsorship of automobile-safety campaigns and research on soft-tissue injury, although this, too, is using what is known to manage the risks better.[11]

The insurance industry may gather data with a singularity of purpose and a seeming absence of theoretical fussiness that distinguish it from most of what the social sciences do. Yet there is something ultimately

10. Ibid., 340, 94. It is worth noting that the police are not totally comfortable with their info-work: "The police see themselves," Ericson and Haggerty observe, "as deskilled servants of the insurance companies and their knowledge needs." They provide a steady flow of information to other agencies as well, in health, public welfare, finances, and education. Still, it should be reported in the taxpayers' interest that police accident-reconstruction reports in Canada are sold to insurance agencies for $1,500 and in other cases the police charge insurance companies $75 per hour for their information, which may seem a reasonable rate for professional, rather than deskilled, knowledge work.

11. Ericson and Haggerty, *Policing the Risk Society*, 109; François Ewald, "Insurance and Risk," in *The Foucault Effect: Studies in Governmentality*, ed. Graham Burchell, Colin Gordon, and Peter Miller (Chicago: University of Chicago Press, 1991), 197–210. On causality, compare Andrew Tish, of the Lorillard Tobacco Company, who was g(r)asping at epistemological straws when he testified before Congress in 1994 that "the data that we have been able to see has all been statistical data that has not convinced me that smoking causes death": cited in Barry Meier, "Among Cigarette Makers, Old Habits Die Hard," *New York Times*, September 7, 1997, E3. No one needs to tell people that life is too short to wait for what it will take to establish the chemical causal chain for cancer. The better rule of thumb is to go forward, knowing the posted odds.

sensible in staying focused on knowing what will protect one from risks of calamitous chance. The industry goes after what it needs to know in order to manage its own risks. The social sciences could further focus their work to play a similar role of protecting the public's investment in social policies and programs. It can learn from the insurance industry's innovative tapping into public-sector information sources to further what can be learned of life's risks. This concept of insurance and risk management already has inspired a history of state-run efforts at social-insurance schemes intended to protect otherwise unprotected segments of society from calamity, a history to which I now turn.

SOCIAL INSURANCE

People have long gathered together to conspire against chance, learning how to protect themselves from unpredictable losses through coopera-tives and forgivable loans. Since the sixteenth century, for example, the English organized forms of public welfare and social policy to protect against poverty and plague through a mix of state and church, public and private, national and local initiatives. The state's hand in risk man-agement slowly developed, largely through the sale of annuities to its citizens. The English, Dutch, and other European governments sold annuities to raise money for state coffers, in a form of borrowing that could pay a higher rate of return to the citizen than Christian prohibi-tions against usury would otherwise allow. Until 1789, in the case of the British, these guaranteed incomes for life were priced without regard to the purchaser's age.[12]

By the nineteenth century, however, a particular form of widespread risk had emerged. The human damage rendered by a loosely governed industrial revolution was becoming increasingly public and publicized. Liberal-minded citizens were alarmed by the risks to body and soul faced by the majority of the nation. It was becoming increasingly clear that staffing the satanic mills simply cost everyone too much, in a moral sense. Not the least consideration was that it did not do for a nation intent on leading the greater colonized world through its civilized example to have its own children work themselves to disfigurement, if not death, in the cotton mills. The damning data, often compiled and made public by amateur statistical societies that had sprung up in London, Manchester, and other European cities, pointed to a nation at risk. In fact, the talk was

---

12. Paul Slack, *From Reformation to Improvement: Public Welfare in Early Modern England* (Oxford: Oxford University Press, 1999).

of two nations, the rich and the poor (as captured in Benjamin Disraeli's 1845 novel *Sibyl, or The Two Nations*). This risk was not simply to the safety and health of the poor. It lay, as historian Gertrude Himmelfarb describes it, in "the kind of poverty that threatened to reduce the laboring poor to a state of dependency and degradation." Action had to be taken as a matter of both self-interest and altruism on the part of the governing classes.[13]

Here, then, was the power of public knowledge at work. Government-sponsored commissions were producing all too vivid stories and statistics in their blue books on the social devastation wreaked by the Industrial Revolution. The press picked up the harrowing tales, which were further augmented by early social surveys such as Henry Mayhew's *London Labour and the London Poor*. Writers such as ex-reporter Charles Dickens and Elizabeth Gaskell turned the distressing facts into popular fiction, and Marx transformed them into political economy, working as did Dickens in the British Museum Reading Room with the public records. Statistical portraits continued with Charles Booth's landmark survey of London in the 1880s. Booth developed an "arithmetic of woe," as he called his work, to establish the proportions between misery and happiness among the eight social classes into which he divided London so that compassionate action could be taken within what could be fairly claimed as the bounds of reason. "In its unsentimental mode, compassion seeks above all to *do* good," writes Himmelfarb, "and this requires a stern sense of proportion, of reason and self-control." Is it any less so today as developed nations attempt to construct a reasonable end to the welfare state?[14]

It was Germany that first created an obligatory "public-legal" accident, sickness, disability, and old-age insurance law in 1884, administered by the Imperial Insurance Office. France followed by nationalizing the industrial-accident departments of the private insurance companies, leading to the country's first social-insurance policies. Thus the "providential state" was born, according to François Ewald, and "societies [were to] envisage themselves as a vast system of insurance." Social insurance transformed individual risk into a collective, national

---

13. Gertrude Himmelfarb, *Poverty and Compassion: The Moral Imagination of the Late Victorians* (New York: Knopf, 1991), 13.

14. Charles Booth cited in Himmelfarb, *Poverty and Compassion*, 5. Among the British examples of government reports are the *Report on the Employment of Children in Factories* (1833) and the *Report on the Sanitary Conditions of the Laboring Classes* (1842): see Adam Ashforth, "Reckoning Schemes of Legitimation: On Commissions of Inquiry as Power/Knowledge Forms," *Journal of Historical Sociology* 3, no. 1 (1990): 1–22. Also see Porter, *Trust in Numbers*, 80; Desrosières, *The Politics of Large Numbers*, 257–59

matter of rights and responsibilities. "The first [principle] was the expansion of the concepts of rights to include the obligation of society toward the individual to reduce or minimize risk and inequality," writes historian Anson Rabinbach. "A corollary of this idea was that social responsibility can be grounded scientifically and demonstrated by statistical laws." Here was the national proving ground of an emergent social science. The knowledge it afforded was as critical for initiating progressive reforms and achieving a more humane state as it was for keeping a watch, and thus a political hold, on the state of the nation.[15]

In America the concept of social insurance was slow to take hold. In 1906, an American Association for Labor Legislation formed with the help of social scientists, and within two years' time a workers' compensation program for federal employees was enacted by the government. Moved by the statistical research accumulated on child labor and its associated abuses that was gathered by reformist groups and philanthropies, the U.S. government formed a Children's Bureau in 1912. Progressive women's groups, such as the Federation of Women's Clubs, proved a strong moral force in advancing social-welfare policies. Although women did not yet have the vote, these groups succeeded during the early decades of the twentieth century in having a mother's pension established on the model of the Civil War veterans' pension.[16]

Still, the comprehensive Social Security Act—which eventually covered retirement pensions, disability insurance, unemployment insurance, Medicare, public assistance, and child welfare—was not introduced until 1935. Although the debate continues over how to ensure a sustainable future for social security—whether through stock-market investment or individual management of pensions—there is little question that the nation bears some responsibility for insuring its citizens against the risks they face. As risks go, only "national security" commands a greater portion of the federal budget than social security. This concept of risk also mobilizes additional educational support for students designated "at-risk," just as it led in the 1920s to the cost–benefit analyses of government policies to reduce the risk of loss and waste.[17]

15. Ewald, "Insurance and Risk," 210; Anson Rabinbach, "Social Knowledge, Social Risk, and the Politics of Industrial Accidents in Germany and France," in *States, Social Knowledge, and the Origins of Modern Social Policies,* ed. Dietrich Rueschemeyer and Theda Skocpol (Princeton: Princeton University Press, 1996), 48.

16. John R. Sutton, "Social Knowledge and the Generation of Child Welfare Policy in the United States and Canada," in Rueschemeyer and Skocpol, *States . . . ,* 202; Theda Skocpol, *Protecting Soldiers and Mothers: The Political Origins of Social Policy in the United States* (Cambridge: Harvard University Press, 1992).

17. From 1937 to 1994, social security collected $4.9 trillion and paid out $4.5 trillion. Its provisions for old-age pensions now cover 90 percent of senior Americans, keeping

Safety regulations in the workplace, dating back to the establishment of the Bureau of Mines in 1910 in the wake of a major coal-mining disaster, have contributed to a 90 percent reduction in job-related deaths since 1913. A similarly dramatic drop in risk has been experienced by women in childbirth, which began to improve only after 1940 in the United States, with the number of deaths dropping from 1 woman in 200 dying in childbirth in that year to the current figure of less than 1 in 10,000. The figure is more than three times as high for black women, with this and similar figures leading the government to make it a goal to eliminate racial disparities on health care by 2010.[18]

While the social sciences have developed the means of assessing risk within most every area of our lives, the politics of public concern, or more specifically interest-group lobbying, dictate what becomes the focus of risk-managing programs and policies. For example, proposals for publicly financed health insurance, designed to protect uninsured people from the devastating costs of illness, have failed, although the health costs of uninsured children are covered. In all of this, social-science research must continue to inform prevailing perceptions of how well and fairly the state is helping its citizens to manage the risks it faces.[19]

By contrast to the American situation, for example, the French have introduced remarkably far-reaching social programs, none more so perhaps than the GAMIN system of automated maternal and infantile management, which since 1976 has amassed data on parents and infants, based on examinations at a few days after birth, a few months, and two years of age. This enables the state to manage the physical, psychological, and social risks that the young face. The system is set up to auto-

roughly half of them, it has been estimated, from falling below the poverty line: Marvin Mandell, "In Defense of Social Security," *New Politics* (summer 1997): 23; J. Madrick, "Social Security and Its Discontents," *New York Review of Books* 43, no. 20 (1997): 68–72. In 1997, social security accounted for 23 percent of the U.S. federal budget at $323 billion, up from 14 percent in 1967: see Public Agenda, http://www.publicagenda.org.

18. See Porter, *Trust in Numbers*, 148–89. In the early 1950s, Porter reports, economists and other social scientists started to play a much larger part in this analysis: Associated Press, "Job Related Deaths Fall by 90 percent since 1913," *New York Times*, June 11, 1999, A24; Janna Malamud Smith, "Now That Risk Has Become Our Reward," *New York Times*, July 25, 1999, WK15; Sheryl Gay Stoberg, "Black Mothers' Mortality Rate under Scrutiny," *New York Times*, August 8, 1999, Y17.

19. Gigerenzer et al. raise the interesting case of the tension between equality and fairness in social-insurance plans exemplified by the suit brought in the 1970s by female employees against the Los Angeles Department of Water and Power. The women won, because their pension plan required higher contributions, expecting that they would, in all probability, live longer. The courts ruled that fairness to individuals ranks above fairness to classes, while allowing that this outcome was not meant to affect the insurance industry as a whole: *Empire of Chance*, 259.

matically alert the appropriate social services to visit all at-risk children "to confirm or disconfirm the *real* presence of a danger," in the words of French sociologist Robert Castel, "on the basis of the *probabilistic and abstract* existence of risks." GAMIN completes a long loop in the history of probability. After centuries of gathering information on populations, the state now directs those data at the surveillance and management of individuals. Such are the trade-offs of risk are between the knowledge of populations and the "protection" of individuals.[20]

When it comes to the knowledge that moves states, institutions, and industries, that shapes policies and programs, one finds the world compellingly framed by concepts of risk and probability. At this level, probability may seem to stand in our world as beauty stood for Keats: "—that is all / Ye know on earth, and all ye need to know." Risk gives a particular focus to probability, and if it is not all that we know or all that we publicly fund (allowing, for example, for the much-contested National Endowment for the Arts budgets) or all that we line up to take of the world (whether in movies or Monet exhibitions), it nevertheless holds the lion's share of attention and funding (what with the combined risk-management interests of social and national security).[21]

Certainly art and literature seem to hold a brief candle to the public and private concerns of risk as ways of knowing and working with the world. The complex constructions of risk that prevail in the political and private spheres today make public access to this form of knowledge all the more critical to people's informed participation in social processes. This way of thinking about how risk prevails in our private and public lives, as a business enterprise and social mission, offers one way of bringing into focus the knowledge that the social sciences have to offer, one way of grasping the relative urgency of issues and augmenting the process of arriving at personal and political decisions. Yet this broader approach to risk needs to be set in relation to the idea that we now live within a risk society.

A RISK SOCIETY

As risk has become the most prominent aspect of probability within the realm of public knowledge, so "risk management" has become our way

---

20. Robert Castel, "From Dangerousness to Risk," in *The Foucault Effect: Studies in Governmentality*, ed. Graham Burchell, Colin Gordon, and Peter Miller (Chicago: University of Chicago Press, 1991), 287–88, original emphasis.
21. John Keats, "Ode on a Grecian Urn." Note that the urn filled with a ratio of blue and white balls plays a critical conceptual role in the study of probability. See Marquis de Laplace, *A Philosophical Essay on Probabilities*, trans. Frederick William Truscott and Frederick Lincoln Emory (New York: Dover, 1952).

of taking this dangerous world in hand. In a press conference on the eve of the 1999 NATO bombing of Yugoslavia intended to end Serbian ethnic cleansing of Kosovo; President Clinton explained that "we must weigh the risks [of bombing] against the risks of inaction.... If it spreads, we will not be able to contain it without far greater risk and cost." This is the popular logic of risk today. Risk is often the answer to the question of what is knowledge about in this knowledge economy. In the meantime, we have come to think that "our society is riddled with random risks," as Ulrich Beck, a University of Munich sociologist, puts it—coining the phrase "risk society" to describe our current state of affairs. It is worth considering, however, whether earlier efforts at minimizing risk have now given way to an "incalculability" of consequence, as Beck claims, with a political economy, deeply mired in risk exploitation, leaving in its wake the desolation of Chernobyl and the depleted parking lots of corporate downsizing. We may well be living within what Beck calls "forms of organized irresponsibility." It certainly seems that postindustrial economies devote a great deal of attention to limiting their liabilities and managing their risks.[22]

For that reason, a risk society requires greater public understanding of the risk-management industry itself, which in the United States is largely concentrated in America's health and environmental regulatory agencies, such as the Environmental Protection Agency. To Stephen Breyer, associate justice of the United States Supreme Court, who has been deeply involved in presiding over the legal end of things, the frustrations are all too apparent. Breyer has come to wonder at the proportion of money that goes into legal fees and into cleaning up toxic-waste sites to unrealistically high standards, compared to what might help people improve the quality of their lives in more direct ways. Breyer

---

22. Bill Clinton, cited in William Saletan, "The Kosovo Question," *Slate* (March 24, 1999), http://www.slate.com/FrameGame/99-03-24/framegame.asp. Cass R. Sunstein claims that "the diminution of social risks has been the most novel and important task of the national government since the late 1960s": "Health-Health Trade-Offs," in *Deliberative Democracy*, ed. John Elster (Cambridge: Cambridge University Press, 1996), 232–33. Ulrich Beck, *Risk Society: Toward a New Modernity*, trans. Max Ritter (London: Sage, 1992), 21. Beck writes that "under the surface of risk calculations new kinds of *industrialized, decision-produced incalculabilities and threats* are spreading within the globalization of high-risk industries" (22, original emphasis). Cambridge sociologist Anthony Giddens, who worries about the angst produced by this modern obsessing with risk, points to how this concern with risk "is bound up with the aspiration of control and particularly with the idea of controlling the future," and with how such control might hold out "the expansion of choice." A key element of *public* control and choice, I would hold, is the state of public knowledge: Anthony Giddens, "Risk Society the Context of British Politics," in *The Politics of Risk Society*, ed. Jane Franklin (London: Polity, 1998), 27. See also Anthony Giddens, *The Consequences of Modernity* (Palo Alto, Calif.: Stanford University Press, 1990).

specifically mentions "overkill and random agenda setting" as current threats to risk management's regulatory agencies. Yet for all of his concerns about the inconsistencies and politics of the current "regulatory gridlock"—concerns he feels can be met only by the establishment of a new, politically insulated risk-management superagency—my interests remain with how we can bring the study of risk back within the realm and reach of common understanding.[23]

The study of risk provides insight into just how politically directed social-science knowledge can be. The risks are only as real as the politics that drives the investigation into those risks. For example, the basic unit in doing a cost–benefit analysis of risk regulation is "cost per premature death averted." This figure is arrived at by setting differences in pre- and postregulation mortality against the cost of regulating the risk. For example, the Children's Sleepwear Flammability Ban of 1973 is assessed as having saved one child's life for every $800,000 spent by consumers and taxpayers as a result of banning flammable sleepwear.

If these life-to-dollar ratios have any meaning at all, it is in how they can facilitate deliberations, comparisons, and budgetary allocations within public and political contexts. This knowledge is but a way of mobilizing and informing political action, and as such is very much a part of the public-knowledge enterprise. Such calculations, as Breyer suggests, enable "the nation to buy more safety by refocusing its regulatory efforts."[24]

This purchasing of public safety and refocusing of regulation should be as public a process as possible, given that risks, as we saw with maternal health, are not borne equally across society. Risk management is implicated, much as issues of education and justice are, in the struggle for social justice. Yet as things stand, regulatory information tends to circulate among the professional circles of government officials and elected representatives. It seems to me democratically insufficient to leave up to experts, regulators, or politicians this knowledge of what is at risk and how that risk can be addressed. So I ask whether the social sciences could support greater public access for its ongoing inquiry into risk. The knowledge developed should be able to facilitate a greater degree of public

---

23. Stephen Breyer, *Breaking the Vicious Circle: Toward Effective Risk Regulation* (Cambridge: Harvard University Press, 1993), 23, 51. Using a New Hampshire example, Breyer points out that the cost of cleaning up the last 10 percent of a toxic-waste site was $9.3 million, enabling a hypothetical child to safely eat small amounts of dirt on 245 days rather than just 70 days of the year (12).

24. Ibid., 24–27. In contrast, the regulation cover by its Hazardous Waste Listing for Wood-Preserving Chemicals of 1990 charges out at an astounding $5.7 trillion per premature death avoided, meaning that labeling creosote from now until the last tree is cut isn't likely to save a life (26–27).

participation in this thinking about how we should approach risk. Studies estimate that 60,000 lives or $31 billion could be saved by improving the allocation of existing risk-management resources, suggesting just how much is at issue (with the question of lives versus dollars itself inviting public discussion). Another study warns that risk regulators may have lost their bearings, as "advances in low-level risk detection threaten to engulf us with information." Risk is a matter of public perception to which the social sciences can contribute reality checks, wake-up calls, comparison shopping, and other modern conveniences.[25]

The public perception of risk certainly follows the political spectrum. On the right, people are concerned with the risk posed by increased immigration for its strain on social services and its potential "disuniting of America." On the left, people see the social safety net at risk in current government downsizing, as well as an undermining of racial equality. Social scientists tend to follow a similar pattern and should not be expected to resolve what is finally and truly at risk, but they may well be able to facilitate a more detailed look at the various risks in any one case, and thereby introduce a reasoned basis into what are still bound to be heated, partisan discussions. One interest of this public-knowledge project is whether and how an increase in the public scale of what is known about risks encourage greater democratic participation in the relevant political processes.

As things now stand, getting the word out on risk has developed into the field known as "risk communication," which is largely assumed to be a matter of public relations. The challenge for such communication is defined as overcoming "the great divide that often separates two evaluations of risks: those of scientific experts on the one hand and those of members of the public on the other," in the words of Douglas Powell, sociologist of science at the Universities of Guelph and Waterloo, and William Leiss, Eco-Research Chair at Queen's University. In their book *Mad Cows and Mother's Milk: The Perils of Poor Risk Communication,* Powell and Leiss describe how this great-divide needs to be addressed by public-relations mediation between expert and public, which poses a particular challenge to the far more direct approach of my public-knowledge project. Powell and Leiss describe "the zone that separates the languages of expert risk assessment and public risk perception" as one that can only be bridged by ongoing public education and public "participatory opportunities," with the experts. I see these as important aspects of "risk

---

25. Ibid., 22; Tammy Teng el al., "Five Hundred Life-Saving Interventions and Their Cost-Effectiveness," *Risk Analysis* 15, no. 3 (1995); Richard J. Zeckhauser and W. Kip Viscusi, "Risk within Reason," *Science*, May 4, 1990, 559.

communication," just as I would hold with delivering a forceful message to those at immediate risk, along the lines of, "Warn your children that this device can kill them if it falls into water," even if such messages are as much about corporate liability as about public understanding of risk. Yet what I want to explore rather than accept is that the public is inherently limited in its understanding of technical language, as well as in its appreciation of probabilities and other scientific forms of reasoning, as Powell and Leiss hold.[26]

The current state of risk communication also troubles Jane Franklin of the Institute of Public Policy Research in London. Franklin finds risk "a dynamic force for change in our individual lives," yet she fears that we are forced to act on risks "in light of conflicting information from experts and politicians, whom we can no longer trust to keep us informed." The result is that experts and politicians themselves become sources of risk, adding to the anxieties of knowing in this Information Age. Certainly, polls indicate that public confidence in experts has continued to fall since the 1960s, suggesting a general communication problem. So it should not surprise us that religious and spiritual sources of understanding thrive, as Franklin also notes, on the insecurities of the age: they suffer few conflicts over the evidence and no lack of clarity or certainty, at least on their own terms.[27]

What can we hope to gain from this extended and coherent access to what is known about risks to our world? University of Toronto philosopher Mark Kingwell has pointed to the consolation such knowledge offers: "The more each of life's myriad risks can be quantified and categorized, the more life in general ceases to seem risky—or at least to seem quite so random." Kingwell contrasts this idea with the alternative case of not knowing, for example, whether power stations increase the risk of cancer, commenting that it is "much scarier still to think that perhaps no one knows what causes [cancer]." Certainly, the public is interested in knowing more about risk, if we are to believe John Graham, founding director of the Center for Risk Analysis at Harvard University, and Lorenz Rhomberg, from Harvard's School of Public Health: "Citizens desire authoritative information about which risks are real, how

---

26. Douglas Powell and William Leiss, *Mad Cows and Mother's Milk: The Perils of Poor Risk Communication* (Montreal: McGill-Queens University Press, 1997), ix, 27, 29–30, 219. Powell and Leiss are encouraged that the current era emphasizes "the development of a long-term organizational commitment and competence in practicing good risk communication" (35). To some degree my public-knowledge project would extend those practices, if on less of a public-relations basis.

27. Jane Franklin, introduction to *Politics of Risk Society*, 1; Breyer, *Breaking the Vicious Circle*, 36.

large or serious these risks might be, and what steps can be taken to reduce or prevent the risks through cost-effective interventions." Graham and Rhomberg warn that although risk assessment can clear the air and "narrow the uncertainty," it can also exacerbate the play of interests and values that lead people to make decisions that fly in the face of the numbers. Writing in the *Wall Street Journal*, Graham gives an example of how risks need to be played off each other, by calculating that proposals to raise new fuel-economy standards to forty miles per gallon will lead to lighter cars, which will increase the hazard of fatal crashes, which will outweigh, in turn, the gains made by airbag technology. Identifying potential risks for the public is only the start of the discussion, not the end of it. I am also proposing that this awareness of risk would be valuable in public-policy areas not only in the environment and health but also in education, welfare, justice, economics, and politics.[28]

Harvard political scientist Robert Putnam, for example, has identified how people are no longer joining churches, unions, or recreational leagues in the same numbers and this may be undermining, he suspects, the trust and cooperation that are critical to democratic processes. Putnam's evocative and much-discussed piece "Bowling Alone" describes, as I am casting things, the risks to democracy posed by changes in patterns of association. The consequences of this "social disengagement" could well affect how we arrive collectively at decisions concerning what is just and how we are to be governed. The risk of this "social disengagement" can be best managed, I think, not by joining a local bowling league, but by understanding how new forms of association, whether in interest groups or through online communities, are developing, as well as by appreciating how new sources of trust and cooperation will be needed to advance this democratic project. In this way, the social sciences have something to offer people in response to the question, "What is happening to the world I knew?" which may creep up on them after an afternoon in the local mall.[29]

Although much risk analysis is directed at managing liabilities, political and financial, the social sciences can offer a corresponding spirit

28. Mark Kingwell, "A Shock to the System," *New York Times Magazine*, August 8, 1999, 16; John D. Graham and Lorenz Rhomberg, "How Risks Are Identified and Assessed," *Annals of the American Academy* 545 (May 1996): 16, 23. On the haphazard tendencies of the risk-analysis field, as well as the public's seeming ineptness in responding to risk through cost–benefit analysis, see Zeckhauser and Viscusi, "Risk within Reason," 559–64; John Graham, "Regulation: A Risky Business," *Wall Street Journal*, May 16, 1994, A14.
29. Robert D. Putnam, "Bowling Alone: America's Declining Social Capital," *Journal of Democracy* 6, no. 1 (January 1995)—http://muse.jhu.edu/demo/journal_of_democracy/v006/putnam.html. Putnam has since discovered a wealth of information,

of concern and responsibility for what is risked on civil rights and obligations. Take the glass-ceiling syndrome that women experience in climbing through the corporate ranks. As long as this practice continues, it places women's rights and aspirations at risk. Named as a risk, this syndrome is more likely to be monitored, whether calculated statistically or tracked through case studies, with the findings used as a public resource in the struggle for equality. An individual can call her boss on this acknowledged risk, and a group of women can take action against an employer. Turning the social sciences' analysis of risk into a public resource is a strategy of hope and advantage, in Laplace's sense, as described in the preceding chapter.

There also remains a risk to knowing. At some point, learning more about a critical issue can lead to greater uncertainty, rather than easing the decision that needs to be made. It is obviously a finely nuanced and carefully calibrated, but no less real, sense of risk that I want to work with in improving the contributions that the social sciences make to public knowledge. The value of going public with social-science research is related to a far more general understanding of the risks related to knowing and knowledge, which this public-knowledge project is also intent on investigating. I want to emphasize that this is not simply about public benefit. The social sciences are just as much in need of this engagement with the public, if not more so, if they are to keep their grip on the meaningfulness of risk, and thus on their very claim to knowledge.

Not many of us have a penchant for uncertainty. Even scientists searching for answers in laboratories prove to be no more inclined toward a vacuum than nature itself. That is, they tend to consistently overestimate the certainty of their findings. We all want to believe that we know enough to rest assured in our knowing, even as experience often proves otherwise. As an educator, I hold that having one's certainties shaken through the availability of new information is one path to learning, to seeing the world anew. Given this society's enormous investment in social-science research, much of which has something to say about the risks people face in their daily lives, the time may well be ripe to see if the public value of that information can be improved as a practical, political, intellectual, and moral resource that people can draw on

---

29. *(continued)* ... gathered by consumer-research firms on people's attitudes and behaviors demonstrating the convergence of private- and public-knowledge interests, which further confirms the decline in civic memberships and public activities more generally: see D. W. Miller, "Perhaps We Bowl Alone, but Does It Really Matter?" *Chronicle of Higher Education,* July 16, 1999, A16.

in making greater sense if the world around them, and in making that sense matter.[30]

As drawn as I am to risk as a way of making sense of chance and probability, it is not the only response to the rarely bearable uncertainty of knowing. I have been struck, for example, by the pluckiness of Gary A. Cziko's approach to probability. Cziko, an educational psychologist at the University of Illinois, concludes that we may not be able to resolve or reconcile the conflicts among research studies of, for example, bilingual education. Any sort of synthesis of results, he holds, is "simply not possible or meaningful." There is too much to measure, he insists, and too much variability in the measures. Not only are we unable "to predict and control human behavior in educational contexts," we are also unlikely to come up with generalizations of any lasting value. Our efforts to tame chance reach their limits, according to Cziko, within the complexity of the daily human activities of teaching and learning. We can identify the risks and learn more about how they operate, but we are not going to arrive at a steadfast knowledge of how to eliminate them.[31]

What is to be done? Cziko opts for what he characterizes as a "method of possibilities," which "specifies desirable goals that previous research has shown to be *possible* in a similar setting." Rather than naming what is at risk, he seeks to combine what is desirable with what has been shown to be possible. This sense of "possibility" seems the perfect complement to "risk." This is why I have put the two together at various points in this chapter. What we risk, it suddenly becomes clear, is often in the name of what is possible. The weighing of probabilities in research can be directed toward assessing the degree of risk just as easily as toward the degree of possibility. What researchers can ascertain of risk, then, should inspire them to pursue the prospects of new possibilities. Their question becomes, "Given what is risked, what are the possibilities?"[32]

30. James K. Hammitt, "Can More Information Increase Uncertainty?" *Chance* 8, no. 3 (1995).

31. Gary A. Cziko, "The Evaluation of Bilingual Education: From Necessity and Probability to Possibility," *Educational Researcher* (March 1992): 10.

32. Gary A. Cziko, "Unpredictability and Indeterminism in Human Behavior: Arguments and Implications for Educational Research," *Educational Researcher* (April 1989): 17–25. For a critique, see Richard Lehrer, Ronald C. Serlin, and Ronald Amundson, "Knowledge or Certainty? A Reply to Cziko," *Educational Researcher* (August–September 1990): 14, 16–19. Cziko's approach is to be distinguished from that of Isaac Levi, who writes of "knowledge as a standard for serious possibility"; Levi considers the possibility of knowledge as opposed to Cziko's knowledge of possibilities: *The Enterprise of Knowledge: An Essay on Knowledge, Credal Probability, and Chance* (Cambridge: MIT Press, 1980), 2–5.

Yet something more is called for with the knowledge of possibilities than specifying reasonably possible goals. If people are going to be able to work with and test the idea of what is possible, they will need a strong guide to what achieving the possible might take. This sort of practical help, however, typically falls outside the scope of what researchers do. Yet it would take little enough effort, within the hyperlinked environment of the web, for researchers to connect their studies on what is at risk and what is possible to sites that can help people implement new programs, obtain grants for innovation, or connect to those experimenting with similar possibilities for practice. The lack of connection between research studies and program materials, between the knowledge of research and experience, has long contributed to the practitioner's sense of the irrelevance of research. Research on possibilities begs for connecting research to practice. I see this not as the total responsibility of the researcher but as a reason to create a public space for connecting research to professional and public interests.

At the University of British Columbia in the spring of 1999, my colleagues and I launched the Public Knowledge website, which aimed to improve the links between research and practice as a way of bringing an understanding of risk and possibility into greater proximity. In conjunction with the *Vancouver Sun,* we created links between a series on technology in education and related online versions of research, policies, programs, and practices. For a *Sun* article on the ongoing gender stereotyping of technology, for example, which featured a young female computer whiz and interviews with Mary Bryson, a colleague of mine at UBC, the Public Knowledge website offered readers links to Bryson's studies, as well as to the website of her ongoing research program, GenTech, and to related sites on classroom practices in which girls have thrived. The Public Knowledge website also had an open forum in which Mary and another GenTech member participated with members of the public. The links to classroom programs for girls in technology included recommendations for providing girls with greater opportunities, and the links to provincial legislation and policies provided a means for fighting gender discrimination, as well as to organizations devoted to working on behalf of gender equity with technology both in schools and workplaces. In this way, the Public Knowledge website tried to connect risk to possibility and to the means to make it happen.[33]

---

33. Vivian Forssman, Henry Kang, Lisa Korteweg, Brenda Trofanenko, and John Willinsky, Public Knowledge Project, in conjunction with the *Vancouver Sun* (April 24–29, 1999), http://www.educ.ubc.ca/faculty/ctg/pkp.

One can see how a much more complex picture among different means of knowing begins to emerge with these links, even as the site posed new challenges to our goal of coherence and intelligibility on a public scale. Our experiment was to closely link works and draw from different categories and genres—research, practice, organization, policy, or news article—while also grouping these works by educational technology topic—gender, educational funding, school curriculum, libraries, and computer implementation. Although we may well have enabled the newspaper readers of the original articles to steer their own course among research studies and other materials related to those articles, we have only begun to explore whether this ability afforded them a greater understanding of the diversity of ideas on the question. Organizing links by genre and topic, even with summaries for each link, is still too simpleminded, and we need to think more about how we connect ideas (which is why the subject of the following chapter is the footnote).

What would happen to this changing representation of knowledge, we have begun to consider, if the people developing these studies and other materials began to prepare them with the possibility of an extensive web of connections in mind. What would happen if the *relation among* these materials could be discussed and challenged on such public-knowledge sites, as well as the *range and arrangement of ideas* that drive the social sciences? Certainly, the tentativeness and diversity of this knowledge would increase, as well as public accountability and engagement. But such a shift could also make something more of the knowledge that so many of us working in the social sciences are paid to produce, and it would do so, in part, by enabling us to attune our work so that others might make more of it.

The risk here is, finally, in the living. There is no ultimate insurance against that risk, no real assurances to be found in the face of it. Still, I am convinced that more could be done with the social sciences' study of risk and possibility to create a coherent and comprehensible public resource. More could be done to help people learn from how research studies work with and against each other, as they extend and push against what has long been assumed, and as they invite people to consider how we are currently handling what is at risk and what is possible. On that basis, one can asses whether all that can *reasonably* be done *is* being done. Having been entrusted by the public to produce a steady stream of knowledge about the social world, social scientists have now to consider how new and old technologies could improve the possibilities of improving the quality of understanding on a public scale.

Footnotes among Fragments   9

This could be a difficult chapter, given its focus on the small-print attributions of the footnote. This twelfth-century invention of the monk's scriptorium may seem an unlikely topic for a work dedicated to improving public access to scholarship through new technologies. After all, publishers today believe that nothing puts a potential reader off faster than the sight of footnotes scurrying along the bottom of the page. As a result, notes are buried at the back of the book deterring all but the determined from exploring the sources and connections behind their reading. I am here to defend and revitalize the footnote in its new hypertext guise. The footnote has long served scholars well as a device for augmenting knowledge. Recall Bacon, who was far from bookish or pedantic in his efforts to advance learning, in a line I quoted in chapter 4: "It is no easy matter even to teach what I am proposing, for things new in themselves will still be understood by reference to things already known." These annotated maps to things already known can guide the public to all that connects social-science research and the larger world.[1]

The footnote did have a recent and brief moment of public glory in 1998, with the publication of Kenneth Starr's *Report of the Independent Counsel*, as readers were drawn to the prurient details of President Clinton's affair that were duly recorded in the footnotes. As things now stand, however, whether relegated to a book's end-matter or demoted as a system of referencing, as in the social sciences, the footnote is an atrophied organ of citation and commentary.

The style manuals that currently govern publishing practices in most social sciences discourage the use of footnotes. It is seen as inefficient compared to the now prescribed use of parenthetical citation—inserting

---

1. Francis Bacon, *Novum Organum,* trans. P. Urbach and J. Gibson (1620; reprint, Chicago: Open Court, 1994), 52. On the origins of the footnote, see Ivan Illich, *In the Vineyard of the Text: A Commentary to Hugh's Didascalicon* (Chicago: University of Chicago Press, 1997), 98–100.

(Willinsky, 2000), for example—with a complete bibliographical listing at the end of the text. The footnote may have lost its hold as a scholarly universal, but with the introduction of hypertext environments, I think it stands as the perfect device, both medieval and postmodern, for extending the coherence and connections that exist within bodies of research. The footnote has always been used to stitch scholarly works together, binding what has come before to what others are even now working on. To follow yet another metaphorical route, the footnote has always offered a guided footpath—pedestrian and accessible—through the groves of scholarship, at least for those able to consult a full-scale research library. With the Internet, we suddenly have the capacity to open that path still wider, allowing virtually anyone with access to a computer terminal to reach the whole of what will only grow to be a greater proportion of current and past academic work, notwithstanding licensing agreeements. And however limited access is to computers on a global scale, it is still much greater than access to an adequately equipped library. This improved public access offers a new opportunity for the thoroughly academic apparatus of the footnote, namely as a public guide to social-science research.[2]

To that end, this chapter is taken up with the need to expand the scope and scale of scholarly reference in the social sciences against a background of technical possibilities. Once researchers are convinced that public access is worth supporting, it will take little effort to add a series of footnote or hyperlink icons to their texts that link to explanatory materials, related projects, and other supportive sources. Certain icons, or colored backgrounds behind a single letter of a word, could indicate that different orders of reference and support are available to the reader. One could indicate that a technical definition of a term or phrase is available, using the equivalent of embedded and multilayered "help screens," which would enable a wider, less experienced set of readers to consult the research. Another type of icon could provide a more complete guide to the background and historical context of a concept or method. A third

---

2. The widespread public interest in the footnotes of Starr's *Report of the Independent Counsel* is exemplified by what became known as "footnote 209," which reads in its entirety: "They engaged in oral-anal contact as well"; *Report of the Independent Counsel* (September 9, 1998)—http://icreport.access.gpo.gov/report/1cover.htm. See also, Alexandra Gill, "Pillow Talk at 100 Decibels," *Toronto Globe and Mail*, December 26, 1998, C7. As for online scholarly publishing, as of January 2000, the New Jour website, "the Internet list for new journals and newsletters available on the Internet," lists 8,000 online titles—http://gort.ucsd.edu/newjour/index.html. The JSTOR (Journal Storage) project, originally funded by the Mellon Foundation to digitize complete sets of "core scholarly journals," going back to the 1800s in a few cases, currently has 117 journals available in its database—http://www.jstor.org.

could offer links to related studies (complete text for some, abstracts for others), with a variety of options for obtaining access to book-length works. A fourth icon could connect readers to relevant policy and legislation, to websites on the practices described, and to organizations involved in supporting such work, in a system of knowledge integration that has formed part of our initial experiment with a public-knowledge website.[3]

Next, consider how the footnote can work in a dynamic and interactive sense with readers, after the manner of the ancient commentaries that sprang up in the margins of sacred texts. That is, a fifth type of icon might lead to a discussion that has been initiated at this point in the text by previous readers, perhaps also involving the authors of the text. A sixth might signal a link to material added by readers that supports, complements, or challenges the work. And lest one envision a text overrun by teeming swarms of icons, I should add that readers, of course, would choose which icons, if any, are visible as they read. After all, there could be more, for another function of footnoting is to indicate the level or degree of information made available. I can foresee links that enable readers to dip into more detailed information about a sample, or a method of analysis, or the data themselves, with additional links to comparative data from other studies. There could also be retrociting, by which a reader could follow a work into the future, leading to works that had cited *it* as recently as that very day. And on it would go in a web of knowledge. Some of these citational links could be part of the automated publishing process that would extend a work's connections within the Internet.[4]

There are numerous reasons, then, to return to the footnote, reviving its role as the original hyperlink of the always virtual, always expansive universe of knowledge. Still, I enter this territory knowing that some will think, "If it isn't broken, then don't try to make it do more than it was intended to do, just because you have the resources to do it." Yet the problem in research is not the referencing but the fragmentation. As I have already indicated, the very scale of social-science research is working against my hopes for turning it into a greater source of public knowledge. New strategies of integration clearly need to be devised and

---

3. See Chapter 1, Public Knowledge Project, fn. 8.
4. In *Technologies of Knowing: A Proposal for the Human Sciences* (Boston: Beacon, 1999), 107–11, I discuss forms of autocitation and Robert Cameron's, "A Universal Citation Database as a Catalyst for Reform in Scholarly Communication," *First Monday* 2, no. 4 (1997), http://www.firstmonday.dk/issues/issue2_4/index.html. Commercial versions of auto-citation software that comb Internet libraries and indexes are available with EndNote, ProCite, and Reference Manager.

tested if a corresponding increase in our general understanding of the world is to develop with any help from the social sciences.[5]

The footnote may seem to operate like no more than a storm sewer, running along the bottom of the page, where it catches and funnels off excess scholarship. Yet it is also all about going public. It puts one's sources and indebtedness on display. It declares the clubs one belongs to or disavows. It holds within it the hope of grasping the lay of this learned land, the accumulation of knowledge in a given field. It directs readers to where a work is heading, by virtue of where it has been. It is little credited for all that it gives, I hold, in the name of knowledge.[6]

As Princeton historian Anthony Grafton explains in his charming history of the footnote, the note was once a literary art form, intended to bemuse and engage, as well as to inform, the interested reader. Public access to the footnote was actually an issue for the great historian Edward Gibbon, as he rued being forced by "public importunity" to place his notes for the *Decline and Fall of the Roman Empire* at the bottom of the page rather than at the end of the book, thereby defacing, in his eyes, the gracefulness of the page. I have petitioned my publishers to bring my notes back to the foot of the page, where the reader can readily judge their value with less interruption of the main text (which is why I also favor placing their numbers at paragraph's end).[7]

More to my point, however, is how a reference linking one study to

---

5. Joseph Ben-David, "How to Organize Research in the Social Sciences," *Daedalus* (spring 1973): 40–42; David M. Ricci, *The Tragedy of Political Science: Politics, Scholarship, Democracy* (New Haven: Yale University Press, 1988), 228: "For total confusion, we need only a sufficiently large number of potential challengers, working on a great many small parts of political life. Where that situation obtains, individual pieces of research will add up to an impenetrable mass of limited findings of such intrinsic inconsistency that even when large-scale coherence might be desirable as the basis of public policy, it will be impossible to draw the pieces of knowledge together and use them effectively."

6. I notice that before I completely cut a passage from my text because it has come to seem extraneous—and I'm hardly alone in treating writing as much a matter of cutting away as of building up—I consider whether I can divert it into a footnote.

7. Anthony Grafton, *The Footnote: A Curious History* (Cambridge: Harvard University Press, 1997), 224. The footnote in the hands of the professional historian, Grafton points out, "identifies both the primary evidence that guarantees the story's novelty in substance and the secondary works that do not undermine its novelty in form and thesis" (5). Or more nobly: "Only the use of footnotes and the research techniques associated with them makes it possible to resist the efforts of modern governments, tyrannical and democratic alike, to conceal the compromises they have made, the deaths they have caused, the tortures they or their allies have inflicted" (233). On the fate of the artful footnote, Stanley Weintraub, in reviewing a volume of Disraeli's letters, notes: "His adroit editors have compensated for contemporary cultural illiteracy with awesome detective work. Their notes are often fun": "The Whole Disraeli," *New York Times Book Review*, August 9, 1998, 22.

another can work with or against the social sciences' service to public knowledge. The argument that I want to put forward here is that nothing is more critical to bringing the social sciences into the realm of public knowledge than this act of citation. Wherever the footnote appears—at the bottom of the page, at the end of the book, or in the text itself—it is vital that readers are able to see that the very claim to knowledge lies in how studies work together. Toward that end, the footnote is only the most typographically obvious of foundation stones for setting a text within the company of other texts. There is no writing, after all (certainly not after Derrida), that is not engaged in an act of reference. When Grafton speaks of modern history writing as "an investigative discipline as well as a form of story telling," he sees the footnote playing its part on the side of history's "coherent literary form." And coherence is one of the necessary themes for improving the social sciences' contributions to public knowledge.[8]

Yet the literary form of the narrative, favored with history, is not a typical component of the social sciences. Nor do the social sciences often use, as history does, other texts or archival materials as sources of original data. Citation in the social sciences is more typically about rooting the concepts, instruments, and assumptions that researchers have applied in their study. That the standards for this form of scholarly citation were set some time ago becomes strikingly apparent from Pierre Bayle's description of seventeenth-century scholars' passion for footnoting in his popular *Historical and Critical Dictionary* of 1697: "They try to make suitable applications, and to link their authorities well. They compare them with one another—or, indeed, they show that they conflict. Moreover, they are people who make it their religion, when points of fact are concerned, to make no assertion that has no proof." This very spirit guides current habits of referencing in the social sciences and elsewhere. I want to apply Bayle's standards to a number of contemporary research studies to demonstrate the shortcomings that mar the intelligibility and diminish the public value of the research.[9]

To test whether the citation can be made to stand against the forces of fragmentation, I turn to three recent research studies drawn from well-respected journals in the study of education. The articles focus on the familiar experiences of junior high schools in one case, and of elementary-school science classes in the other two. They take up critical issues in the education and experience of the children and teachers in those schools. In so doing, the researchers work with difficult, specialized

---

8. Grafton, *Footnote,* 232.
9. Pierre Bayle, *Historical and Critical Dictionary* (1697), cited in ibid., 199.

knowledge, which is nonetheless directed at helping classroom teachers improve their work with students, as well as at ensuring that students and their parents and communities get the education they deserve. I do not intend to judge the quality of the research, but only to comment on how the current approach to referencing, which these studies expertly adhere to, stands to be improved. Is it possible, I am asking, for this system of referral to make a more readily comprehensible contribution to the understanding of those who are both its subject and its hope for change? There are ways, I propose, for improving how such studies work toward forming a larger picture—albeit always *partial*, in the double sense of the term—that will have far more to offer teachers, parents, students, administrators, and elected officials.

THE CASE FOR THE CASE STUDY

The lead article of the *American Educational Research Journal* for April 1997 was "Restructuring in Context: A Case Study of Teacher Participation and the Dynamics of Ideology, Race, and Power," by Pauline Lipman from the School of Education at DePaul University in Chicago. Lipman conducted a case study of a junior high school that attempted to restructure its program to improve the educational opportunities of "at-risk" students. The research was drawn from her doctoral research, completed at the University of Wisconsin in the early 1990s, and it was also about to be published as a book, so in one sense it represents a large part of the publishing activity going on in the field of the social sciences.[10]

Lipman spent a year in the junior high school, studying the change process, before coming to the conclusion that the school's restructuring efforts did not succeed. In her estimation, the restructuring failed because the school staff implementing the changes did not face up to "how existing relations of domination are reproduced." The primary evidence for drawing that conclusion, Lipman argues, was the lack of any noticeable increase in the participation of African-American students, teachers, or parents in the life of the school. She points to how students were being segregated by race through the school's new system of tracking and how the African-American teachers were not invited in to the reform process. Through a detailed analysis of the relevant policy, participants' interviews, and her field notes, she makes apparent how restructuring was made to work within the existing racial structures governing the school.

---

10. Pauline Lipman, "Restructuring in Context: A Case Study of Teacher Participation and the Dynamics of Ideology, Race, and Power," *American Educational Research Journal* 34, no. 1 (1997).

Although this particular school's failure is disheartening, the challenge for the researcher is to identify the larger lesson that can contribute to what is already known about school change and restructuring, so that it can help others facing similar situations in schools everywhere.[11]

It's true that relations of domination were not the intended target of the school's restructuring effort—which set out to improve *performance*, not *participation*—but there is research, which Lipman doesn't cite, that makes the case for how students' greater engagement in school can lead to improved performance. However, Lipman chose to step outside of the school's intended goals and to place the school's efforts within the larger historical restructuring of racial divisions in American education. As one might imagine, the school-district officials were dismayed on hearing Lipman's conclusions. Unfortunately, they responded by restricting community access to, and discussion of, her work. A group of white teachers, on learning about the findings, angrily rejected the charge. Yet it did lead, in Lipman's estimation, to "somewhat more heterogeneous" student groupings the next year.[12]

It then falls to me to establish how improving the way Lipman references other works could do more to help such research support the educational opportunities of African-American students and teachers. My seemingly perverse point of intervention assumes that as knowledge is all about connections, our hopes lie in a closely woven canvas of findings that, when hoisted on the mast of ongoing educational desegregation, will carry the schools forward.

The white teachers in the school Lipman observed spoke of their decisions as "colorblind" and Lipman comments, "This assiduous avoidance of naming students' race was driven by a powerful taboo against discussing racial issues and a widely articulated claim 'not to see color' (Schofield, 1982)." Notice how Lipman's standard method of referencing tells the reader little about the relation of her work to Janet Ward Schofield's 1982 book, *Black and White in School: Trust, Tension, or Tolerance?* One may infer that Schofield used the phrase "not to see color" and presumably found a similiar "taboo" against discussing race in her study. I think there is much more to cite and tell.[13]

---

11. Ibid., 33.
12. On the salutary impact of school engagement in reducing risk behaviors that affect students' achievement, see Michael Resnick et al., "Protecting Adolescents from Harm: Findings from the National Longitudinal Study on Adolescent Health," *Journal of the American Medical Association* 278 (September 1997): 823–32; Lipman, "Restructuring in Context," 13.
13. Lipman, "Restructuring in Context," 19; Janet Ward Schofield, *Black and White in School: Trust, Tension, or Tolerance?* (New York: Praeger, 1982).

Schofield's book has much to offer on the race taboo. It is a study of a school that was intended to be a model of integration when it opened in 1975, and in it Schofield establishes that this taboo was the single most powerful strategy for perpetuating a racial inequality in the school that extended from the student council to expulsion rates. The consistency between what teachers said to Schofield and what they said to Lipman decades later is striking, so much so that I would argue that the knowledge at issue here is largely about the *persistence* of this "color blindness" line despite its racial consequences for children's education. Schofield also shows how the taboo against acknowledging race operates within the school even as race was frequently and openly discussed by school officials and the press. This might form another point of comparison with Lipman's study in helping us understand ongoing discrimination perpetuated in the guise of color blindness.

Schofield offers her own sources for the color-blind concept with three parenthetically inscribed references (Rist, 1978; Sagar and Schofield, 1982; Willie 1973). As it turns out, Ray Rist provides an introduction to Schofield's book, which is part of an early ethnographic series on schools that Rist edited. Rist speaks of Schofield's work as contributing to "perhaps the first 'critical mass' of such studies" on the educational implications of race. "Critical mass" suggests that great energy is about to be released by virtue of the radioactive weight and number of these works, but only in a productive form, I would suggest, if the connections are carefully, thoughtfully aligned. The search I am proposing is for ways of connecting studies so that their cumulative consequence does indeed go "critical."[14]

The standards of citation followed in these two studies by no means signal a failure of scholarship on the part of either Lipman or Schofield. The current standards support a shorthand citation that does little to support a center of gravity emerging among the studies. As an alternative, think of a hypertexted footnote on "color blindness" in Lipman's study that provides an annotated guide back to Schofield and similar studies. The note could possibly open windows on parallel passages in these studies' findings as a way of bringing the mass of evidence to bear on Lipman's analysis. It would situate readers within the cumulative history of this knowing, enabling them to explore the depth of the

---

14. Ray Rist, *The Invisible Children* (Cambridge: Harvard University Press, 1978); H. Andrew Sagar and Janet W. Schofield, "Integrating the Desegregated School: Problems and Possibilities," in *The Effect of School Desegregation on Motivation and Achievement*, ed. David E. Bartz and Martin L. Marhr (Greenwich, Conn.: JAI Press, 1982); Charles Willie, *Race Mixing in Public Schools* (New York: Praeger, 1973).

problem, while adding to the immediate poignancy of Lipman's study. Some readers of her work may, in the world of footnoting that I am imagining, want to append their own note, including commentary or evidence, for or against, Lipman's findings. The footnote provides a guide to how related case studies work with this issue, enabling people to judge the consequences, concerns, and contentions surrounding school talk of color blind educational practices.[15]

This approach to the footnote means shifting the epistemological spotlight, in effect, away from how well an individual study stands on its own with only the attributed phrase, in this case, "color blindness," linking it to another's work at a critical point in the argument. The art of citation needs to be directed at bringing the cumulative weight of this research to bear on the present situation, by the situating the researcher's own findings within this larger body of work. We need to be able see how individual case studies work together by extending and challenging each other's findings. How far the researcher needs to go in securing her work to this cumulative body of related research, without unduly minimizing her contribution or obfuscating the issue at hand, becomes the art of the public footnote, the integrative hyperlink.

What would such hyperlinked footnotes mean for a group of teachers and parents at a junior high school who have come together to consider what school restructuring might hold for them? As part of the deliberative process, both individually and together they could review the related research. They would probably start not with Lipman's study but with the general topic of school restructuring, with links to summaries of works such as Fred Newmann and Gary Wehlage's *Successful School Restructuring*, which reports on school-changing strategies that demonstrate "authentic learning" and "professional community building." In considering potential points of caution, they would come to Lipman's study on the risks and possibilities of this initiative. Parents and teachers visiting Lipman's study could gain a perspective on how race was a notable structural feature of the particular school she studied and at other schools studied, such as Schofield's, dating back decades. While review-

---

15. For example, conservative advocates of color blind policies may append a further note citing, as they have in other circumstances, Martin Luther King Jr.'s dream that we judge his children not "by the color of their skin but by the content of their character." I would add that King's line in "I Have a Dream" needs to be read in light of his later reflections on the need for "radical moral surgery" in America, given the extent of racism among "the vast majority of white Americans"; Martin Luther King Jr. cited in Robert S. Boynton, "Detour to the Promised Land" (review of Michael Eric Dyson, *I May Not Get There With You: The True Martin Luther King, Jr.*), *New York Times Book Review*, January 23, 2000, 12–13.

ing the Lipman study, teachers and parents might be able to listen literally to one of her participants, Larissa, "a critical African-American eighth-grade teacher," explain how we are failing to educate students when we deal only with their immediate and individual problems.[16]

These teachers and parents could sample other compelling experiences, voices, and documents that Lipman gathered during her year's work in the school. Lipman's study could lead, in turn, outward to other programs and organizations that support those working to change the structural role of race. This group of teachers and parents might be able to move from examples of classroom lessons that speak to the realities and challenges of race to school policies that make race the focus of restructuring greater equality of opportunity. They might run into debates, or perhaps initiate them, over the "achievement" implications of such measures, which could lead to still other studies and data. It would be readily apparent that no one study could determine their decision, and they would be left having to come to some agreement about the values and priorities that they would like to see applied to their community. Still, they would come to that process with some confidence that they were acting with an awareness of what is known, at least in a research sense. With each phase of the discussion, people might want to return to the public-knowledge website with a new set of questions and concerns, knowing always that it fell to them to make the choices, for which knowledge is no substitute. Finally, they might want to have their school participate in a proposed or ongoing research initiative that would help them to evaluate the implications of those choices.

Remember, this concern with coherence does not assume that this body of research will be pulled together, footnoted by hyperlink, into a Grand Unified Theory. It holds only that researchers can do more to ensure their contribution to knowledge than merely offering a thin thread of citational links among other works before dropping their own effort into a database like ERIC with nearly a million "abstracts" (an aptly chosen term) of educational research and related materials. I do not imagine that such clustering of works will make them more likely to be universally accepted by the scholarly community, but it may reduce the prevalence of "cliques, coteries, and lone wolves talking past one another or to themselves" that characterized the research community for political scientist Andrew Hacker some years ago. Such a development would begin by improving the level of reference within associated projects with

16. Fred M. Newmann and Gary Wehlage, *Successful School Restructuring: A Report to the Public and Educators* (Madison, Wis.: National Center on Organization and Restructuring of Schools, 1995); Lipman, "Restructuring in Context," 18–19.

an expanding sense of the value of carefully positioning the work in relation to other schools of thought.[17]

I am proposing that we considerably stretch the function of the footnote. I think if it is used in this extended fashion we would be in a better position to judge the value of such knowledge work, including whether we need as much of it as we are now producing. It will use new information technologies that are already exerting an increasing influence on academic publishing to test whether fragmentation among research studies can be reduced in ways that serve the cause of public knowledge.

THE RESEARCH–PRACTICE LINK

If studies continue to move away from each other within a universe of research that we might better connect with stronger links, where does that leave the world they are studying? Far behind, it often seems. In fact, the most common complaint about the fragmentation of knowledge surely concerns the divide between research and practice. If I have any hopes of bringing the social sciences and public knowledge into closer proximity, it must begin with rebuilding the citation as a way of bridging this gap.

To demonstrate what sort of citational work might be needed to address the problem, I offer an exchange between two scholars who disagree over applying lessons from developmental psychology to a science classroom. The exchange, published in the *Review of Educational Research*, takes place between Deanna Kuhn, a professor of psychology at Teachers College at Columbia University, and Kathleen Metz, assistant professor of child cognition at the University of California at Riverside. I should start off by noting that both of their strong research records include the close observation of children working on science problems, as opposed to the armchair analysis that I am guilty of here. And which one of them is right in their debate over the role of developmental

17. Andrew Hacker, "The Utility of Quantitative Methods in Political Science," in *Contemporary Political Analysis,* ed. James C. Charlesworth (New York: Free Press, 1967), 147; Lipman's abstract could be more pointedly helpful, I believe, although it does provide an excellent summary: "My analysis of the data suggests that, if restructuring is to transform the educational experience of marginalized students, it will require both personal and social change—challenging educators' beliefs and assumptions as well as relations of power in schools and communities"; Lipman, "Restructuring in Context," 3. On efforts to improve the abstract in medical journals, see R. Brian Haynes et al., "More Informative Abstracts Revisited," *Annals* of *Internal Medicine* 113, no. 1.

psychology in science teaching is not my issue. My interest is in how, despite their differences, they demonstrate a common pattern of reference. Their work begins, as is common to the research genre, by citing the need to improve the quality of children's educational experiences; they then present data in support of developmental models for scientific thinking among the young; but they finally fall short, I suggest, in completing the cycle. That is, their research fails to adequately reference how the models work themselves out in classrooms, and how they serve those who work in the educational settings that first gave rise to their research program.[18]

Developmental psychology represents one of the most influential theories in education and is considered a crucial component in the education of teachers in most jurisdictions. How this enormous field of research has come to reference the world of teaching and learning and how it follows through on the application of its ideas represents a major test site for the value of research knowledge. It also offers a major point of connection with public knowledge, given the interest in children's development among parents, educators, and child-care workers, not to mention the toy and "edutainment" industries.

The disagreement that I consider here between Kuhn and Metz is over moving theories of child development into classroom practice. Kuhn initiates the exchange by responding to Metz's published critique on elementary school teachers' misunderstanding and misapplication of research on children's cognitive development. The problem, as Metz outlines it in the original piece, is that teachers too often focus in their science classes on what is called the "concrete" stage of children's mental development, following Piaget's categories. This leads, in Metz's estimation, to too many lessons focused on observation, ordering, and categorization. Metz then demonstrates how "neither the Piagetian nor the non-Piagetian research supports the validity of these developmental assumptions."[19]

---

18. Deanna Kuhn, "Constraints or Guideposts? Developmental Psychology and Science," *Review of Educational Research* 67, no. 1 (1997); Kathleen E. Metz, "On the Complex Relation between Cognitive Developmental Research and Children's Science Curricula," *Review of Educational Research* 67, no. 1 (1997).

19. Kathleen E. Metz, "Reassessment of Developmental Constraints on Children's Science Instruction," *Review of Educational Research* 65 (1995): 93. Here would be a good place for a standardized footnote hyperlink on the Swiss psychologist Jean Piaget (1896–1980), of the Académie de Genève, including a review of his child-development theory, which includes the sensorimotor period (from birth to roughly two years of age), the preoperational period (ages two to seven), the concrete-operational period (ages seven to twelve), and the formal-operational period (twelve and up).

In her response, Kuhn takes Metz's position to be a general assault on what developmental psychology has to offer teachers of science. She counters Metz's critique with recent and seemingly effective research contributions to science teaching. Metz, allowed the final say in this exchange, comes back with a further critique of developmental psychology as an educationally useful concept, taking issue with its dependence on stages to explain children's shortcomings, its confounding of knowledge and capabilities, and its neglect of individual variability.

Now, where, one might wonder, is the problem here with the gap between theory and practice? The gap, after all, is precisely what Metz and Kuhn are addressing. Yet at a critical point they lose the connection to the practice, and in ways that I believe could be remedied by the electrofootnote.

In taking exception to how developmental models of children's thinking have been applied to science teaching, Metz is particularly disheartened by the way classroom lessons are shaped and restrained by "seemingly fundamental stage characteristics," which can end up postponing a child's experience of experimental science until adolescence. Metz cites Yale psychologist Robert Sternberg's claim that the real source of "disappointment" in the failure of cognitive theories to improve instruction is "the absence of an instructional theory to mediate the link between cognitive theory, on the one hand, and educational practice, on the other." Forgive me if I find it a little strange to think we are just one more theory short of completing the link from theory to practice. For me, the "fundamentally complex" relationship that Metz sees between research and practice is more fundamental than complex. And fundamentally, critical points of reference are liable to go missing in this research, which brings us back, of course, to the footnote.[20]

Science teaching is a primary point of reference for developmental psychology's research program on children's thinking. How children learn science in school is what gives this research meaning and value. Metz's framing of the problem does not acknowledge that the classroom is the point of reference for this research when she sets the theory of development apart from the practice of teaching. She cites the classroom in the opening of her article but not in closing, when she calls for

---

20. Metz "On the Complex Relation," 153, 161. The way forward that Metz recommends took me rather aback. After all, it might seem as if such research would only make the "seemingly fundamental stage characteristics" all the more fundamental and all the more open to misapplication; Robert J. Sternberg, "Cognition and Instruction: Why the Marriage Sometimes Ends in Divorce," in *Cognition and Instruction*, ed. Ronna F. Dillon and Robert J. Sternberg (New York: Academic Press, 1986), 378.

more and better research on children's mental development, with a special focus on determining what "differentiates relatively robust and immutable stage characteristics from malleable cognitive characteristics." The value of establishing "relatively robust and immutable stage characteristics" and certainly the value of differentiating them "from malleable cognitive characteristics" depend on the difference these ideas make to children's learning in a classroom with a teacher who may or may not have a background in science. This research does not simply use science topics to learn about how the mind develops, but is devoted to understanding how students come to think about science. It is first and foremost about how children think about science in educational settings. This is why I hold that the immutable point of reference for this work is the malleable and robust state of classrooms. The classroom needs to be a point of reference at the beginning and end of this research, just as these ideas about children's thinking need to be judged by how they work themselves out in classrooms. This is also why I think that footnotes can increase the public value of this research in ways that I will illustrate after introducing a second instance of this missing point of reference in the Metz–Kuhn exchange on cognitive development.[21]

In posing her challenge to Metz's critique, Deanna Kuhn introduces another aspect of this citational responsibility. Among the points Kuhn raises in defense of developmental psychology's contribution to education is its identification of the scientist in the child. The "origins of scientific thinking competencies" emerge in children, according to Kuhn, "somewhere between the ages of three to five." Kuhn supports this claim by citing David Olson and Janet Astington's study on how young children, in Kuhn's words, "acquire the understanding that statements are expressions of someone's belief." Children can see, she also draws from their study, that statements about the world are "subject to verification and potentially disconfirmable," which is, after all, "the hallmark of sci-

---

21. Kathleen E. Metz, "Preschoolers' Developing Knowledge of the Pan Balance: From New Representations to Transformed Problem Solving," *Cognition and Instruction* 11, no. 1 (1993): 34. After giving detailed analysis of preschoolers' problem-solving experiences with a pan balance, Metz recommends that schools offer a physics laboratory for young children to learn in, as a way to build from tacit to explicit understanding of scientific principles. Again the original point of reference is not the final one, when it comes to judging the efficacy of the ideas presented: "In short, a physics laboratory for young children can provide opportunities for children to apply proprioceptive, tacit knowledge of physical phenomena. Children's tacit knowledge can then be gradually transformed from this point to the externalized knowledge of scientific canon" (90).

ence." Kuhn cautions that young children are "far from effective or efficient scientists." Yet this is where developmental psychology can help educators "to know what skills they [junior scientists] do not yet have and how these evolve and can be developed."[22]

Kuhn extends the child-as-scientist metaphor by insisting that the child requires informed, selective cognitive nurturing to eventually acquire mature adult-as-scientist manners of thinking. Much as Metz presents cognitive characteristics removed from educational contexts, so Kuhn treats scientific thinking as an abstract quality of mind rather than a cultural practice that schools seek to structure and develop. Kuhn also claims that this manner of scientific thinking, consisting of "the coordination of theories and evidence," prevails in medical and legal thinking as well. And although she concedes that scientists' actual thinking is poorly understood, she sees nurturing ideal forms of "scientific thinking" in the young as clearly a global priority in education.[23]

Kuhn's treatment of children's "scientific thinking" without direct reference to science teaching is an example of the "naturalistic fallacy" identified some years ago by the Cambridge philosopher G. E. Moore. It is fallacious, Moore suggests, to treat a cultivated and refined quality, such as scientific thinking, as a natural attribute of the brain. This is much like describing the driving of a golf ball far down a tree-lined fairway as a natural stage in human physical development without making reference to the game of golf. Kuhn would do better to treat the child-scientist as a metaphor that can clarify children's potential for educators and the public rather than as a proven concept to now be applied to classrooms. The proof and value of this idea, much as with Metz's idea about cognitive

---

22. Kuhn, "Constraints or Guideposts?" 143 For a similar view on children-as-scientists, see Patricia Kuhl, *Scientist in the Crib* (New York: Morrow, 1999); "Babies revise their views about people and things in the world based on new information just as scientists do. A difference is that babies do it more quickly and profoundly than adults, because their brains are less committed—literally less cluttered—than ours are," cited in Erica Goode, "Mozart for Baby? Some Say, Maybe Not," *New York Times*, August 3, 1999, D9; David Olson and Janet Wilde Astington, "Thinking about Thinking: Learning How to Take Statements and Hold Beliefs," *Educational Psychologist* 28, no. 1 (1993); Kuhn, "Constraints or Guideposts?" 143–45. See also Deanna Kuhn, "Children and Adults as Intuitive Scientists," *Psychological Review* 96, no. 4 (1989).

23. Kuhn, "Intuitive Scientists," 674. Compare to pragmatist-philosopher Richard Rorty's take on scientists and their thinking: "They use the same banal and obvious methods that all of us use in every human activity.... They check off examples against criteria; they fudge the counter-examples enough to avoid the need for new models; they try out various guesses, formulated within current jargon, in the hope of coming up with something which will cover the unfudgeable cases": "Method, Social Science, and Social Hope," in *The Postmodern Turn: New Perspectives on Social Theory*, ed. Steven Seidman (Cambridge: Cambridge University Press, 1994), 48.

characteristics, lies in how it helps teachers think of ways to improve science teaching and learning.[24]

In both cases, Kuhn and Metz's conclusions would support a wider readership with footnotes that guide readers back to the classroom, whether to additional research on the impact of these ideas or to examples of the ideas at work in curriculum policies, plans, or practices that integrate this knowledge into the world. Later examples could be retroactively linked by two-way footnotes to their work, which would be especially helpful in the early days of such research. Other footnotes could invite educators to submit their own examples, collaborate with teachers working with these ideas, or join further research projects. The public-knowledge ecology and ethic of citation that I am proposing here is simply that from where the research first cites, so must it return as a point of reference.

Recalling that I am proposing that this referencing process is a two-way street, some readers of this literature may wish to draw links between the concept of children's scientific thinking as part of the natural unfolding of the brain, and the feminist critiques of science posed, for example, by Evelyn Fox Keller and Sandra Harding. This is another way of asking after the implications of these developmental models for a girl's experience in science class or a woman's in graduate school, as well as for the practice of science itself. What do the "successful" programs that Kuhn describes, which fill gaps in a child's scientific competency, mean for that basic divide described by Keller, for example, between traditional scientific models of domination and feminist alternatives? "In our zealous desire for familiar models of explanation," Keller warns, "we risk not noticing the discrepancies between our own dispositions and the range of possibilities in natural phenomena." Moving this cognitive research into the realm of public knowledge may open such challenges and debates to a wider audience that would include educators interested in having a choice in thinking about how to study science.[25]

Although my faith in footnotes as a force against one of the impediments to knowing well may seem a little extreme, the fragmentation of knowledge continues to keep us from realizing the connections and coherence within and among schools of thought. I think we need to push the technologies at our disposal, from the footnote to the hyperlink, so

---

24. For Moore's naturalistic fallacy, see chapter 7 of Bernard Williams, *Ethics and the Limits of Philosophy* (Cambridge: Harvard University Press, 1985).

25. Evelyn Fox Keller, *Reflections on Gender and Science* (New Haven: Yale University Press, 1985), 157; Sandra Harding, *Whose Science? Whose Knowledge?* (Bloomington: Indiana University Press, 1991).

that what the social sciences produce in the name of knowledge offers greater public value in this age of information. Anything less may seem epistemically irresponsible on the part of those who imagine that their contribution to humankind lies in just such knowledge.[26]

What I have sketched here is one possible path for extending the public reach of knowledge, and I am hardly alone in such speculations. The technology of citation is currently a focus in refining World Wide Web search engines that attempt to find order within an otherwise chaotic ever-expanding library. One innovative and relevant approach is that of the Clever Project, from the IBM Almaden Research Center in San Jose, California. Here is a search engine designed to identify works that are often cited and works that are reliable citers of these recognized works. The Clever Project team has created a "hypersearch" tool that scours websites, deciding which ones qualify as, either "authorities" or "hubs." An "authority" is defined as a site to which a number of other sites point, through their hyperlinks. The number of citations linking to an authority gives a measure of its standing in the field. The sites that point to these authorities may qualify as "hubs," based on the number of attested authorities to which it points. The result is an iterative process that, by comparing sites, ranks the strongest authorities and hubs on a given topic.[27]

The Clever search engine is designed for the web as a whole, but its benefits for searching within a body of research that has been posted on the web should be obvious. The Clever engine identifies the impact or authority of a study by tracking how often it is cited by other works, and Clever's approach to the hubs—works that connect these authoritative works—should also make possible a ready mapping of schools of thought and influence. By examining the leading authorities and how they are linked through a series of hubs, one sketches, in effect, an epistemic mapping of a domain. Where the footnote, as I am proposing it, can provide a more detailed description of a relationship linking one study to another, a future version of this Clever engine will be able to automatically index a given research field by mapping the strength and clustering of citation patterns. In the midst of one's inquiry, one would be able to "rise up" and, propelled by the search engine, do a "flyover" of a field of related studies, lighting on the footnotes behind the links to learn more of the intentions behind the connections. Here, then, is an old

---

26. See Lorraine Code, *Epistemic Responsibility* (Hanover, N.H.: University Press of New England, 1987), on why it is undeniable that human flourishing is deeply dependent upon knowing well (9).

27. The Clever Project, "Hypersearching the Web," *Scientific American,* June 1999.

scholarly apparatus teaming up with a new publishing medium, with the combination contributing to making the coherence and divisions within the field that much more available.

Having offered a glimpse of the future, let me now return to where this chapter began, with a final retrofootnote for my conclusion. The great French essayist of the sixteenth century, Michel de Montaigne, readily conceded that the reason he was so quick to cite other authors in his work was that their virtues might serve as a "cloak for my own weakness." In his essay "On Books," he goes so far as to propose that his own work "be judged from what I borrow whether I have chosen the right means of exalting my theme." He offers the image of the thoughtful writer fishing for knowledge, suggesting the patient and contemplative search among sources that is required of writers and readers. Yet in this same piece Montaigne offers a hymn to the fragmentation of knowledge, in his praise of Plutarch and Seneca: "The knowledge I seek there is treated in disconnected pieces that do not demand the bondage of prolonged labor, of which I am incapable." How might I hope to please this impatient Montaigne, as he stands at the origins of our modern quest for knowledge? On the one hand, he wants "discourses that plunge straight into the heart of the perplexity," and on the other, he knows that we must address that body of "children and the common people, with whom nothing must be left unsaid, in the hope that something will hit the mark."[28]

Given all that I have argued in this chapter, I trust that the footnote's potential contribution to public knowledge is readily apparent. Here is an intellectual resource that stands to be revitalized with hyperlink technologies, offering great prospects of weaving together bodies of knowledge. It can guide readers through the array of social-science research on any topic plunging into the heart of the perplexity while leaving nothing unsaid or unexplained—as Montaigne insisted on behalf of the people—or at least almost so, with options of always supplementing the existing story. Even as readers of this literature would find greater support for their inquiry with these technologically revitalized footnotes, they would also have greater control over the direction followed, in pursuing their interests from one study into another. They might proceed from lessons afforded by school-restructuring initiatives to the lessons learned in a quiet classroom corner where children experiment with the density and displacement of plasticine boats. What the

28.   Michel de Montaigne, "On Books" (1580), in *Essays*, ed. J. M. Cohen (Harmondsworth, England: Penguin, 1958), 160, 159, 165, 166.

social sciences know, in all of its expansive speculations, limitations, qualifications, and critiques, can stand as a public resource for those whose education, health, welfare, work, and governance are this field's very subject. This is a lot to ask of the modest footnote, I know, even within hyperlinked technologies. But my theme throughout this book has been that humanity's knowledge project has always been conceived within such ambitions and has always been looking for ways and means of taking yet another step toward realizing them.

Section III
Politics

A Knowing Democracy 10

Thinking through the idea of going public with social-science research has much to teach us about the politics of knowledge. At one level, this book has been about little else than the association of knowledge with power. Think of Bacon's imperial quest to house the known world, Leibniz's census proposals to the Prussian state, Nader's fight to preserve the Washington archives, interest-group referenda on social policy, the search for a post–cold-war research rationale, efforts to strengthen the link between research and policy, Dewey's public philosophy, Gandhi's social theory. It seems important, then, to propose something of a political theory of public knowledge at this juncture.

A political consolidation can be organized around three broad questions: What role has knowledge played in democracy? What could it do to extend democratic participation? What could this greater political engagement do to knowledge? My starting assumption is that the democratic role of knowledge extends beyond what people need to know in order to vote, just as the political aspect of their lives is about so much more than this. Whether that knowledge, which touches on so many areas of our lives, can contribute substantially more to what people appreciate, challenge, and refute is what needs to be tested by experimenting with how that knowledge can be structured and presented in the new online publishing medium.

Such experiments will enable us to appreciate the potential contribution that knowledge can make to people's thinking and acting. It can help us to see what knowledge offers to people seeking to advance their interests, protect their rights, and take political action. At issue is whether this body of social-science research can be made into more of a democratic resource that encourages greater participation not only in formally political settings but in all walks of our lives. It may well be that the public value of this knowledge will prove to lie not only in what it contributes to people's understanding but also in what it makes apparent of their rights and responsibilities, their powers and obligations.

Whether in visiting a doctor, lawyer, or our children's school, the ability to tap into an accessible source of the relevant research (or the lack of it, or the contradictory results it has produced) could encourage greater participation in the decisions affecting us. Knowing that one has ready access to the knowledge that underwrites modern systems of governance could encourage a more critical interest in how one is governed. One could turn passing concerns into inquiries on, for example, "What do we know or think we know about mental illness, deinstitutionalization, and the homeless, and what are the different ways in which communities are responding?"

This still leaves the question of what technology's got to do with it. Can new information and communication technologies extend the reach of public knowledge and democratic processes? Is there a will to do so? That, too, has yet to be decided, and it needs to be explored and tested by pushing ahead with the capabilities of the machines to connect people and to support new ways of organizing information and ideas. This is not about software upgrades or memory expansions, of course, but about directing the technology toward public ends, using it to support public exchange and deliberation. The technology has already proved to be a boon in connecting people and information, reaching well beyond traditional means in speed, reach, and interactivity. The Chinese Democratic Party, prior to the arrest of its leaders in 1998, found that the Internet could be used with great speed and reach to organize branches throughout China. The Zapatista movement in Chiapas, Mexico, was able to build an international constituency of support online, and the antisweatshop movement has spread across American university campuses through website activism.[1]

Still, in this case of increasing the contribution of social-science research to public knowledge, I am assuming that the qualities of the knowledge at issue (reliability, accessibility, intelligibility, etc.) and the way they relate to political and the public affairs are far more critical than the quality of the technology. The politics of knowledge, as I will show, provides the very reason for initiating a project among the social sciences that is aimed at contributing more to the realm of public knowledge, yet this self-same politics will also make changing the way that people go about doing social-science research a project of extreme hope

---

1. Barbara Crossette, "The Internet Changes Dictatorship Rules," *New York Times,* August 1, 1999, WK1. See also Douglas Kellner, "New Technologies, the Welfare State, and the Prospects for Democratization," in *Communication, Citizenship, and Social Policy: Rethinking the Limits of the Welfare State,* ed. Andrew Calabrese and Jean-Claude Burgelman (Lanham, Md.: Rowman & Littlefield, 1999), 246–50.

and pigheadedness, if it is ever to be more than an experiment in understanding the ways in which what we call "knowledge" works within our lives.

KNOWLEDGE IN DEMOCRACY

Given that the political hopes of this project depend on improving the role of knowledge in democratic processes, it is fortunate, perhaps, that we know a fair bit about people's current political understanding. I say "perhaps" because, as Harvard political scientist Jeffrey Friedman shows, the "overwhelming ignorance" of the public on political matters is "one of the strongest findings that have been produced by any social science—possibly *the* strongest." The bad news for projects and hopes such as mine is the public's stunning lack of knowledge about politics and political processes. The good news is the amount of room for improvement. Earlier in this book, I raised Walter Lippmann's notion from earlier in the twentieth century of a "phantom public" incapable of directing a democracy and therefore dependent on the wisdom of professional expertise. Yet what Lippmann took as the fixed and overwhelming capacity of the public is, for me, the eternal educator at heart, but a starting point. Still, I do not want to downplay the challenge.[2]

Just how ignorant is the public? It may sound like the opening line of a bad joke, but the research of an earlier generation tends to read this way. In a recent summary of this work, Harvard doctoral student Ilya Somin catalogs the extent of public ignorance, pointing out, for example, how easy it is for Americans to believe simultaneously that the government is too large and that it should increase spending in almost every major area, or for a majority not to have any idea who Newt Gingrich was, only a month after he led the Republicans to a majority victory in Congress in 1994. This ignorance spans domestic politics, foreign affairs, and policy issues, as well as the basic structure of government, such as which branch has which powers. The evidence of this ignorance dates back, with only slight gains, to the beginnings of mass survey research in the late 1930s, leading Somin to conclude that "a relatively stable level of extreme ignorance has persisted even in the face of huge and widespread increases in educational attainment and an unprecedented expansion in the quantity and quality of information that is available to

---

2. Jeffrey Friedman, "Introduction: Public Ignorance and Democratic Theory," *Critical Review* 12, no. 4 (fall 1998): 397; Walter Lippmann, "The Phantom Public," in *The Essential Lippmann: A Political Philosophy for Liberal Democracy* (New York: Random House, 1963).

the public at little cost." This "deliberative incapacity" of the ignorant voter clearly poses a serious threat to a public-knowledge project: Social-science research turned into a new, improved public resource? Why would anyone care?[3]

The other side of this ignorance issue is that it may only make sense to stay dumb. Anthony Downs, economist with the Brookings Institution, influentially argued some four decades ago that within the information economy of a democracy, the payoff of putting any energy into learning about politics is so slight, given the ineffectiveness of any single vote, that it raises the question, "Why bother?" This version of the rational-choice model is undone by the fact that people do bother to learn and vote, if never at very high levels of voter turnout. They also end up making "reasonable choices" in voting, according to the analysis of political scientist Bernard Grofman, consistent with how they would have voted if they had been "perfectly informed." People also have an influence despite their political ignorance it would seem, judging by other studies that point to how closely government policy tends to follow public-opinion polls, which in turn are said to fall under the influence of informed elites. These findings may not add up to a very encouraging picture of democracy or public knowledge, but that is hardly reason to leave things as they are, especially for a social scientist who believes in the public value of research.[4]

The media are bound to take part of the rap for public ignorance. One problem, according to UCLA political scientist Richard D. Anderson, is the press's increasing tendency to treat elections as a "horse race" between canidates rather than a public forum for reviewing the issues and manner in which we are governed. The public continues to be influenced by the media's coverage of the issues, however inadequate,

---

3. Ilya Somin, "Ignorance and the Democratic Ideal," *Critical Review* 12, no. 4 (fall 1998): 419. Somin goes on to argue that our only hope is to limit the very size of government, bringing it down to a more comprehensible scale, and he uses the nineteenth-century example of a smaller government accompanied by a more informed public, evidenced by the Lincoln-Douglas debates. On a related argument, based on empirical studies of modern-day town-hall democracy, defending the effectiveness of reestablishing and reempowering "governments of human scale—the thousands and thousands of little governments that serve the parts of America": see Frank M. Bryan, "Direct Democracy and Civic Competence: The Case of the Town Hall Meeting," in *Citizen Competence and Democratic Institutions,* ed. Stephen L. Elkin and Karol Edward Soltan (University Park: Pennsylvania State University Press, 1999), 222.

4. Anthony Downs, *An Economic Model of Democracy* (New York: Harper & Row, 1957); Bernard Grofman, introduction to *Information, Participation, and Choice: An Economic Theory of Democracy in Perspective,* ed. Bernard Grofman (Ann Arbor: University of Michigan Press, 1993), 7; Robert Erikson, Gerald Wright, and John McIver, *Statehouse Democracy: Public Opinion and Policy in the American States* (Cambridge: Cambridge University Press, 1993).

and other studies show, with the media's tendency to pursue the electoral race rather than the issues, narrowing the field of ideas at play.[5]

A more serious charge against the press's political coverage—that it feeds a "spiral of cynicism"—is found in a study by Joseph Cappella and Kathleen Hall Jamieson, both of the Annenberg School of Communication at the University of Pennsylvania. Cappella and Jamieson found that the press's coverage of political news was "highly focused on tactics, maneuvers, and positioning" rather than substantive issues and that this contributed to readers' cynicism toward both press and government. Cappella and and Jamieson feared that it was enough to "shut down the question, 'How can we do democracy better?'" Yet they do point to encouraging examples of cooperative efforts among the press, public, and politicians in Minnesota directed at improving the quality of public discourse, as well as to promising shifts in the increased use of historical contexts and original sources in the *New York Times*. Their study certainly provides a more precise sense of how the very form and framing of knowledge can work for or against the public good.[6]

A fuller study of the public play of political ideas is found in Erik Åsdard and W. Lance Bennett's *Democracy and the Marketplace of Ideas.* Out of an analysis of political communication in Sweden and the United States, these two political scientists, the former at Uppsala University and the latter at the University of Washington, identify "four broad regulatory mechanisms" that they claim govern the marketplace of ideas: electoral and party systems, campaign-finance practices, interest-group systems, and the mass media. These principal mechanisms appear to be providing increasingly poor service to public interests, leading to the "spiraling discontent of publics and the fragmentation of traditional forms of governing powers." They place the blame on "the lack of guiding visions and the reluctance of parties and leaders to engage in searching national debates." Åsdard and Bennett hold that current social and political institutions, as well as "finance arrangements and media formats" that "link citizens, ideas, [and] governments together are insensitive to new ideas, and in other cases are openly resistant to political invention." They are no less concerned with financial inequities among interest groups, providing some with a much louder and better-informed

5. Richard D. Anderson, "The Place of Media in Popular Democracy," *Critical Review* 12, no. 4 (fall 1998); W. Russell Neuman, Marion R. Just, and Ann N. Crigler, *Common Knowledge: News and the Construction of Political Meaning* (Chicago: University of Chicago Press, 1992), 10.

6. Joseph N. Cappella and Kathleen Hall Jamieson, *Spiral of Cynicism: The Press and the Public Good* (New York: Oxford University Press, 1997), 231, 238, 242, 244–45.

voice on matters of, for example, the environment over child poverty, despite the availability of a wealth of understanding on both.[7]

Not surprisingly, I take Åsdard and Bennett's work, along with that of Cappella and Jamieson, as a call for a fifth estate that goes beyond the press in providing an alternative source of public reflection and analysis that might revitalize the play of ideas in political processes and the life of citizens. I hold no illusions about the social sciences possessing the intellectual resources to end the spiraling public discontent and cynicism, but given that such knowledge appears capable of addressing the shortage of new ideas and guiding visions cited in these studies, as well as fostering national debates and relieving inequities in access to information, it seems only responsible for the social sciences to at least test the value of what it envisions it already has in abundance. If one foresees a general lack of interest in any such public-knowledge ventures, it may only be, as Åsdard and Bennett hold, that the public-relations industry—"the merchants of meaning"—has succeeded in undermining what these scholars perceive, based on their analysis of the New Deal in the United States and a similar history in Sweden, to be an earlier and stronger public interest in new ideas.[8]

Åsdard and Bennett's recommendations for improving the marketplace of ideas are intended to offer greater public access to the broad range of ideas that hold the possibility of guiding voters in evaluating policy proposals. My hope, in contrast, is to explore whether greater public access to the social sciences' detailed and fine-grained analysis of ideas and their consequences could provide a greater sense of why it is worthwhile to work out the larger "thematic agendas" that give shape to our day-by-day lives.

Yet, as I have also mentioned, I think this politics of knowledge goes well beyond people's interests in voting. Voting is but one aspect of public engagement, a potentially powerful moment but nonetheless not the whole of the opportunity for working on political processes when one considers the commissions, hearings, policy reviews, lobbying campaigns, referenda, and other political opportunities, not to mention the politics of the workplace and home, the neighborhood and the family. Politics is about how lives are controlled, opportunities expanded. And the politics of knowledge to which social-science research can contribute is broadly based in that larger sense.

---

7. Erik Åsdard and W. Lance Bennett, *Democracy and the Marketplace of Ideas: Communication and Government in Sweden and the United States* (Cambridge: Cambridge University Press, 1997), 177–78, 47, 7, 41.

8. Ibid., 15, 20.

Shrinking the scale of government to reduce the information demands on people, as Ilya Somin proposes at the conclusion of his analysis of voter ignorance, is not going to reduce the political scope of our lives or the potential value of having knowledge that bears on the political and personal states in which we live. The introduction of this knowledge into the public sphere is intended to shift democracy's knowledge economy, to return to Downs's metaphor. If it is truly rendered in a readily intelligible form, the public can be expected to at least test the value of this knowing in claiming rights, reducing risks, ensuring opportunities, gaining understanding, and generally being reassured that the possibilities have been considered.[9]

There are also encouraging rebuttals of the voter-ignorance thesis, of which two especially bear on this public-knowledge project. The first, by Arthur Lupia and Mathew McCubbins, political scientists at the University of California at San Diego, addresses what they term the "democratic dilemma" of whether citizens can learn what they need to know to justify democracy. Lupia and McCubbins establish that citizens can make perfectly sensible decisions based on a combination of partial information and informed delegation. This is made necessary by the size and scope of modern democracies and can be supported by the development of institutions that "facilitate reasoned choice and successful delegation by helping people choose whom to believe." This seems a fair balance, and I think the social sciences could respond to it by doing more to inform the choices, even if that complicates rather than facilitates those choices. After all, more information from the diverse and divergent research of the social sciences will certainly not simplify the democratic dilemma. Yet additional information can still contribute to a greater sense of people's control, if only over the depth to which they want to go and the degree to which they want to delegate.[10]

A second tempering of the electoral-ignorance thesis comes from the "common-knowledge" research of W. Russell Neuman who teaches communications at Tufts University, and two political scientists, Marion R. Just at Wellesley College and Ann N. Crigler at the University of Southern California. Their work demonstrates the critical role played by people's interest in determining what they learn about complex political issues. A little motivation or interest on the public's part can go a long way, making up for a lack of "cognitive ability ... in the acquisition of knowledge." From the media's perspective, efforts to provide greater

9. Somin, "Voter Ignorance," 446.
10. Arthur Lupia and Mathew D. McCubbins, *The Democratic Dilemma: Can Citizens Learn What They Need to Know?* (Cambridge: Cambridge University Press, 1998), 227.

context and background in reporting the news can also "compensate" for "deficits in cognitive skills or motivation."[11]

Although these suggestions for improving the depth of information complement the structures that I am proposing—which would link related research, theories, and measures with the relevant policies, practices, programs, and organizations—I would not label them "compensatory." Rather, they are better thought of as simply taking advantage of existing resources to improve the quality of public knowledge. The common-knowledge study also identifies acute differences between the media's emphasis on the day's story and the public's interest in the larger issue and opportunities for action. This speaks to the value of establishing forums for sharing and understanding the different interests of the public; the media; and, given my project, the social sciences, which, after all, work to connect the immediate with the general. At issue here are participation and power, with knowledge once again the mediating factor. What is clearly needed for a convergence of democratic interests is a revitalized public sphere, because a vital and informed public sphere initially gave rise to democracy.[12]

The public sphere, as a source of political and public reason, has been much lauded by political philosopher Jürgen Habermas, who continues the social-theory legacy of the Frankfurt school with his theory of communicative action. Habermas worries that in recent times, as the public sphere came "to penetrate more spheres of society [work and family], it simultaneously lost its political function, namely: that of subjecting the affairs that it had made public to the control of a critical public." The critical public that has been lost dates back to the origins of the public sphere in the seventeenth century, when it consisted of the bourgeoisie using what it knew to challenge and debate the authorities through its unending correspondence, emerging political journalism, and coffee-house chatter. Publicity became the bourgeois political weapon of choice against the arbitrary use of power, at least as it affected bourgeois interests. Thus writers such as Joseph Addison directed their work in the *Tatler and Spectator* "toward the spread of tolerance, [and] the emancipation of civic morality from moral theology and of practical wisdom from philosophy of the scholars." The French philosophes later contributed their great *Encyclopédie* to the furthering of this informed public sphere and throughout Europe subscription libraries, book clubs, and reading circles took root. Soon there was talk of a "public" and of "public opinion." By

---

11. Neuman, Just, and Crigler, *Common Knowledge*, 106, 109.
12. Ibid., 110–11.

the close of the eighteenth century, Charles J. Fox advised his fellow members in the British House of Commons that "it is certainly right and prudent to consult the public opinion," to which he added that "one thing is most clear, that I ought to give the public the means of forming an opinion."[13]

If this public was but an expression of an emerging political and economic force of the bourgeoisie, it was nonetheless critical by the turn of the eighteenth century to the development of democratic ideas of governance, both conservative and revolutionary. Edmund Burke insisted that in free countries the "real public wisdom and sagacity in shops and manufactories" was greater than "in the cabinets of princes in countries where none dares to have an opinion," and the delegate Bergasse in the National Assembly of France held "that before public opinion all authorities become silent, all prejudices disappear, all particular interests are effaced." This was democracy's path to legitimacy, its hope that a broadly based sovereignty could guarantee a greater measure of justice. This faith in the public situation of politics and the inherent value of having people engaged in public concerns soon evolved into a "regime of publicity," as Jeremy Bentham called it in the nineteenth century. If the scope of the public has only expanded, it has been in the face of an increasingly constrained public sphere.[14]

Today, rather than strolling down to the civic square to deliberate and be counted, we tune into carefully orchestrated electronic town-hall meetings, take in the Ping-Pong of political sound bites on the evening news, and catch a phone-in talk show's caricature of public deliberation. The "general will" is in the hands of the next caller, the next voter, lined up like so many customers waiting to go through the checkout till of democracy.

The public sphere has been replaced by the "New Public," as sociologist Leon Mayhew names it. It is the product of media and public-relations professionals who since the 1950s have assumed control of older forms of public participation. Mayhew has little trouble portraying how the New Public (really a public-less-ness) is increasingly manipulated by spin doctors and idea marketeers. It represents an evolving democracy of market share. The public has little ability to interrupt the process, to stop and ask for the facts, to call for a full discussion in a

---

13. Charles J. Fox, cited in Jürgen Habermas, *The Structural Transformation of the Public Sphere: An Inquiry into a Category of Bourgeois Society*, trans. Thomas Burger (Cambridge: MIT Press, 1989), 140, 43, 66.
14. Edmund Burke, Bergasse, and Jeremy Bentham, cited in ibid., 94, 99.

public forum: "The rise of the New Public has made information-rich, issue-joining debate progressively difficult."[15]

One could argue, although I think it an unfortunate argument, that the social sciences bear no responsibility for this deterioration of public life, nor need they do anything in response except to write the sort of critical and timely analysis that Mayhew manages. I obviously think they have opportunity and motive to do more than that. As it is, the media wizards who direct the New Public are themselves social scientists of a sort, equipped with market research and economic models. They have made it their business to study and shape the public, and the proof of their knowledge is evident in the price they can charge for it. They have even created an alternative model community for those suffering the loss of that old public space, or so I would interpret Disney's gated-community, front-porch approach to consumer democracy in its new town of Celebration, Florida.[16]

Certainly, efforts are always afoot to revitalize public life, with many organizations using new media to support public-spirited sources of knowledge. For example, the Center for Democracy and Technology, with a focus on "free expression and privacy in global communications technologies," lobbies for the release of further sources of government information, the Congressional Research Service reports topping its list. Another strong organization is Public Agenda, which conducts opinion-research and citizen-education programs across a range of social topics that it then makes available online, in hopes of informing leaders as well as citizens. The goal is to keep alive the unfinished project of democracy, in Abraham Lincoln's phrase, which calls for the continuing articulation of and deliberation over what this political project is about.[17]

DELIBERATIVE DEMOCRACY

This case for improving the social sciences' contribution to public knowledge fits very neatly within the current body of thought promoting the political ideal of "deliberative democracy." This idea, which draws inspiration from the political theory of John Dewey and Hannah Arendt, and more recently Jüngen Habermas and John Rawls, dates back to democ-

---

15. Leon H. Mayhew, *The New Public: Professional Communication and the Means of Social Influence* (Cambridge: Cambridge University Press, 1997), 12.

16. See Douglas Frantz and Catherine Collins, *Celebration, U.S.A.: Living in Disney's Brave New Town* (New York: Holt, 1999).

17. Center for Democracy and Technology, http://ctd.org; Public Agenda, http://www. publicagenda.org. See also Stateline.org, Politics1.com, Policy.com, and the Milken Exchange.

racy's earliest days. It posits that what democracy requires, now more than ever, are ways for citizens to participate in the decisions and policies by which they are governed. This process of deliberation will strengthen the quality of politics, the legitimacy of the state, and the education of the citizenry. This model of a deliberative democracy is often contrasted with market and consumer models of democracy, in which one's political shopping around is a private affair, an expression of individual interests, decided ultimately by market share. By contrast, deliberation refers to a coming together to think through, learn from, and become part of the political process. Deliberative democracy invokes ideals of "rational legislation, participatory politics and civic self-governance," to borrow from the introduction to the topic by James Bohman and William Rehg, in one of a spate of recent books on deliberative democracy.[18]

If the argument has a certain familiar ring, it may be because it parallels my discussion of John Dewey and the ethos of the social sciences in chapter 5. Dewey's call for developing deliberative structures, as it names what is required so forcefully, bears repeating: "The highest and most difficult kind of inquiry and a subtle, delicate, vivid, and responsive art of communication must take possession of the physical machinery of transmission and circulation and breathe life into it." Dewey sets the tone and criteria for the public's engagement in this democratic process. More than a century earlier, Immanuel Kant was promoting "the public use of reason" as critical to the success of the Enlightenment. Kant spoke of the obligations of the citizen-scholar and the scholar-citizen, as they have "the complete freedom, even the calling, to communicate to the public." The public use of reason was, for Kant, a human-rights issue tied to our autonomy and to what he saw as human progress. "Citizens learn and profit from conflict and argument," writes the modern-day champion of public reason, Harvard philosopher John Rawls, "and when their arguments follow public reason, they instruct and deepen society's public culture.[19]

This theme of the educational benefit of greater deliberation was first observed by Alexis de Tocqueville as a lesson that nineteenth-century

---

18. James Bohman and William Rehg, introduction to *Deliberative Democracy: Essays on Reason and Politics,* ed. James Bohman and William Rehg (Cambridge: MIT Press, 1996), ix–x. On the comparison of market versus forum, see Jon Elster's essay in that collection, "The Market and the Forum: Three Varieties of Political Theory," 3–34. Also see Carlos Santiago Nino, *The Constitution of Deliberative Democracy* (New Haven: Yale University Press, 1996); and Jon Elster, ed., *Deliberative Democracy* (Cambridge: Cambridge University Press, 1998).

19. John Dewey, *The Public and Its Problems* (New York: Holt, 1926), 184; Immanuel Kant, *Was ist Aufklärung?* trans. Lewis White Beck, in Michel Foucault, *The Politics of Truth* (New York: Semiotext[e], 1997), 12, 15; John Rawls, "The Idea of Public Reason," in *Political Liberalism* (New York: Columbia University Press, 1996), 213, xxvi, lvii.

America had to offer the world. In America's "extreme equality" and "confused clamor," Tocqueville noted, "it is incontestable that the people often manage public affairs very badly, but their concern therewith is bound to extend their mental horizon and shake them out of the rut of ordinary routine." The effect of these deliberations, which Tocqueville also noted in the jury system ("the most effective means of popular education at society's disposal"), stands a strong chance of increasing concerns over the common good even as the public place of politics grows. In this way, the quality of politics and knowledge, of community and its concerns, can be extended by this political process. This public engagement was a source of hope against what Tocqueville found to be the "strange power" of public opinion: "It uses no persuasion to forward its beliefs, but by some mighty pressure of the mind of all upon the intelligence of each it imposes its ideas and makes them penetrate men's very souls." A lack of deliberation continues to reduce the political value and legitimacy of public opinion.[20]

In thinking about how to foster greater deliberation, Habermas has turned his attention in more recent work from the regulated structures of governance to the "informal processes of opinion-formation in the public sphere" linked to "the thick networks of interaction found in families and circles of friends as well as to looser contacts of neighborhoods, work colleagues, acquaintances, and so on." Habermas sees this unregulated public sphere—which he identifies as "a network for communicating information and points of view"—as a critical site of both dangerously "repressive and exclusionary effects" and, more promisingly, "new ways of looking at problems." He offers the examples of feminism and the labor movement as deliberative breakthroughs that took place in the "'wild' complex that resists organization as a whole," even as some feminist scholars criticize his utopian hope that traditional power dynamics can be overcome. Rather than somehow transcend power relations, the social sciences can improve the public distribution of one of their critical contributions—knowledge. The public-knowledge project is, after all, about experimenting with ways of improving the distribution and exchange around social-science research

---

20. Alexis de Tocqueville, *Democracy in America*, trans. George Lawrence (Garden City, N.Y.: Anchor, 1969), 243–44, 275, 399–400. See also Jürgen Habermas on the theme of deliberative democracy invoking "a rationalization of the lifeworld reaching far beyond the political," in "Popular Sovereignty as Procedure," in *Between Facts and Norms: Contributions to a Discourse Theory of Law and Democracy*, trans. William Rehg (Cambridge: MIT Press, 1996), 489. John Stuart Mill drew on Tocqueville in his defense of representative government in 1861, advocating that "the whole public are made, to a certain extent, participants in the government, and sharers in the instruction and mental exercise derivable from it": *Utilitarianism, Liberty, and Representative Government* (London: Dent, 1910), 243.

that enables it to grow, in the process, more attuned to how knowledge can support deliberative forms of democracy.[21]

Habermas certainly recognizes that "unavoidable asymmetries in the availability of information" currently persist, just as he is concerned that "reasonable or fair results are obtained insofar as the flow of relevant information and its proper handling have not been obstructed." He is also aware of the potential "*cognitive overburdening* of deliberative politics," which limits citizens' ability "to take in and digest the *operatively necessary* knowledge," as Habermas emphatically puts it. Of course, this is where I want to jump in and insist that social scientists are in a position to do far more about such asymmetries and overloading than to elaborate, in the demanding style of Habermas, ever more complete and comprehensive deliberative processes.[22]

The social sciences, after all, possess the very thing that may be needed to tip the balance in deliberation's favor—knowledge that bears on the decisions that need to be made—and the power, presumably, to render that knowledge manageable, intelligible, and less than cognitively overwhelming. This is to say that social scientists could, in this way, better serve Habermas's notion of the political role of the public sphere: "From the perspective of democratic theory, the public sphere must, in addition, amplify the pressure of problems, that is, not only detect and identify problems, but also convincingly and *influentially* thematize them, furnish them with possible solutions, and dramatize them in such a way that they are taken up and dealt with by parliamentary complexes."[23]

This names precisely the contribution intended for my public-knowledge project. Yet to say that "the public sphere must ..." still leaves open the questions of exactly who is going to introduce these procedures into public life, where are these changes going to be initiated, and who is going to remove the obstructions and create the opportunities. For my part, I am asking social scientists to set their own example by rebuilding at least a portion of the public sphere by experimenting with new ways of getting their own house of knowledge in better order, that it might less obstructively provide opportunities for people to turn to what researchers believe to be important sources of understanding.

21. Habermas, *Between Facts and Norms,* 307, 308, 365–66, 374; Mary P. Ryan, "Gender and Public Access," in *Habermas and the Public Sphere,* ed. Craig Calhoun (Cambridge: MIT Press, 1992).

22. Habermas, *Between Facts and Norms,* 325, 320. Robert Dahl insists that "insofar as a citizen's good or interest requires attention to a public good or a general interest, then citizens ought to have the opportunity to acquire an understanding of these matters": *Democracy and Its Critics* (New Haven: Yale University Press, 1989), 112.

23. Habermas, *Between Facts and Norms,* 325, 359, original emphasis.

Social scientists could take a lesson from the community-based research movement that currently operates out of roughly fifty centers in the United States, from the Good Neighbor Project in Cambridge, Massachusetts, to the Applied Research Center in Oakland, California. These research projects, staffed by community members and funded by government and foundations, are aimed at action and have produced results that inform new health programs for refugee women in Chicago and a moratorium on logging, pending negotiations between Alaskan legislators and activists. Community-based research finds its champion in Richard Sclove and his associates in the Loka Institute, itself a nonprofit research and advocacy organization devoted to "making science and technology responsive to democratically decided social and environmental concerns." This form of civic knowledge-work represents a political response to the failure of academic research to connect, as Sclove, Madeleine L. Scammell, and Breena Holland make apparent in their report on the need for more such work: "Our analysis of community-based research reveals a striking mismatch between the United States' generously endowed, mainstream R&D agenda and the urgent needs of countless communities across the country. By expanding the social infrastructure for conducting community-based research, thereby making empowerment-through-mutual-learning universally accessible, we can better direct our nation's prodigious capabilities toward our most urgent social and environmental needs. We can help alleviate suffering, revitalize democracy and community."[24]

These sentiments would find much sympathy among social scientists, many of whom already work hard to ensure that their research is responsive to the communities in which it is conducted. It would seem to me that bringing different forms of social-science research into greater proximity and allowing these forms to complement, augment, and challenge each other within the public space proposed by this public-knowledge project would increase the public value of this knowledge. The critical need here is to explore how these forms of knowledge can work together in this deliberative and thus democratic fashion.

Another, perhaps more obvious source of deliberative structures is the government itself. Robert B. Reich proposed, before he was called on to serve as the secretary of labor in the Clinton administration, that those who deal in public policy—elected officials, administrators, policy

---

24. Richard E. Sclove, Madeleine L. Scammell, and Breena Holland, *Community Based Research in the United States: An Introductory Reconnaissance, Including Twelve Organizational Case Studies and Comparison with the Dutch Science Shops and the Mainstream American Research System* (Amherst, Mass.: Loka Institute, 1998), viii.

analysts—should lead a deliberative movement by engaging "the public in rethinking how certain problems are defined, alternative solutions envisioned, and responsibilities for action allocated." This, Reich held, could only "strengthen the public's capacities to deal with similar problems in the future" while providing a check on the temptations of bureaucratic efficiency and pure utilitarian calculations. What policy analysts should do, according to Reich, is point out inconsistencies in assumptions and metaphors, as well as apparent patterns, while offering novel interpretations. Such thought-provoking analysts may raise the public's level of "social learning," if not its ire and interest in greater bureaucratic efficiencies. This process should engender a form of "civic discovery," as he puts it, which augments policymaking and review. He offers the example of William Ruckelshaus, who, as an Environmental Protection Agency official, held deliberative meetings in Tacoma, Washington, over local toxic emissions, which produced "social learning about the health risks of pollution and the enormous cost of eliminating them altogether, not only in Tacoma but also in other communities that saw what occurred there." And although Reich allows that such opportunities for social learning rarely lead to consensus and "may exacerbate divisions within the community," such are the risks of ideas coming to the fore and such is a place where the contribution of a coherent base of research would be welcome.[25]

Of course, it was Reich's rare privilege to have the chance to apply his ideas about government structures in more than a token way. As secretary of labor, Reich contributed to the national agenda on the new work world, but the degree to which he could foster a deliberative atmosphere among the public appears to have been relatively limited: "For four years, my days were broken into 15- or 20-minute segments," he wrote after returning to his academic career at Brandeis University. "My time wasn't my own. My self wasn't my own. I had to be extremely careful about what I said and to whom I said it. I was in a bubble." His experience points back to how the academic life offers greater opportunities for fostering forms of civic discovery and social learning. Yet Reich's advocacy of deliberative bureaucrats suggests that it might be worth exploring a dynamic integration of public-knowledge interests among government officials and social scientists, along with community-based research activists.[26]

Whether the political uses of this knowledge can be expanded defines one of this project's research questions. Would a public-knowledge

25. Robert B. Reich, "Policy Making in a Democracy," in *The Power of Public Ideas*, ed. Robert B. Reich (Cambridge: Harvard University Press, 1988), 5, 149, 154.
26. Robert B. Reich, "My So-Called Life," *Fast Company*, June 1998, 142.

website invite further participation by public and social sciences in formal and informal political processes? Would it lead to forms of civic discovery as a point of civic participation? Would it have an impact on democracy's deliberative strand and the public play of reason? Would this public interest affect the research?

Research on such questions has already begun with the work of James Fishkin, a political scientist at the University of Texas. Fishkin has drawn on George Gallup's initial inspiration of using polls to "restore" town-hall democracy, in creating his own experiments with "deliberative polls" in England and America. Fishkin's deliberative polls bring people together for a weekend to discuss specific social issues among themselves and with experts of differing viewpoints, before being polled on what this deliberation has left them thinking, with a televised summary of the process later broadcast to reach a wider public. He makes the case that this process transforms the participants into more thoughtful and engaged citizens, both during the process and, some initial signs indicate, afterward. The participants are first given briefing materials and then meet together to generate what they want to know about the issue, before consulting with the "competing experts," as Fishkin calls them, that have been assembled. The people, rather than the organizers or experts, set the agenda. Although the three hundred participants in the British deliberative poll on crime proved just as tough on criminals following the discussion as they were going into the process, Fishkin found that they were prepared to support a far more subtle and sophisticated approach to criminal law. Fishkin offers a model of limited participation, even with the television support, especially given what newer technologies have to offer in connecting people and ideas.[27]

The need to continue the democratic experiment, while striving to achieve its highest political ideals in the face of social changes and new technologies, is obviously part of what my public-knowledge project is all about. In another variation on this theme, we on the Public Knowledge Project team at the University of British Columbia are working on extending this deliberative political theme to the web. As this book goes to press, we have worked with the British Columbia Teachers Federation and the British Columbia Ministry of Education to design a public-knowledge website to enable greater participation by British Columbia teachers and the public in the educational policy initiatives of the Ministry of Education. The website has at its center the Ministry's proposed policy, which

---

27. James S. Fishkin, *The Voice of the People: Public Opinion and Democracy* (New Haven: Yale University Press, 1995).

in this case deals with the use of technology in education. The site provides access to a major background paper that has informed the policy process, as well as to related research, practices, policies, and organizations that are further organized by the major topics covered by the background paper and policy. The site allows teachers, ministry personnel, and the public to initiate discussions on various points in the policy, whether to comment, challenge, question, or propose. Contributors to the discussions are able to support their positions by posting educational examples from their own or others' programs. They are able to link their comments to related policies and research. At this point, midway into the policy review period, we still only have a small proportion of visitors to the site participating in the open forums, where they raise issues of teaching conditions, budgets, curriculum, and professional development. We have had high school students join in with their technology experiences (with a nudge from their teachers), and teachers who asked that their messages not be publicly posted, as they are not, or at least not yet, comfortable going public with their views. What remains to be seen, this far into the process, is how this experience will move from public deliberation to political action, which is always a challenge for deliberative democracy. It could take the form, in this case, of the development of further iterations of the policy, the setting of collaborative research agendas, or the striking of committees to examine specific issues. At the same time, the project team will evaluate how well the different structures and organizing principles for the site work with different forms of knowledge and different communities of interest.[28]

Technical and design challenges continue to confront us over how to organize both the mix of genres and the ongoing dynamics of public discussion with easy reference to comments previously made, indexes of cited research and programs, and summaries of the discussion thus far. To turn the ongoing and varied contributions into a more coherent and comprehensive picture may require, for example, additional layers of commentary and knowledge maps. Guides or standards might be needed to help people judge the quality of research. The research and evaluation of this and future public-knowledge sites will be intensely focused on how effectively different designs extend the scope of deliberation and the potential for participation. This experimenting with how best to put together public-knowledge sites cannot help but teach us more about the civil, political, and professional role of knowledge and learning.

---

28. Glynis Andersson, Vivian Forssman, Henry Kang, Shula Klinger, John Willinsky, and Paul Wottenholme, *Public Knowledge Policy Forum* (1999), http://pkp.bctf.bc.ca.

Such an engaging political process should contribute to who we are and how we understand the risks and possibilities afforded by this life, even as it is likely to change both, as increased knowledge enables one to realize how the personal is political and how personal that political is. Whether such deliberations and realizations will lead people to be more civic-minded or otherwise improved has yet to be established in the research literature, as is noted with some regret by Jane Mansbridge, a political scientist at Northwestern University, although she feels certain that such activity changed her own civic disposition for the better. This still leaves the question of what all of this proposed political activity will do to knowledge, which may be the line of real risk for social scientists keen to improve public knowledge and democratic deliberation.[29]

POLITICAL DEMANDS ON KNOWLEDGE

In October 1998, the United States Senate passed a four-thousand-page appropriations bill that contained a two-sentence amendment designed to enable the public to "get all data produced" by federally funded research studies. Although the final wording of this amendment, an extension of the Freedom of Information Act, is still being worked out, as I write, it appears that researchers will be obliged to open their laboratory notebooks, computer disks, tapes, survey forms, and other data records to public scrutiny. The amendment was introduced by Senator Richard C. Shelby, a Republican from Alabama, and when it finally came to light and drew the ire of research scientists, he held forth that "experience has shown that transparency in government is a principle that has improved decision-making and increased the public's trust in government." It seemed to him simply unfair that for too long the American people had been "unable to access federally funded research data despite the significant impact of this data in the policymaking process." It represented "a first step in ensuring that the public has access to all studies used by the Federal Government to develop Federal policy."[30]

29. Jane Mansbridge, "On the Idea That Participation Makes Better Citizens," in Elkin and Soltan, *Citizen Competence*, 291.

30. Philip J. Hilts, "Law on Access to Research Data Pleases Business, Alarms Science," *New York Times,* July 31, 1999, A1, A9; "Uniform Administrative Requirements for Grants and Agreements with Institutions of Higher Education, Hospitals, and Other Non-profit Organizations," *Federal Register* 64, no. 23 (1999): 5684–85. Senator Shelby did not mention that he had unsuccessfully introduced such an amendment earlier, after a congressional fight over accessing the data from a Harvard study that influenced 1997 federal regulations on emissions from cars and power plants. The amendment was publicly opposed by Alabama Power.

The United States Chamber of Commerce was quick to celebrate the proposed law, casting it as a tool for fighting "the bureaucracy [that is] imposing $700 billion in annual regulatory costs on us," as the Chamber's website explains. Not so happy with the proposal is Nils Hasselmo, president of the Association of American Universities, who has interpreted it as supporting "a broad political attack on both science and on the Federal regulatory apparatus." His concern is that "such an effort could involve actions designed to discredit scientists and discourage researchers from addressing controversial topics." Why this opposition? Because, as George D. Thurston, in environmental medicine at the New York University School of Medicine, puts it, "past history would indicate that [such a law] could be used to undermine the research results that they [business interests] don't like." In addition, "it would take a substantial amount of time from my research," adds Elliot R. McVeigh, a biomedical engineer at Johns Hopkins School of Medicine, thinking of how he might have to "keep separate notebooks for all activities." And to think that all that Senator Shelby is concerned with is that "the American people have not been given an opportunity, up to this point, to review such data for themselves."[31]

The Shelby motion will be settled anon, but its focus on the politics of raw data neatly captures the major challenge my project faces, which is strengthening access to knowledge amid existing struggles over intellectual property, traditions, and economies. What this research defensiveness can look like in the social sciences is illustrated by no less a notorious figure than the former advertising icon Joe Camel. It began with the research of Paul Fisher, at the Medical College of Georgia, which established how effective tobacco advertising was with children. Fischer's 1991 study, published in the *Journal of the American Medical Association*, made it clear that children as young as six years old knew Joe Camel as well as they knew Mickey Mouse, and they knew that this very cool dromedary was all about cigarettes and smoking. Expressing its incredulity over these findings, the R. J. Reynolds Corporation asked to see the original data, including the names and addresses of the children who participated in the study, apparently for purposes of reinterviewing them. Fischer rightly said no, and the case went to court, with his college's president finally agreeing that the information should be turned over to the Reynolds Corporation. Although the children were not contacted,

---

31. United States Chamber of Commerce cited in Hilts, "Law on Access," A9; Nils Hasselmo, George D. Thurston, and Elliot R. McVeigh are cited in Paulette Walker Campbell, "Budget Law Forces Scientists to Release Data Gathered While Using Federal Grants," *Chronicle of Higher Education,* February 5, 1999, A34.

Fischer resigned from the college, declaring he would not do research on tobacco again.[32]

One might think that tobacco-company executives would want to steer clear of an image of themselves tracking down and cross-examining children ("Now kid, tell me again, just what did you say to that researcher fellow about Joe Camel?"). One might also think that tobacco-industry executives, whose record on research suppression makes its own devastating case for the public obligations of researchers, would want to steer clear of the research issue altogether. But this industry's ongoing, death-defying macho has helped reinforce the ethical limits of Shelby's proposed extension of the Freedom of Information Act. The proposal would protect trade secrets and financial data, as well as private information such as "personnel and medical files and similar files the disclosure of which would constitute a clearly unwarranted invasion of personal privacy." Making the data public does not necessitate making the identity of the research subject public. Precautions can be taken even as challenges are posed, for example, by the use of video to gather data.[33]

The ability to review, share, and variously analyze data—whether from censuses, surveys, interviews, or ethnographic records—can clearly contribute, as I have argued elsewhere, to the value and coherence of social-science research. For the public, the opportunity to dip into the data, to appreciate the basis of a study's probable knowledge, and to witness disputes over its interpretation can only lead to a better understanding of the value of research. Maintaining that the public is not

---

32. The lesson in public knowledge here, and part of the ludicrousness of Reynolds's fight, is that brand awareness is not brand usage. Richard Kluger reports that Camel's share of the declining cigarette market, after investing $75 million a year to put Joe in the minds of children and adults alike, was a 1 percent gain, which had disappeared by the time the government drove Joe off the streets: *Ashes to Ashes: America's Hundred-Year Cigarette War, the Public Health, and the Unabashed Triumph of Philip Morris* (New York: Vintage, 1996), 703. Paul Fischer, "Brand Recognition by Children Aged 3 to 6," *Journal of the American Medical Association* (December 11, 1991).

33. In 1995, the Brown and Williamson Tobacco Corporation told the editors of the *Journal of the American Medical Association* that it was not giving up the "privilege or confidentiality associated with these documents [including research results] and we are taking every step to preserve those rights": cited in Stanton A. Glantz, John Slade, Lisa A. Bero, Peter Hanauer, and Deborah E. Barnes, *The Cigarette Papers* (Berkeley and Los Angeles: University of California Press, 1996), 443. Research privacy could be addressed by, for example, the United States Office for Protection from Research Risks, operated by the National Institutes of Health, which has brought entire federally funded programs of research on human subjects to a halt on university campuses: Jeffrey Brainard, "Watchdog Agency Halts 1,000 Human-Research Projects at U. of Illinois at Chicago," *Chronicle of Higher Education*, July 23, 1999, A41. Shelby motion found in "Uniform Administrative Requirements for Grants and Agreements with Institutions of Higher Education, Hospitals, and Other Non-profit Organizations," *Federal Register* 64, no. 154 (1999): 43786–91.

qualified to handle such information and that industry will abuse access to it does not seem a healthy stance to take on the place of knowledge within the deliberative aspects of democracy.[34]

Among the eight thousand comments that the government received on the Shelby motion during the sixty-day "public comment period," only 8 percent were opposed to its substance (with 36 percent of all comments coming from identifiable university researchers). At the same time, the government reaffirmed its commitment to "(1) further the interest of the public in obtaining the information needed to validate Federally-funded research findings, (2) ensure that research can continue to be conducted in accordance with the traditional scientific process, and (3) implement a public-access process that will be workable in practice."

After the review, the government narrowed the focus of the proposal from research "used by the Federal Government in developing policy or rules" to research "used by the Federal Government in developing a regulation," with a further provision that the regulation have "a $100 million dollar impact threshold." Although I recognize that this change is the result of business going after the regulatory agencies, I think it unfortunate to reinforce an image of the scientist as one who should be kept at a remove from the world, absentmindedly working among ill-sorted stacks of data, with a Do Not Disturb sign on the door. It would seem that the public's interests lie in how research operates, much as a legal trial is considered necessarily public. As justice must not only be done but must be perceived to be done, so we might demand in regard to other trials of a wider truth. I wonder whether there is not some way for researchers to call on the senator to support the idea that research isn't research if it isn't as public as it can possibly be. Why not knock on the doors of the Chamber of Commerce and the Republicans to ask for greater support in taking this research public and creating new standards and formats for representing and sharing more of this inquiry, including the data? Why wait for the subpoena or demands made under the Freedom of Information Act? Let us build new infrastructures for this knowledge work that open the entire range of elements—research initiation, design, data, results, applications, and consequences—for it will be researchers, above all, who will take advantage of it.[35]

---

34. John Willinsky, *Technologies of Knowing: A Proposal for the Human Sciences* (Boston: Beacon, 1999), 103–7. Especially worth noting in the social sciences is Richard Rockwell's work with the Inter-University Consortium for Political and Social Research at the University of Michigan.

35. "Uniform Administrative Requirements for Grants," 43786–91.

One of those who expressed qualified approval of the government measure was Wendy H. Baldwin, director of extramural research at the National Institutes of Health (NIH). Baldwin called herself "a strong supporter of clear policies in regard to data-sharing." She acknowledged that data sharing can be a burden but concluded, "That's fine. We all have burdens to bear." As it turns out, the NIH is at the center of its own politics-of-knowledge controversy regarding its electronic archives, known as E-biomed and PubMed Central. The NIH is about to set up "a Web-based repository for barrier-free access to primary reports in the life sciences" that will "archive, organize and distribute peer-reviewed reports from journals, as well as reports that have been screened but not formally peer-reviewed." The NIH has assumed responsibility for "the technology for enhanced retrieval, presentation, and navigation" and for improving "access and utility." Here will be a place for a much broader expanse of information, including reports on experiments that found no effect. Yet some question whether "a monopolistic archive under government control by the major research funder enhance[s] science progress better than the existing multiple alternatives of journals?" as Floyd E. Bloom, editor in chief of *Science*, puts it. The editor of the *New England Journal of Medicine* is no less suspicious of this open and free access.[36]

Although there are clearly commercial interests at stake in these editors' responses, the fears of centralization, as an abuse of economic and political power, are going to remain a serious impediment to any efforts to increase the coherence and coordination of the research enterprise. The independence of researchers combined with the competitive hierarchy of journals within the marketplace of ideas add up to a substantial cultural investment in current structures. There may be some eight thousand refereed journals now online, but the basic structure of the journal and the research article has changed little. The exception and model for the NIH initiative is the now famous arXiv.org website at Los Alamos National Laboratory, run by Paul Ginsparg. It began as a preprint service, and now posts some twenty-four hundred papers per month in physics, mathematics, nonlinear sciences, and computer science, and logs 100,000 connections per weekday, attesting to the vital usefulness of this no-muss, no-fuss approach to research dissemination.[37]

36. Wendy H. Baldwin, cited in Campbell, "Budget Law Forces Scientists," A34; National Institutes of Health, "PubMed Central: An NIH-Operated Site for Electronic Distribution of Life Sciences Research Reports" (August 1999), http://www.nih.gov/welcome/director/ebiomed/ebiomed.htm; Floyd E. Bloom, cited in Vincent Kieran, "Editor of 'Science' Voices Doubts on NIH's Proposed On-Line Archive," *Chronicle of Higher Education*, July 23, 1999, A41.

However, I am asking for something more than easing the journal-subscription price crisis with economical online publication. What sets my project off from arXiv.org and the NIH's E-biomed proposal is the idea that the online coordination of resources and restructuring of knowledge is justified only insofar as it improves the public value of this knowledge, and that improvement is what needs to be closely evaluated and experimented with. That can happen only if we overcome the initial resistance to the interest of a "meddling public" in what the research community learns.

The NIH's E-biomed and the Shelby amendment are but two steps in what is becoming a footrace between private and public interests in the political economy of this Information Age. Other senators have put forward a Collection of Information Antipiracy bill that would protect those who assemble data for commercial purposes, and a Consumer and Investors Access to Information act that would open such sources to researchers and brokerages. The public as consumers and investors in social-science research will need its defenders at a time when information is becoming *the* commodity of choice? I see an opportunity for the research community to demonstrate both greater leadership and more scholarly inquiry focused on realizing the public value of research.

This still leaves at least one major question about the politics of knowledge. What, amid all of this public and political activity, are the possibilities of a value-free science? It should be a nonissue, according to Robert Proctor, historian of science at Pennsylvania State University. In his history of "purity and power in modern knowledge," Proctor argues that science's claim to neutrality has always been directed, dating back to Bacon, at protecting its own project from what were seen as the undue and often threatening incursions of outside authorities. In securing its self-interested state of neutrality, science has, according to Proctor, deployed a number of tactics that fall within four themes: Science has kept itself at a distance from the demands of *utility* and avoided taking a stance on matters of *value*, all the while holding itself to the rigors of a *method* that, along with institutional protection of the laboratory and classroom, offered it a measure of *security* in pursuing knowledge apart from the political and economic interests of this world. Rather than expose science's self-interested claim to neutrality, as Proctor does, I

---

37. See arXiv.org, http://xxx.lanl.gov. On the International Consortium of Alternative Academic Publication, "a scholar-led initiative designed to build a low-cost but professional quality scholarly journals infrastructure," see Mike Sosterig, "The International Consortium of Alternative Academic Publication: An Idea Whose Time Has Come," *Feliciter*, no. 1 (1999); and http://www. iccap.org.

propose that social scientists continue to honor these four themes, as a means of fulfilling their public responsibilities rather than protecting their interests.[38]

I would not ask the social sciences to succumb to *utility,* although the public-knowledge project obviously has a place for utility. Yet this project also seeks something more from knowledge, as utility lacks a concern for understanding, for adding to the sense of the world, in all or its earnestness to be a source of action. Utility also has little patience with diverse ways of knowing, which I see as central to what the social sciences currently have to offer. This diversity also protects the social sciences against the undue influence of *value.* The social sciences reflect the same play of values as the larger world, which will become increasingly public with a greater sharing of this knowledge. Not all human values will be represented, or represented equally in this knowledge. But that will, in itself, be open to engagement and challenge in discussing how well the social sciences are fulfilling their public responsibilities. Human values are the source and subject of the social sciences' research project. This research can be judged by how it adds to the richness and clarity of our thinking about these values and their consequences.

The scientific fortress of *method,* as protection against the fallibility of human habits and judgments, would remain central to the public-knowledge project. Method would continue to loom large, not only in the integrity and ingenuity of individual studies but in efforts to improve the coherence and comprehensibility of the larger body of knowledge. And finally, the *security* of the sciences will not be jeopardized by this public-knowledge project. The project will be unable to "meddle in matters of Moralls, Politics, or Rhetorick," as Bacon declared the basis of scientific neutrality, because of, I would argue, its increasingly open and public contribution to these human endeavors, with far less of the meddling, behind-the-scenes, exploitation of expertise.[39]

---

38. Robert N. Proctor, *Value-Free Science: Purity and Power in Modern Knowledge* (Cambridge: Harvard University Press, 1991), 262.

39. Bacon cited in ibid., 263, 264. It is worth noting that Galileo was among those who used this neutrality to protect himself from undue interference in the form of, in his case, the Inquisition. Max Weber's famous call for neutrality in the social sciences was intended to censure professors who were casting political struggles as technical or academic problems with the support of a less-than-liberal state in early twentieth-century Germany. Had Weber been as free to express his own liberal sentiments in the universities, Proctor suggests, then value-free science may not have been such a strong theme with him (265–66). See also Max Weber, "The Meaning of 'Ethical Neutrality' in Sociology and Economics," in *The Methodology of the Social Sciences,* trans. Edward S. Shils and Henry A. Finch (New York: Free Press, 1949).

Science is always already political in the modern world. It is a state apparatus, Proctor notes, taught in school systems, funded by the military establishment, shaped in its social practices, and given to studying vital human matters. There is no point in worrying about preserving science's neutrality. It has secured its place in society and now must do more to meet its social obligations. Nor does dropping the shield of neutrality mean giving up on objectivity, Proctor helpfully points out. After all, "neutrality refers to whether a science can take a stand; objectivity, to whether a science merits certain claims to reliability." He goes on to remind us that "certain sciences may be completely 'objective'—that is, valid—and yet designed to serve political interests." This leads Proctor to suggest that the important questions about knowledge are, why do we know this and not that; who gains from knowledge of this and not that; and what is to be done—or undone?[40]

For me, the main point is to make this no-longer-neutral science far more an open part of the political process so that then such questions contribute more to the public's engagement with what is known. I take this as a call for experimenting with new kinds of public spaces that will add to the quality of public knowledge and its pursuit, setting it within the scope of people's experience rather than the parameters of a philosopher's epistemology. As the social sciences have rarely played the neutrality card, they should be that much better prepared for a political engagement of utility, method, value, and security.

Former Speaker of the House Tip O'Neill famously held that all politics is local. Then came the feminist version, that the personal is political. What we have with the politics of knowledge is the local, personal work of researchers struggling to fund and conduct their studies and then have them published. Changing this politics may pose a fundamental, near-intractable cultural issue, held by habits of mind and a honed language, and wrapped in the highest principles of an academic mission of epistemological consequence. None of this will be turned by a simple trick with a computer, nor will it be changed by compromised amendments to the Freedom of Information Act that pit the rights of industry against those of research in the context of regulation. Yet the technology can at least demonstrate how that change can happen and happen in ways that improve the value of the research for researchers as well as for the public.

Social-science research will begin to operate as if it were part of the main, rather than an island of discrete intellectual integrity, only when

---

40. Proctor, ibid., 267, 270, 10.

researchers put to the test the typical research rhetoric about contributing to the public good, by watching a lot more closely how their research works in public. Given the chance for ongoing public engagement with their work, some researchers will reorient their research projects and language. The recognition of the larger world adds to the meaning of their daily struggle over the interpretation of data and the validation of conclusions and claims. Others, perhaps, will rethink how their not-so-neutral research could better speak to public projects and political acts and how their research could be taken up within the larger political spectrum. This knowledgeable exchange could draw the public into a similar kind of experiment with the potential value and contribution offered by this knowledge.

If the public-knowledge project needs an inspiring phrase in this age of trademarked slogans, it might be "More than research for researchers" or "Making good on knowledge's public good." The political scope of this project is, first, to move this potentially powerful knowledge into public realms in new ways, as an experiment in the prospects of power. The second move is then to observe how that knowledge works and how it can be structured to work better, in moving toward more deliberative, more democratic goals in life and work. The politics of this knowledge will add to what we know of this political world and, perhaps more important, to our hopes for a more knowing public participation in it.

The Next Incunabula 11

After two years of uninspired and uninspiring study for a first degree, I left university and, on what then seemed something of a whim entered a teachers college in North Bay, Ontario. It was during the final years of Ontario's tuition-free normal schools, open to high-school graduates and university dropouts who wished to teach in the elementary schools of that province. My thinking was that teaching the young, now that the 1960s had come to a close, might be a way to continue the dream for a new world that had been that decade's hope-filled project. Like many before and after me, I found myself determined during that one-year teacher education program to make teaching into something more like the learning that went on outside of my school days. The "master teachers" there advised me that it would be better for me and the students if I went with the standard behavioral objectives and learning outcomes after two of us led an unsuccessful boycott of an education course that would have us determine our teaching day by pre-defined behavioral outcomes for our students. Teaching jobs were scarce then, perhaps more so for failed boycott leaders. After I finished the program, I was working in a neighbor's barn stacking the summer's first cut of hay, when I finally got a call to come fill an opening in Sault Ste. Marie created by the suicide of a science teacher who was famous in town for being a one-armed church organist. After Labor Day, at the age of twenty-three, I entered the classroom to begin teaching with all the excitement and apprehension of the young taking that first serious step into a world suddenly made real.

I taught in the schools of Sault Ste. Marie for eight years with something of the same excitement and apprehension, occasionally supervising the creation of a minor masterpiece in a morning's collaboration among children, only to spend a disruptive afternoon disciplining them, for reasons that seemed to elude me. At the same time, I was slowly catching up on my university education in the evenings and summers. I distinctly remember asking myself, more than once in those classroom days, why my best-laid plans failed to change students' minds about the world. Why was it so hard to do what I would have thought enjoyable to do, in working with books, brushes, numbers, musical instruments, and children? As I continued my part-time university studies, I continued to imagine that the social sciences held out the promise of at least more of an answer than I could muster on my own in the midst of my teaching day. I finally decided to go to graduate school full-time, and I approached Edgar Z. Friedenberg, whose research—his writing, really—as I noted earlier, seemed particularly adept at understanding the loss of hope and recovering a knowledge of youth's lost dignity in schools. I can still vividly recall how, after flying out to Halifax to meet him, he confronted me in his kitchen with what seemed unanswerable questions on what my educational ideas had to do with the ayatollah's revolution in Iran and other global matters of the day, before agreeing to supervise my doctoral program in the sociology of education at Dalhousie University.

It was no coincidence that my hopes and frustrations as a schoolteacher aspiring to educational reform paralleled by those of the social sciences, which came out of the 1960s having contributed to "a remarkable burst of social reform," as Nathan Glazer names it. Glazer was among the economists, political scientists, anthropologists, and sociologists who worked on the reform programs of the Kennedy and Johnson administrations. These academics saw themselves as fully part of what Glazer on looking back, recollects as "a new era in which we would rationally and pragmatically attack our domestic social problems." Theirs was "the optimistic vision of social science guiding policy," which ended up teaching Glazer and others hard lessons on "the limits of social policy." Even the best-laid social programs created and compounded problems while undermining what Glazer later came to see as the real means—traditions of family and community—for redressing them. He allows that, of course, there remains the need for more research, given the complexities introduced by policy initiatives. But that knowledge needs to serve, for this latter-day Glazer, "the creation and building of new traditions."[1]

Between then and now, I moved from the school to the university classroom where I began to teach students who wanted to be teachers,

---

1. Nathan Glazer, *The Limits of Social Policy* (Cambridge: Harvard University Press, 1998), 1, 142, 7, 8. Glazer's later change of heart and mind, from opposition to affirmative action to a qualified support for it, shows a shift in his faith in social policy that should be noted: see "The Case for Racial Preferences," *Public Interest*, no. 135 (spring 1999).

while conducting research in schools about how they might bring more of their own love of literacy and learning to the young. All of this gave me more knowledge about classrooms and schools than I had possessed when I was a schoolteacher, although whether I knew or understood the children in those classrooms any better is another question. The research questions that I pursued seemed to speak to the schoolteacher that I had once been and to the teachers, students, and parents who had filled my life in those days. Whether the schoolteacher that I once was and the people I knew then have reason, at the end of their long days, to attend to the knowledge resulting from this research is yet another question, but it is one that I have now turned around with this public-knowledge idea, by asking instead whether I and my colleagues in the social sciences have done enough to support and warrant that attention.

This is, for me, where the social contract for the social sciences that I described earlier enters the realm of a more personal obligation. I think of my research as a trust, undertaken in having left teaching, as I did, to see whether some greater help was to be found among those who profess to find out things and to know about them. For what drives this public-knowledge project is the trust and good faith that needs to exist between those who inquire and those who live within the scope of that inquiry. Where Glazer came away from his earlier period of public engagement with a sense that he and his colleagues had run into the limits of social policy, I want to push, in yet another direction, against the seeming limits of our own work with knowledge, to risk testing whether we have exhausted the public value of knowing what is known as a result of the social sciences. Where Glazer saw the hopes of an era dashed as social scientists struggled with the making of social policy, I have taken up another theme from the 1960s—namely, a concern with extending public *participation* as a means of expanding the democratic basis of our daily lives. To engage people in these forms of knowledge, which were once far more of a social force in the hands of Glazer and others during the 1960s than they are today, is part of a democratic experiment based on the public value and force of this knowledge. Now, most of the tie-dyed communes and cooperatives have faded, worker ownership is about stock options, and the referendum politics of interest groups is on the rise. Still, I have argued throughout this book that it is the social sciences' turn to test whether they have been holding all along—given the relation of knowledge and power—a means for increasing public participation. I am calling on social scientists to experiment with their own assumptions about the value of their work, their own sources of authority and power. I am asking that we together explore what this knowing can do for public participation and understanding as people come to see the scope and limits of the social sciences' vast and varied research program. Such an experiment will have much to teach us about the role of knowledge in democratic, public life.[2]

It may become apparent, through this experimentation and testing, that the public value of this knowledge cannot reasonably be increased, that nothing the social sciences can say or do will convince people that ready access to this form of inquiry adds something important and worthwhile to their understanding of how the world works. This, too, we need to know. For if that proved to be the case, it would then be time for the social sciences to rethink their social contract and find new ways to reestablish the basis of the public trust implied by the current sponsorship of their work by governments, educational institutions, and foundations.

Up to this point, I have taken a threefold approach to persuading both social scientists and the public that something needs to be done, given the amount of research available and the technologies at hand. I began with *Technologies of Knowing*, a book much inspired by my work with Vivian Forssman on designing collaborative websites and educational programs with the not-quite-for-profit Knowledge Architecture venture. The book represented a thought experiment, a (social) science fiction using the corporate guise of an Automata Data Corporation, in which the cyberdata really mattered as it rarely does in cyberpunk noir. The book explored how an imagined corporation for public knowledge could fill the gaps, reduce the contradictions, and generally improve the quality of research by compiling public data on an ongoing and global scale, comparable to the massive private assembling of marketing data already under way. I drew examples from the development of evidence-based medicine and corporate data mining to demonstrate the effective integration of research into professional and business practices. Yet even as I explored the technical wonders of data mining and autocitation, I realized that the social sciences' support for public knowledge was a far more complex issue than managing the technologies. The challenge would be in convincing both social scientists and the public of the possibilities and obligations in improving the public value of largely state-subsidized work with knowledge.[3]

---

2. Three decades ago, Carole Pateman, a political philosopher now at UCLA, declared greater public participation to be a source of critical and realistic hope for extending democratic possibilities, not only within the scope of government and social policy but also in such areas as the workplace: *Participation and Democratic Theory* (Cambridge: Cambridge University Press, 1970).

3. John Willinsky, *Technologies of Knowing: A Proposal for the Human Sciences* (Boston: Beacon, 1999).

This development led me to fall back on old scholarly habits in this the second phase of my venture, by assembling a historical, philosophical, and political argument for the social sciences to get behind public knowledge. The issues addressed in this book have been directed at understanding how this project is part of a long tradition within knowledge work. I have considered why and how social sciences can improve their contribution to public knowledge, largely through their constant themes of probability and reference. Risk is already a constant point of reference for people in assessing their situation and making sense of the world. Within the scope of this public-knowledge project, the social sciences can explore ways of helping people work with this understanding by demonstrating the various ways in which risk and possibility can be conceived, studied, and connected. The social sciences can make apparent how risks and possibilities are acted on and realized by connecting these different forms of knowledge and action. Among professionals and practitioners, this integration of knowledge has already begun through the action-research model that makes research the practice of professionals. But the fact that more people are doing research, even research directly related to their work, still leaves the challenge of creating a public space for engaging this knowledge. This is the motivation for my extended argument on behalf of experimenting with a greater democracy of knowledge.[4]

What I have tried to make relentlessly apparent in this book is not just the obligation but also the opportunity, at this point, for initiating a public-knowledge project. Certainly, the launching of new Internet technologies on an almost daily basis defines this moment of opportunity. However, we have this opportunity not only because this technology can enable us to do things that the printing press cannot, but also because the technology commands people's attention. The motto among researchers in my field is that whatever you are studying, "Wrap it in technology and they will fund." People are curious; institutions feel compelled. The questions are everywhere: What can these machines do for me? What am I about to miss?

The private sector has wasted little time in pursuing potential avenues of opportunity, from domestic cyberpets to restaurant-locating cars. My case is that the public sector could use some boosterism and bolstering by the social sciences, principally in testing whether their particular

---

4. See, for example, Cynthia D. Bisman and David A. Hardcastle, *Integrating Research into Practice: A Model for Effective Social Work* (Belmont, Calif.: Wadsworth, 1999); and "Web Links to Participatory Action Research Sites," http://www.goshen.edu/soan/soan96p.htm.

approach to knowledge could do a good deal more for people, public life, and democratic processes. This is not about the social sciences closing the research–policy gap or providing performance indicators of research effectiveness. It is not about testing the limits of social policy. It is about the social sciences becoming more of a source of understanding and knowledge for more people. We can test the public value (and the underlying rhetoric) of this knowledge, or we can wait and watch the new medium gradually reshape it as it inevitably will. I propose that those with a strong interest in the public contribution of the social sciences join in the experimentation with these technologies to see what they can do with our ideas and ideals of knowing. This is what the third phase of my project is about.

In pursuing the third phase of this public-knowledge project, the team at the University of British Columbia is engaged in using new technologies to build and test online models that restructure the representation of research as knowledge for a range of communities. If *Technologies of Knowing* and the present book have raised the prospect of greater convergence between public knowledge and the social sciences, the next logical step is to demonstrate a workable, engaging public space needed for working it all out in practice. The team's current work includes inviting a wide a range of interested parties to test the promise and premises of this new interactive broadcasting system with the team, while investigating what this does for people's understanding of how knowledge works and how such knowledge might serve them better. We hope the resulting designs will be further explored, stretched, and tested by those working in other social sciences.

These new approaches for organizing knowledge include such structures as metadata classification systems, which enable documents posted on the web to be automatically referenced and indexed, wherever they reside, across a number of predetermined fields. The use of markup languages, such as XML (Extensible Markup Language), which involves the tagging of different aspects of a document according to standards that might be set by, for example, the American Psychological Association (much as it sets standards for bibliographies). As more and more research is posted on the web, the use of only a small set of identifying XML tags in these documents would enable them to be found, wherever they sit, perhaps according to research topic, method, location of study, age group studied, program used, and whatever categories were decided as valuable ways of linking studies, including validated peer reviews. New tags and refined categories among existing tags could be introduced into existing documents. Readers would be able to determine whether they looked at research, policies, programs, or organizations related to a topic, as well as how the material was displayed, whether by title, abstract, results, or full-text. In this way, public-knowledge websites, whether in education, welfare, justice, health, or another area, would be little more than engines of public inquiry and forums of public reflection, with a wide range of possible links to the expanding realm of knowledge on their sites.[5]

Metadata tagging also enables the user to access a lot of the knowledge in new ways, as I discovered a decade ago when an early version of this tagging system was applied to the *Oxford English Dictionary* (*OED*) at the University of Waterloo. At the time, I happened to be researching how the editors of the *OED* put the language together, and this new way of merging text and database with embedded tags that identified the different parts of the dictionary (word, definition, supporting quotation, date, author, etc.) enabled me to turn the *OED* inside out as a source of knowledge about the English language. I was able to use those tags to ascertain the most influential authors and books that shaped the editing of the dictionary in both the late Victorian edition (1888–1928) and the modern supplement (1957–1985). To dynamically reconfigure the knowledge so that it can demonstrate new sorts of connections, including a connection to its own construction, is to approach Leibniz's "demonstrative Encyclopedia"—introduced in chapter 4—which would link in "an exact chain" demonstrations and observations that would provide the truths "the public would like to learn." The power of every document to form part of that exact chain, through metadata tagging, introduces elements of Borges's library of Babel.[6]

Given the onrush of new technologies, we need to design and create experimental online settings to see how these innovations might begin to connect the interests of those who are traditionally thought of as producers and consumers of knowledge. This means bringing people together to talk about how this knowledge works for them—how it connects, serves, consoles, and confounds. The political dimensions of this knowledge are played out in the deliberations over the potential for restructuring knowledge and using it in new ways. The project continues with the political economies of intellectual property, research ethics, funding and reviews, as well as editing and publishing that this restructuring

5. On the *Dublin Core Metadata Initiative*, see http://purl.org/DC/index.htm; on XML, see http://www.xml.com.
6. John Willinsky, *Empire of Words: The Reign of the OED* (Princeton: Princeton University Press, 1994); Gottfried Wilhelm Leibniz, "Precepts for Advancing the Sciences and Arts" (1680), in *Leibniz: Selections*, ed. Philip P. Weiner (New York: Scribner, 1951), 38–40; Jorge Luis Borges, "The Library of Babel," in *Labyrinths: Selected Stories and Other Writings* (New York: New Directions, 1962).

will raise. Interaction will need to take place among researchers, editors, reviewers, librarians, publishers, international scholars, professionals, policy makers, and a variety of public participants. In the process, we on the team have been working up sets of potential components that could go into a public-knowledge website that would be used to test ways of improving the public value of research in the study of education (see the appendix).

For all the connecting, collaborating, and communing among people, this project is still about what we know. It is still about the trouble and comfort, the challenge and assurance afforded by that knowledge. What we stand to learn is more about what can be made of knowledge, not only through this new technology but also as we direct that knowing at extending participation in political (public and personal) processes. I don't have to wait for the launching of this project to get into the politics of knowledge. I have found the politics of knowledge invoked at each step of the way, in working with colleagues and professional associations that have first to get comfortable with both the idea of focusing attention on what we do with knowledge, and the prospect that we should be testing whether we could be doing it better from a public perspective.

Our goal is not, as is sometimes assumed, simply to build a website through which all knowledge must pass. To be a clearinghouse or knowledge broker is not our goal. Others are doing this, and we are learning from their efforts at managing this knowledge. Our work, instead, is about researching the possibilities for the public, professional, and political play of knowledge in this new medium. It is about placing this knowledge within public reach and testing ways of making it contribute more to a sense of public space and public sector, to a sense of public engagement in this area of knowledge production. It is directed at testing whether the public value of research in the social sciences can be increased in ways that, I realize, will challenge the nature of this academic calling. It pushes at knowledge and knowing as means of political participation, which is only to take Carole Pateman's point that a participatory theory of democracy has as a necessary condition a participatory society, one in which people have the resources to play a more active role in shaping social structures. If knowledge can support that participation, if it can give people a greater sense of what can be done, then the social sciences, among all research endeavors, should be able to offer critical support for that increased participation.[7]

When it comes to making a claim to knowledge, the assumption in

---

7. Pateman, *Participation and Democratic Theory*, 102.

the sciences has long been that the proof for a given study lies in the ability to replicate the results, use them to predict future events, and establish the causal sequence within them. Those conditions have been understood as the necessary and sufficient conditions of knowledge, and thus they warrant conducting the research and claiming that it adds to the body of knowledge. The only problem is that replication, prediction, and causal determination is not what social scientists do (nor is it what most scientists of any sort do). They do, however, try to make greater sense of the world by connecting their studies to others, sharing research methods and providing critiques of existing work. I think these activities should be extended and more closely connected to the larger common project of making sense.

There remains to be explained how knowledge, for all that I have made of it, is also the central philosophical paradox of this era. For what the economy thriveth on, the philosophers cannot wait to sweep away as being neither here nor there. The dominant institutional form of our lives is staffing up with chief knowledge officers devoted "to creating [in corporate settings] a legitimate knowledge sharing culture," according to John Peetz, CKO for the global consulting corporation Ernst and Young. And at the same moment that knowledge is having its inestimable economic value heralded, philosophy's new chief postepistemology officers are triumphantly completing their excavation and removal of the last of its very foundations.[8]

Among the leading CPOs, Richard Rorty speaks openly of philosophy writing off as simply a bad intellectual investment its endless search for a theory that guarantees knowledge. We can know employment rates and a child's attitude toward reading, but that knowledge does not come, as we once struggled to establish, with the guarantee we once thought it did. What is true and what we know, Rorty argues, are both ways of describing how the world works for us. What we call knowledge is what helps us to make sense of things, including a sense of how to make things happen. For Rorty, knowledge is all about supporting "edifying" conversations, conversations about, for example, "the social justification of belief," which enable "new, better, more interesting, more fruitful ways of speaking." Freed from pursuing a general theory of knowledge, we can work with the public on establishing what it is useful to know in helping us to do what we as a community have decided to do. Rorty is not so much rejecting the study of philosophy as taking it public, which seems all the more critical in these knowledge-privatizing days. And so I would

---

8. John Peetz, cited in *Emerson's Professional Services Review*, March–April, 1997.

hold that the social sciences have much to offer to this conversation, especially as they can track the social consequences of those beliefs in policies and programs, as well as in the daily course of people's lives.[9]

While working on this book, I was disappointed to discover that I had missed out on a wonderful grant opportunity offered by the Alfred P. Sloan Foundation. The foundation awarded $1.5 million for studies on the "limits of knowledge" confronted by a number of disciplines. The awards were made in anthropology, cell biology, computer science, economics, historical linguistics, science, oceanography, and population genetics. The limits of knowledge at issue for Sloan are about the farthest reaches of scientific inquiry, as if those scientists working at the edge might then peer off to the horizon or perhaps into the abyss. To take one instance of what they did pursue, the Sloan study on the limits of historical linguistics was directed by Colin Renfrew, an archeologist at Cambridge University. By archeologists' drawing on the findings of other disciplines, those limits have now been pushed back to a time before the origins of the Indo-European tongue, some five thousand years ago, Renfrew points out. Using DNA studies, for example, archeologists have been able to trace humanity's prehistorical migration patterns and thus can speculate knowledgeably on the spread and development of languages before the invention of writing. This interdisciplinary linking of research allows scholars to gain extra ground on the elusive and ultimately unknowable origin of language. The state of knowledge is defined, with this approach, by the image of knowledge's expanding frontier that is continually being extended into the reaches of the unknown, like the great world maps of early Europeans' Western adventure that trailed off into emptiness. This definition suggests that the limit of knowledge is all about what we have been able to uncover thus far, and perhaps what we will yet uncover. Up to those limits, we can assume, knowledge is singular and whole.[10]

My idea is that there is another critical dimension to these limits. It makes as much sense, when it comes to appreciating the limits of knowl-

---

9. Richard Rorty, *Philosophy and the Mirror of Nature* (Princeton: Princeton University Press), 170, 360. Rorty's reservations with research also include a concern that the element of conversation, of public discourse, will be lost to it: "One way to see edifying philosophy *as* the love of wisdom is to see it as the attempt to prevent conversation from degenerating into inquiry, into a research program" (372, original emphasis). Charles Taylor traces this anti-foundational critique of epistemology back to Hegel's work of nearly two centuries ago, and forward through Heidegger, Wittgenstein, and Merleau-Ponty in this century: "Overcoming Epistemology," in *After Philosophy: End or Transformation?* ed. Kenneth Baynes, James Bohman, and Thomas McCarthy (Cambridge: MIT Press, 1987), 472–73.

10. Colin Renfrew, cited in Sarah Boxer, "Science Confronts the Unknowable," *New York Times,* January 24, 1998, 15, 17.

edge, to think about restrictions in the way knowledge works among people. Those limits have much to do with ways to reconcile and represent the diversity of what is already known. These limits of sense and sensibility (indeed, of pride and prejudice as well) in appreciating what this knowledge contributes to our wonder and hope suggests to me the scale of this public project for the social sciences. The goal is not to make this knowledge useful so much as knowable and explorable, probable and probe-able; not to make it unified or singular so much as comprehensible in its divergence, as if the edge of the difference were the most edifying aspect. This public engagement is about extending the value and claim of knowledge as knowledge. In saying this, I am risking that, as in the case of eugenics earlier in the twentieth century, the popular embrace of science might be as dangerously wrong and wrongheaded as the science itself. There are no guarantors of goodness, neither in people nor in the science. Yet rather than forsaking current standards for verifying knowledge claims, such as the not-infallible peer review used by journals and granting agencies, I argue only that this act of public trust could be of more direct public benefit. That letting too many people in on our knowledge could lead to its manipulation and abuse strikes me as a necessary risk that will be kept in check at least partially by the very openness for which I am calling. Still, it may be that organizations much like the Anti-Defamation League, which keeps an ear tuned to excessive assertions of freedom of speech, will arise in the interest of questioning how far we can go with these open intellectual resources.

I have no idea how close we are to the limits of public knowledge, limits to the value of what people can hold in their heads, books, and computers—if limits in that way make any sense at all—and I have been careful to hedge my bet by speaking of *improving* the contribution of the social sciences to public knowledge. The public's exasperation with the current state of research in many areas is exacerbated not simply by conflicts among studies but also by the lack of apparent effort to make clear why this divergence is critical and by the continuing false hope that each question can be resolved by a further and well-funded definitive study. To say that there are insufficient data on the value of using Piaget's developmental stages in science teaching is one thing, and it may well be true; to say that there are two schools of thought on the question, here is why there are two, here are the studies to which these schools have given rise, and here are the consequences at work in actual classrooms, is another.

This is why I am experimenting with structures and mechanisms that not only will lay out the scope of research on a given topic but will also juxtapose the inevitably divergent claims around different facets of the topic. Some of the conflicts, whether in results or interpretations, may be resolved through reanalysis and further study, but the assumption will always be that this sort of resolution of discrepancies is not necessarily going to be the case. Many more of the conflicts, representing the plurality of goals within the social sciences, will be shown to reflect basic differences in values, which occur wherever people gather to share ideas. That is, I want to bring to public knowledge an understanding of the *pluralism* that currently exists within the social sciences and to treat that pluralism as a signal of our human autonomy rather than as the current and temporary state of scientific failure.

The great defender of liberal pluralism Isaiah Berlin makes his case for this necessary range of human values by suggesting that the differences among us are a function of people having a choice and of such choices becoming a part of who we are. Berlin also manages to step around the charges of relativism that follow on this advocacy of pluralism by contrasting its sense of arbitrary choice to the reasonable pluralism that he advocates in the spirit of the philosophers Johann von Herder and Giambattista Vico: "'I prefer coffee, you prefer champagne. We have different tastes. There is no more to be said.' That is relativism. But Herder's view, and Vico's, is not that: it is what I should describe as pluralism—that is, the conception that there are many different ends that men may seek and still be fully rational, fully men, capable of understanding each other and sympathizing and deriving light from each other." The principle of understanding, as well as of sympathy and light, would be supported by a pluralist public-knowledge project by the very contrast of ideas and interpretations. The aim would be to assist people in making choices through a greater understanding of what is at stake in adhering to different values and concepts, just as the rivalry of ideas can encourage greater participation in thinking through the limits of a knowledge worth pursuing. We have to imagine a public-knowledge website that would both demonstrate this pluralism and be open to critiques of pluralism and its relativistic tendencies.[11]

I realize that this embrace of pluralism flies in the face of what seems to be the goal of creating a public space for social scientists to bring greater coordination and coherence to their work. It might seem that what I want is much the same thing Harvard zoologist Edward O. Wilson wants when he writes of "the unity of the sciences" and the "intrinsic unity of knowledge" in his widely reviewed book *Consilience.* He chose the archaic term *consilience* ("literally a 'jumping together' of knowledge")

---

11. Isaiah Berlin, "The Pursuit of the Ideal," in *The Crooked Timber of Humanity: Chapters in the History of Ideas* (New York: Vintage, 1992), 11.

over the related *coherence* because coherence fails to follow his penchant for a singularity of meaning. Now, it's true that we both worry about reducing the fragmentation in research as a means of assisting the public in political matters, the educated public as he would name his audience: "How wisely policy is chosen," Wilson writes, "will depend on the ease with which the educated public, not just intellectuals and political leaders, can think around these and similar circuits" connecting, for example, social science, environmental policy, ethics, and biology.[12]

Wilson and I both draw on the Enlightenment. He is taken by its pursuit of intellectual unity, which only now can be realized, he offers, through the merger of the natural sciences with the social sciences and the humanities; and I am taken by the Enlightenment's intellectual interests in the greater equality and autonomy to be achieved through the powers of reason and knowledge, which I hope to support on a larger scale. We are both inspired, as well, by the perception that the public is not particularly pleased with what the social sciences have offered up to this point. We share a concern with the sense that a footnote can add to a text, with Wilson demonstrating in his book what I find to be a very eloquent version of referencing. Finally, we both see an advantage in borrowing ideas from other disciplines, even if this is convergence toward the underlying unity of knowledge for him, and plain eclecticism that speaks to the artifice of disciplinary conveniences for me. We differ, with far less in common, on whether sociobiology can unlock "the foundations of human nature," in its "deep origins," in ways that offer a "true science of human behavior" within a "seamless web of cause and effect," promising great gains "in predictive power."[13]

12. Edward O. Wilson, *Consilience: The Unity of Knowledge* (New York: Knopf, 1998), 184, 191, 193.

13. Ibid., 181–82, 266. By way of a footnote sample from Wilson's book, indicated at the end of the text with only a page number: "Isaiah Berlin praised the **achievements of the Enlightenment** in *The Age of Enlightenment: The Eighteenth-Century Philosophers* (New York: Oxford University Press, 1979)" (300, original boldface). Stephen T. Emlen, an evolutionary biologist at Cornell University, refers to how awareness of "inherited genetic risks" can be used to "head off trouble before it happens," using the example that children are much more likely to be abused by stepparents who lack genetic connections to stepchildren. As if to prove the unquestionable utility of this discovery, Emlen recommends that "single parents consider emulat[ing] female baboons, which do not accept a new male partner unless he demonstrates parenting skills": cited in Jane E. Brody, "Genetic Ties May Be Factor in Violence in Stepfamilies," *New York Times*, February 10, 1998, B9, B12. On Wilson's hopes of a true science of humankind, see, for example, Richard Rorty, "Against Unity," *Wilson Quarterly* (winter 1998); and Niles Eldredge, "Cornets and Consilience," and Stephen Jay Gould, "In Gratuitous Battle," *Civilization*, October–November, 1998. For the social Darwinist arguments that undergird the conservative dismantling of social-welfare programs, see Michael Epstein, *Welfare in America: How Social Science Fails the Poor* (Madison: University of Wisconsin Press, 1997), 38–55.

Yet I want to leave aside what I find to be Wilson's questionable science of humankind and stay with the specific, although still related, question of whether my concerns with coherence and fragmentation are better addressed through Wilson's consilient unity of knowledge. Any public-knowledge website devoted to the social sciences would provide plenty of room for addressing the research and discussion around sociobiology, and indeed for much discussion of Wilson's ideas in *Consilience*. The need for such public debate becomes all the more critical as the successes of the Human Genome Project bring us closer to a potential era of "volitional evolution," as Wilson puts it. His concluding depiction of the sorry state of the future, due to overpopulation and environmental destruction, provides still further incentive for public engagement with the probabilities and possibilities.

Can the social sciences better address these issues by integrating with the natural sciences, following Wilson's proposal, or by pursuing greater public intelligibility, following mine? The consilience that I am looking for, the reader may recall, is between social-science research and other forms of knowledge and action, whether in policies, journalism, the practices of professionals, or open forums with the public. Issues of genetic intervention and environmental sustainability both strike me as hinging on public intelligibility far more so than on a true science of human behavior rooted in evolutionary forces, unless one holds out some hope of manipulating our genes in order to make us somehow more ecologically simpatico.

Wilson's consilience project of a social–natural science could be made subject to its own form of a public-knowledge project. The advantages of this may become apparent as we begin to explore, within the scope of this public-knowledge project, different ways of structuring, organizing, representing, referencing, and supporting knowledge to improve its public value. Yet I cannot help feeling that at issue between us, at issue in whether energies and talents should be invested in consilience or in public knowledge, is Wilson's idea of the "intrinsic unity of knowledge."

Consider Wilson's claim that "most of the issues that vex humanity daily—ethnic conflict, arms escalation, over-population, abortion, environment, endemic poverty, to cite several most persistently before us—cannot be solved without integrating knowledge from the natural sciences with that of the social sciences." Of course, on one level, the natural sciences often offer relevant information on these vexing issues, but Wilson is talking here specifically about factoring in genetic and epigenetic ("hereditary regularities in development, including mental") influences, and he is talking about a singularity of knowledge that is so powerfully determined and definitive that it solves a problem by the force of its analysis. But knowledge does not solve problems, I want to Ping-Pong back to him—people do. The knowledge afforded by the social sciences, even enriched with the genetic and epigenetic knowledge recommended by Wilson, can helpfully alert us to risks and possibilities. It can offer not just a single point but many points of reference in making decisions and in taking action. The coherence at issue is not about reducing the complexity that we face. It is not about simplifying decisions. The coherence afforded by this public-knowledge project is about relating and integrating different forms of knowledge while giving some direction about how they are divided and distinct.[14]

In this I am with Rorty, as he sees knowledge as a potentially helpful way of talking about the world. The public-knowledge project is all about revitalizing that talk in ways that help us to make greater sense of and to take greater hold over aspects of our lives. It is about expanding the public space for such conversations among people who are drawn to certain issues researched by the social sciences, just as it seeks to inform that conversation, turning it into a point of action and participation, as much for the research community interested in responses to its work as for practitioners and the public who want to draw connections for others to see. Rorty has a way of promoting the promise of a great conversation without giving much apparent thought to where and how it would take place outside of the graduate student seminar and the dinner party of friends, on within the shrinking public spaces of modem life.

Fragmentation among ideas, studies, and practices will be reduced not by finding the unity of the knowledge but by people connecting ways of understanding and interpreting phenomena. I am treating "knowledge" here as a form of human expression, much like art, and not as a Platonic idea—unified, whole, and awaiting consilient realization and uncovering. I do not find it makes much sense to talk of the universe as being subject to a comprehensible body of unified knowledge. The strand of a hair from my child's brush is always open to myriad forms of human expression and knowing, and I am richer and wiser for that.

It is well to recall that after much debate, the editors of *The Encyclopedia of Unified Science*, which was initiated in 1938, decided that they would attempt no more than a bringing together of various types of work between a single set of covers. One editor, Otto Neurath, explained it this way: "If we reject the rationalistic anticipation of *the* system of the

---

14. Wilson, *Consilience*, 13.

sciences, if we reject the notion of a philosophical system which is to legislate for the sciences, what is the maximum coordination of the sciences which remains possible? The only answer that can be given for the time being is: *An Encyclopedia of Unified Sciences.*" The scientific desire for the unity of knowledge is but a "metaphysical sentiment," in Ian Hacking's phrase, and those scientists whom Hacking spoke to as part of his research on the concept saw the prospect of unity as simply irrelevant to their work. "Personally, I applaud the divergence of language in science and find in it no grounds for skepticism or pessimism about the continued growth of the science," Patrick Suppes has written. "The irreducible pluralism of languages of science is as desirable a feature as is the irreducible plurality of political views in a democracy."[15]

"The world henceforth will be run," Wilson observes toward the end of his book, "by synthesizers, people able to put together the right information at the right time, think critically about it, and make important choices wisely." The crux of the politics of public knowledge for me is global access to what we can only hope is the right information at the right time. The social sciences are in a strong position to help people put together information so that more of them can think critically and choose wisely in deciding which information at that time is right for them. Otherwise, the social sciences will fail to support—and Wilson's statement suggests it is already too late—greater opportunities for democratic participation through access to at least one source of potentially powerful knowledge. The world does not need to revert to synthesizers, a unified body of knowledge, or a single way of knowing. It needs much the opposite: more people working on more ways of understanding how to make a better world for each other. At least, I am proposing that it would be worthwhile to research the risks and possibilities, the politics and economics, of improving people's opportunities to play a greater part in the knowledgeable improvement of this world.[16]

---

15. Otto Neurath, "Unified Science and Its Encyclopedia" (1937), in *Philosophical Papers, 1913–1946,* ed. and trans. Robert S. Cohen and Marie Neurath (Boston: Riedel, 1983), 194; Ian Hacking, "The Disunities of the Sciences," in *The Disunity of Science: Boundaries, Contexts, and Power* (Stanford: Stanford University Press, 1996), 58; Patrick Suppes, "The Plurality of Science," in *PSA 1978,* vol. 2, ed. P. D. Asquith and Ian Hacking (East Lansing, Mich.: Philosophy of Science Association, 1978), 2–16. It is worth noting that the editors of the encyclopedia solicited Thomas Kuhn's *Origin of Scientific Revolutions,* which did so much to temper our idea of the sciences as engaged in rational and cumulative knowledge building.

16. Wilson, *Consilience,* 269. See John Dupré for why "only a society with absolutely homogeneous, or at least hegemonic, political commitments and shared assumptions, could expect a unified science": *The Disorder of Things: Metaphysical Foundations of the Disunity of Science* (Cambridge: Harvard University Press, 1993), 261.

For all of my talk about websites and hyperlinks, this experiment with public knowledge doesn't need to be a technical feat. All it takes is a researcher who attempts, by the design and write-up of a research study, to speak to a wider public about the coherence and connection of this work, about how it augments, tests, and challenges existing ideas and practices. This is already going on with diligent and dedicated researchers, the reader may say, and I would agree; but it is not yet going on as part of a conscious and common effort at improving the public value of the research, not yet as part of an experiment in whether and how that public value can be enhanced. These experiments in the ability of research to extend public knowledge, directly and as research, are also found in such areas as the anthropological background provided to museum exhibitions and the use of social-science research in the graduate programs of professional disciplines. Still, I imagine that more can be done with new technologies to make this research work better for those outside, as well as those inside, the research community.

Books that were produced during the half-century following the invention of the printing press, circa 1455, are known as incunabula. The earliest of these look much like the illuminated manuscripts they were based on, from letters cut to look like the writing of scribes and with illustrations by the same illuminators. The Latin illuminated manuscript was all that anyone understood a book could be. But it was not long before new standards for texts emerged. Books were printed in local languages, as well as in Latin. Books had title pages establishing their "civil status," chapter and paragraph breaks and page numbering, and even came in portable editions. Many of these developments were designed to ease the reading process and expand the market. It was a period of experimentation with graphic design. The new title page, for example, grew in the early years of the sixteenth century into a page filled with a laudatory title that included the parts of the book, and perhaps verses (rhyming blurbs) by author and friends.[17]

The Internet offers us another era of incunabula. It may be difficult to imagine current webpages having the same potential collectors' value that those early books possess. Yet there is the same sense of a conservative momentum that is simply carrying the old form of the printed page into the new medium unchanged. Then there's the fact that rather than publish on the Internet, I am turning to that old form to make my case for how the new medium can improve the situation of knowledge, miss-

---

17. Lucien Febvre and Henri-Jean Martin, *The Coming of the Book: The Impact of Printing, 1450–1800*, trans. David Gerard (London: Verso, 1990), 77–108.

ing my chance, perhaps, to speak to the already thoroughly converted. Still, I am also experimenting with hypertext, links, and markup languages. Even though it is impossible for us to know what will stick, we are no less compelled to experiment, to assess opportunities and evaluate options, with an eye to promoting, in this case, the agenda of increasing the social sciences' contributions to public knowledge and deliberative democracy.

What we do know is that a new medium can have a significant impact. Luther's idea of printing the Bible in the people's language was part of a revolution in textuality and the written word. He sensed an opportunity to push the boundaries of the old patterns of knowledge and power, to challenge what was given as known, as did so many others, whether out of scholarly concerns with knowledge, out of religious passion, or out of seditious interests, with no small part played by the commercial possibilities of new markets. Although my book has focused on what might be done with the social sciences and their responsibilities to public knowledge, it is part of a larger project concerned with participating in what comes next in the distribution of word and idea.

This book is offered, finally, as an invitation and a challenge. It invites readers to take hold of a history of possibilities and responsibilities that point to the prospects of expanding the quality and reaches of public knowledge. It invites those researchers with more than a passing interest in this knowledge to become involved in testing ways of making their research a more connected and more integrated aspect of what the public and the professions can readily access. The challenge that follows from this invitation is over the future and fate of public knowledge in an era and an economy driven by efforts to capitalize on intellectual properties. This challenge has everything to do with the future of the university and its research activity as a source of leadership in the public service, and everything to do with the political potential of a digital era to reverse declines in public participation and community.

Neither the accrued knowledge of the social sciences nor the new technologies of the Internet will deliver us once and for all from the social dilemmas we now face, nor will they return us to what we imagine we have lost by way of community and environment. Still, that is no reason not to invite the social sciences to do more with what they know and to challenge the social sciences to make clear how this knowledge can contribute to the quality of life and the future of democracy on a global basis. It means developing and testing new kinds of public resources and public spaces that can better serve people's interest in governing both their own lives and this globe in ways that will ensure mutual well-being for generations to come. Such claims for the potential of knowledge are now ours to put to the test. Improving the public contribution of that knowledge has much to teach us about the difference that knowing can make. It is a project that can help us with fundamental questions of why it is worth knowing.

Potential Components
of a Public-Knowledge Website

PROPOSAL FOR A PUBLIC-KNOWLEDGE WEBSITE FOR EDUCATION

The following components, with a brief description of their possible functions, represent a starting point for a prototype Public Knowledge website for social-science research in education (PK/E) that seeks to improve the research process as a public and professional resource. These components will be assessed, modified, added to, or deleted through a collaborative process conducted with the participating communities of interest in the Public-Knowledge Project. This appendix was developed to accompany proposals seeking support for researching the development of a public-knowledge website for educational research.

(1) Agenda Setting

This section of the PK/E website will test ways of supporting funding agencies and other bodies engaged in the process of setting research agendas. The goal is a more open and coordinated sharing of information, with links to various initiatives and opportunities for discussion of research-funding programs among funding bodies and participating communities of interest. This component may result in a more accurate picture of research programs that are current, ongoing, and under development.

(2) Research Initiation

This section of the PK/E website will test ways of improving the initiation of, collaboration with, and joining in on research projects. Its goal will be to ensure more coordination of programs of comparable research on a global basis. It may be able to support a meeting of research interests from very diverse methodological and ideological approaches to similar questions, with an aim of providing a more comprehensive picture of critical educational issues as a result of this collaboration. It may enable practitioners and related professionals to join research projects and programs.

(3) Literature Review

This section of the PK/E website will test ways of improving (using database features of metadata and markup languages) literature reviews by topic, method, and current status of research programs. Its goal is to facilitate greater coherence within related research programs. The Literature Review component, which can be used by researchers, professionals, and public, should be directly linked to Agenda Setting and Research Design, as it can be used to map the distribution and development of research attention.

(4) Research Design

This section of the PK/E website will test ways of improving the review of current, proposed, and pending studies in the early stages to ensure greater synergy and connection among research designs. Among its goals could be the formation of research programs on a cooperative, international basis. It may offer new ways of making the data widely available for analysis and use by researchers, students, and others.

(5) Format

This section of the PK/E website will test ways of improving the structuring of the research write-up to facilitate different levels of access to the research (abstract, method, data, conclusions, references, etc.). It may support more direct linkages to related theoretical and empirical research as well as to related policies, practices, projects, organizations, and issues. It may facilitate the use of knowledge-management tools (metadata, etc.) to support the Literature Review and Research Design goals of data sharing, while enabling the representation of very different and diverse forms of knowledge.

(6) Publication

This section of the PK/E website will test ways of improving the submission, editorial, and peer-review process to ensure that it is more closely channeled to serve participants' interests and more closely directed at improving the value of the research. It may enable readers to assemble various documents in the creation of virtual journals to match special interests. It may support reader interests with guides to theories, traditions, methods, and language. It may test and assess new formats and open forums that support questions and collaborations that, in turn, can feed into the Agenda Setting and Research Initiation sections.

(7) Application

This section of the PK/E website will test ways of improving the role of research in educational decision making at parental, school, school-district, and state levels. It may enable various communities to participate in state and local policy initiatives and reviews by drawing on its integration of research with other knowledge domains (practices, projects, and organizations). It may enable the PK/E site to be integrated into professional-development programs (both credit and noncredit) that allow practitioners to paritcipate in the creation and review of knowledge components in the site. It may enable the PK/E site to provide an effective knowledge resource for program development and implementation in schools and teacher-education programs.

(8) Archiving

This section of the PK/E website will test ways of improving the dynamic accessing and constructing of knowledge-sets that can be maintained and referenced through mark-up languages (XML) and user portfolios. Voluntary tracking of archive use, supported by formal user surveys, may be used to monitor the public and professional value of the knowledge and the different knowledge structures used by the PK/E website.

Index